NATIVE AMERICANS
A Portrait

The Art and Travels of
Charles Bird King, Geoge Catlin, and Karl Bodmer

STEWART, TABORI & CHANG
NEW YORK

Text
Robert J. Moore

Graphic design
Patrizia Balocco Lovisetti
Clara Zanotti

Editorial Realization
Valeria Manferto De Fabianis
Laura Accomazzo

CONTENTS

Published in 1997 and distributed by
Stewart, Tabori & Chang.,
a division of U.S. Media Holdings, Inc.
115 West 18th Street, New York, NY 10011

Distributed in Canada by
General Publishing Company Ltd.
30 Lesmill Road
Don Mills, Ontario, M3B 2T6, Canada

Library of Congress Cataloging-in-Publication Data

Moore, Robert J. (Robert John), 1956—
    Native Americans : a portrait: the art and travels of Charles Bird King, George Catlin, and Karl Bodmer / by Robert J. Moore, Jr.
        p. cm.
    Includes bibliographical references (p.   ).
    ISBN 1-55670-616-2
    1. Indians of North America—Pictorial works.   2. King, Charles Bird, 1785–1862.   3. Catlin, George, 1796–1872.   4.Bodmer, Karl, 1809–1893.   5. United States—Description and travel.   I. Title.
EE77.5.M67   1997
973'.0497—dc21   97-8563

Printed in Italy by Pozzo Gros Monti, Torino.
Color separations by Fotomec, Torino.

10 9 8 7 6 5 4 3 2 1

The Publisher would like to thank the following for their precious help: Maria Lane, Bernard Shapero, and Achille Castelli.

2-3 *Karl Bodmer's prolific output during the course of his long life included stunning American Indian portraits and genre scenes.*

4-5 ***Bull Dance, Mandan O-Kee-Pa Ceremony, 1832.*** *George Catlin illustrated the Okeepa ceremony, which dramatized the Mandan account of the creation of the earth.*

6-7 ***Young Omaha, War Eagle, Little Missouri, and Pawnees.*** *This group portrait of the heads of five Indian men was realized by Charles Bird King.*

PREFACE

This is a book about a moment in time. Unlike many other books about American Indian people that try to cover their entire history and culture throughout North America, this book focuses on the twenty-year era between 1820 and 1840, an era during which Euro-Americans stepped up the pace of their conquest of the entire continent.

This book is also about art. During those two decades, three diverse artists–Charles Bird King, George Catlin, and Karl Bodmer–undertook lengthy projects to chronicle the cultures and appearance of American Indian people. We are fortunate that they did so, because once the final conquest began, Indian cultures would never be as pure, as independent, or as abundant. This is not to say that Indian cultures were not already touched by Europeans during this period. No culture remains in stasis at all times. Myriad changes in Indian cultures had taken place long before European contact, and Indian cultures continued to evolve even as European technology and ideas began to have a greater effect upon them. But after 1492, the rate of cultural change for both Indian and European cultures quickly accelerated. By the 1840s, this rate of change became so swift that no one and nothing could stop it.

Within the covers of this book are found the very best pictorial representations of Indian life made in the era before photography. Most historians, ethnologists, and anthropologists agree that they are possibly the best pictorial representations of American Indians in any medium. To feature in one book the work of Charles Bird King, George Catlin, and Karl Bodmer makes all their art feel more electric and absolutely comprehensive. Together these three artists chronicled the great majority of the tribes in what is now the continental United States, from Florida to New York, from Virginia to Idaho, as they appeared and lived in the 1820s and 1830s. (Gaps in their artistic witness do exist, however. None of the three artists painted the Indians of the Pacific Northwest, or the Great Basin, or the Pueblo people of the Southwest. No Navajo

9

or Apache were represented, nor were Mexican tribes, Inuit, or Eskimo.)

Within these pages may be found all of the lithographs from Thomas McKenney and James Hall's *Indian Tribes of North America,* as well as reproductions of many of Charles Bird King's surviving original paintings; a substantial representation of paintings by the prolific George Catlin; a nd a fine selection of the watercolors produced by Karl Bodmer in the Far West, including all his best Indian portraits. Books are available that present the work of each of these individual artists, but this is the first to offer high-quality color reproductions of the art of all three in one volume. The titles of the original

lithographs and paintings (which appear in boldface and quotation marks in the captions) have been left as the artists originally named them, complete with spellings of the names of individuals and tribal groups as they were applied in the 1820s and 1830s. The names used in the text and captions themselves conform to modern usage. In addition, the text establishes a context for their art, examining the events that took place during the era in which the paintings were made. Particular attention is given to the relocation of Indians enforced by the U.S. government, which led to the ultimate conquest of much of the continental. The cultural intrusions made upon on American

Indian people are also examined in some detail. The text draws extensively upon quotations from George Catlin, Bureau of Indian Affairs commissioner Thomas L. McKenney, and Karl Bodmer's patron Prince Maximilian of Wied-Neuwied, as well as U.S. Presidents and American Indian people themselves, so that the reader hears from those who made and witnessed the era's history.

Through their works of great historical testament and artistic vision, Charles Bird King, Karl Bodmer, and George Catlin allow us to travel back to a specific moment in time, when many aspects of American Indian cultures had been stable for fifty, or one hundred, or in some cases

10-11 *"Dance of the Mandan Indians," Lithograph after Karl Bodmer's Watercolor.* The Mandan people were hunters and farmers of the upper Missouri River who lived in what is today North Dakota. Their conical lodges, made of wood and earth, set them apart from the stereotypical concept of Indians who lived in tepees. The extremely hospitable Mandans were very open about their culture with European visitors, enabling the creation of images like this one by Karl Bodmer.

11 BOTTOM *"The Bear Dance," Lithograph After Catlin.* This lithograph is taken from a painting by George Catlin, who made his original sketches for it in the field in 1832; the painting was completed in 1835. It depicts an important dance among the Lakota or Teton Sioux people. Catlin's notes on the scene state that "the Sioux, like all others of these western tribes, are fond of bear's meat, and must have good stores of the 'bear's-grease' laid in, to oil their long and glossy locks, as well as the surface of their bodies. And they all like the fine pleasure of a bear hunt, and also a participation in the bear dance, which is given several days in succession, previous to their starting out." Catlin described the way the dance made contact with the spirit of the bear, and the way in which the dancers, some wearing bear masks, imitated the movements of the animal to be hunted.

two hundred years. The text and the colorful pictures presented here show us a world about to be overcome by drastic change, a world inhabited by native peoples who had their own forms of government, warfare, shelter, recreation, humor, and worship. Through the eyes of Indian people and the Euro-Americans who wished to save them, we can recognize how destructive and petty human beings can sometimes be. And we can be uplifted by the realization that, despite the odds, American Indian people and their vibrant cultures survived the onslaught of the nineteenth and early twentieth centuries and continue to exist today.

INTRODUCTION:
THREE ARTISTS MEET
THE WEST

It was not until the 1820s that a few visionary men began to realize that American Indians and their entire way of life were changing forever. Between 1820 and 1840, in the era before photography, three artists—Charles Bird King, George Catlin, and Karl Bodmer—set out to chronicle the faces and lives of American Indian people. Their very different lives and backgrounds converged in the patronage of Thomas L. McKenney, a man who had personally observed the rapid changes in American Indian life during the 1820s, in his role as the first U.S. commissioner of Indian affairs. Using his government position to advantage, McKenney commissioned King to paint portraits of Indian leaders who had been invited to Washington, D.C., to meet the president. When a young artist named George Catlin wanted to travel to the American West to paint Indian people, he sought out McKenney's advice and letters of introduction. Karl Bodmer, a Swiss-born artist who accompanied Prince Maximilian of Wied-Neuwied on his 1832-34 trip to America, also consulted with McKenney, after viewing lithographic prints of the Charles Bird King paintings in Philadelphia.

Although the three artists never met one another, they were familiar with each other's work. Their accomplishments were little appreciated during the 1820s and early 1830s, as a bustling, burgeoning America thought more about its own economic,

12 LEFT *Charles Bird King, Self-Portrait. Painted in 1855 when King was 70 years old, this self-portrait shows the artist many years after his major portraits of American Indian chiefs and warriors had been painted. It depicts King as a man of means, a cultured and refined member of the American art world.*

12 RIGHT *Portrait of Thomas L. McKenney, by Albert Newsam. This lithograph, made about 1837 by the same man who prepared the Indian prints for* Indian Tribes of North America, *served as the frontispiece for McKenney's memoirs. American Indians can be seen behind McKenney's chair, but it is unclear whether they are real*

Indians in McKenney's office, or Charles Bird King portraits. McKenney was noted for his tall, ramrod-straight physique, military bearing, and prematurely white hair. He came to know and respect Indian people and became an advocate for their welfare in the halls of government.

industrial, and cultural growth than about the original inhabitants of the continent, who were being pushed aside. Yet all three artists were equally important in chronicling the American Indian people.

King, Catlin, and Bodmer were not the first artists to penetrate the West or to depict the continent's original inhabitants. From the time of the first sustained contact with the native peoples of the Americas, many Europeans were consumed with an overwhelming curiosity about these hitherto unknown people. Europeans, and later Euro-American immigrants, were fascinated with descriptions, both verbal and pictorial, of "Indians"–the name mistakenly applied to them by early European explorers eager to reach Asia. As far back as the sixteenth and seventeenth centuries artists had recorded their appearance, some with sketches made in America, others with portraits painted during visits by Indians to Europe. But few of these pictorial representations were accurate or sympathetic to the cultural differences of Indian people, much less to the characteristics that distinguished one tribe from another. Nonetheles prints and engravings that supposedly showed American Indians in their native surroundings sold briskly. Nor did most early representations of Indian people take into account the effects of Europeans on the forms and substance of Indian cultures–least of all their devastation of Indian populations through disease and warfare.

The importance of the work of King, Catlin, and Bodmer lies in its general accuracy, its comprehensive scope, and the concepts that shaped it. Like their patron McKenney, they became aware before most of their contemporaries that the lifeways of American Indian people were in danger. They were insightful and bold enough to undertake an important mission and to preserve pictorially as much as they could of cultures that they believed to be vanishing. The immensity of their task, coupled with public apathy about the real problems suffered by Indian people, were realities that would affect the later lives of Thomas McKenney and George Catlin in particular.

Were Indian people really in danger, and were they about to disappear from the American scene in the 1830s? Were the artists and the commissioner justified in hastening to record and preserve information about American Indians? What was it that these men saw that their contemporaries missed?

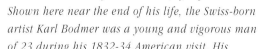

13 LEFT *George Catlin, Self-Portrait, 1824. This self-portrait shows the idealistic young artist at the outset of his career, prior to the formulation of his plan to record the likenesses of the various tribes of North America. Much of his handsome self-assurance comes through in this painting—an attitude that he must have had in large doses. Catlin traveled over most of the American continent and so far as we know never had a major disagreement with an Indian. Further, he was able to convince Indian people, who were suspicious of his artistic powers, to pose for him, to tell him about their tribal customs and ceremonies, and to take him along to festivals, religious rites, and buffalo hunts. Catlin, a salesman and a showman, had a personality people nonetheless trusted, even across cultural divides.*

13 RIGHT *Portrait of Karl Bodmer, by Loys Delteil. Shown here near the end of his life, the Swiss-born artist Karl Bodmer was a young and vigorous man of 23 during his 1832-34 American visit. His illustrations of the American landscape and American Indian people are perhaps the most accurate and beautiful depictions ever made of these subjects.*

14 TOP *Portrait of Thomas Jefferson.*
Jefferson, third President of the United States, was a visionary who imagined the American continent peopled with yeoman farmers, eventually sharing their country with assimilated American Indians. In 1803, Jefferson ensured the purchase of the Louisiana Territory from France, a tract of land extending from the Mississippi River on the east to the crest of the Rocky Mountains on the west. The $15 million purchase doubled the size of the United States, and for Jefferson it represented land enough for Americans to expand westward "to the thousandth generation." But the oldest tenants of the land called Louisiana were neither the French nor the Anglo-Americans, but the Native Americans. Resolving questions of land ownership and use between Euro-Americans and American Indians would be the overriding theme of the nineteenth-century West.

When President Thomas Jefferson authorized the Louisiana Purchase in 1803, doubling the size of the United States, he felt that the new territory would provide land for yeoman farmers to the "thousandth generation." Yet by the early 1830s, only one generation later, Americans were already pushing beyond the bounds of the original purchase into lands claimed by Mexico and Great Britain. Jefferson had felt that the United States was destined to span the continent from the Atlantic to the Pacific, but despite his reputation as a visionary, he was unable to predict the swiftness with which this settlement took place. The westward expansion of the United States was unprecedented in world history, not only in its pace and its permanence but also in its ruthlessness. For in the wake of settlement lay the ruins of hundreds of different cultural groups, more than five hundred nations composed of indigenous people.

King, Catlin, and Bodmer were correct in thinking that change was coming swiftly to American Indian people during the 1820s and 1830s. In every corner of North America, the pace of change was accelerating. Due to the fertility and richness of the continent, people in America were better nourished and healthier than their Old World counterparts; they grew taller, lived longer, and multiplied in greater numbers. This new and healthy land proved increasingly attractive to emigrants, who freely came from Europe to settle in the United States, attracted as well by the promise of state-endorsed religious tolerance and, by the 1830s, by the boast of suffrage for all white adult males.

The burgeoning population continued to move westward, where land was often obtained simply by the practice of "squatting." A squatter was a frontiersman who advanced to the edge of the last piece of privately owned land and began setting up a homestead on unsurveyed federal territory. Even before the Homestead Act of 1862 legalized it, squatters were allowed, more often than not, to retain their plots when

14

14 BOTTOM *Photograph of Frederick Jackson Turner.* Turner, the "father" of the study of the history of the American West, underscored the declaration by the U.S. Census of 1890 that the frontier was closed. One of the first historians to write about the frontier, he developed a cohesive theory about why the West was important to Americans. Born in 1862, Turner was a professor of history at the University of Wisconsin and later at Harvard. Although his "frontier thesis" has been debated by scholars for over a century, it remains a potent force in any discussion of the American West.

14-15 *"Fort Union," Lithograph After Karl Bodmer's Watercolor.* Fort Union, a fur-trading post established in 1829, was located on the Missouri River near the mouth of the Yellowstone. In 1833, when Karl Bodmer and Prince Maximilian visited the fort, it was one of the westernmost outposts of Euro-American culture, and a trading center for the area tribes, particularly the Blackfeet and Assiniboin.

15 RIGHT *"The Bellevue Agency Post," by Karl Bodmer.* Maximilian and Bodmer arrived at the Bellevue Agency, in present-day Nebraska, on May 3, 1833. The unfortified trading post included a church and a blacksmith's shop. Trade was carried on primarily with the Omaha tribe, after whom the modern city of Omaha, which grew up near the post, was named.

15 BOTTOM *"The Hunter Russell," by Karl Bodmer.* This watercolor is a fine example of Bodmer's talent at rendering character sketches. It is one of the few non-Indian portraits he made while in America. It was made on February 18, 1833, during the sojourn of Prince Maximilian at the New Harmony community in Indiana.

federal land offices opened an area for settlement. In the 1830s, it rarely mattered to the squatters or to the government that these lands were often reserved for Indian tribes by treaty. The white population was growing swiftly, a restless people who needed more "elbow room," and the Indians were expendable.

Such appropriatory attitudes toward the lands of the Indians were not motivated solely by racism, hatred, or greed. They often sprang from the completely different world-view held by Euro-American people. One of the first tenets of land ownership in crowded Europe was the rule of wise use: Land not used effectively and productively was being wasted. Land was meant to feed people, to increase exports and commerce, and to produce food during famines and wars. It was true that landed barons in Europe locked up vast tracts for private hunting preserves, and that large forest tracts had been cut before Europeans learned the virtues of

reforestation. But in America the forests seemed endless, and no landed barons held exclusive title to the territory. The application of English land law in America had long ensured that even squatters who filed a claim could keep their lands.

Encountering the frontier with these preconceptions, Euro-Americans were appalled by how American Indians used the land. Particularly in the Midwest, Indians were living in widely scattered villages, their small populations encompassing large tracts

tribes as sovereign nations, for many tribes were powerful enough to challenge U.S. military power. The United States would continue to negotiate as long as Indian tribes were strong enough to win on the battlefield or at least provoke an expensive war. For the most part, the U.S. government negotiated with Indian tribes for cessions of their land, trying to placate them with trade goods and eventually with annuities of food, clothing, and manufactured items. Altogether, at least 370 separate treaties were negotiated with Indian tribes following the Revolution, until

as hunting grounds and buffer zones against enemy tribes. By European standards, the land was not being used productively, and the amount of land compared to the number of people utilizing it was appalling. Why not make better use of the new continent's abundant promise?

*

Three overlapping and sometimes conflicting policies were employed by the U.S. government in reference to Native American people and their land. These policies can be described as negotiation, acculturation, and relocation. The United States began to establish its own Indian policy after the Revolutionary War, guaranteeing that Indians would keep their lands. "The utmost good faith shall always be observed towards the Indians," stated the Northwest Ordinance of 1787; "their lands & property shall never be taken from them without their Consent; and in their property, rights and liberty they shall never be invaded or disturbed, unless in just and lawful ways authorized by Congress." Those promises would soon prove hollow.

During this early period, the new and weak national government treated Indian

Congress abolished the practice of making such treaties in 1871.

Negotiation was not the only way that Euro-Americans in power dealt with Indian people. What the government could not win by war or treaty, it would achieve by acculturation. In 1819, Congress authorized an annual sum of $10,000 as a "civilization fund" to teach agriculture, reading, writing, and arithmetic to Native Americans, in hopes that they would adopt the ways of white society. The prevailing national attitudes assumed that Indians would either have to assimilate or be pushed westward as Caucasian civilization advanced. Few thought that Indians and non-Indians could successfully live side by side. As the nineteenth century wore on, the government was assisted in its goal of "civilizing" the Indians by Christian missionaries and the founders of private schools for this purpose, such as those at Hampton, Virginia, and Carlisle, Pennsylvania.

After the Louisiana Purchase in 1803, President Jefferson developed a third way of dealing with the Indians. The concept of relocation must have appealed to orderly eighteenth-century minds such as his, for it possessed a measure of logic. Since the land

16 LEFT *Portraits of Meriwether Lewis and William Clark by Charles Willson Peale. Lewis and Clark were the first explorers from the United States to cross the continent. Their expedition fulfilled a long-standing dream of Jefferson, and because it happened to coincide with the Louisiana Purchase, most of the land they explored actually belonged to the United States. Leading a contingent that included 29 soldiers, an Indian woman, and an African-American slave, they followed the Missouri River to the Rocky Mountains, and navigated the Snake and Columbia to the Pacific Ocean between 1804 and 1805, returning to St. Louis in 1806. They made first contact with many Indian tribes and tried to lay the groundwork for a fur-trading empire based in St. Louis.*

16 RIGHT *"Lewis and Clark Meeting the Indians on the Lower Columbia," by Charles Russell, 1905. Although Russell lived a hundred years after the Lewis and Clark expedition, his depictions of incidents on their "voyage of discovery" are some of the best ever made.*

17 *"Pet-A-Le-Shar-Ro, A Pawnee Brave." This image of Petalesharro, a lithograph after King's painting, is a prime example of the romanticization of Indian people.*

18 *"Po-Ca-Hon-Tas."* One of the most famous American Indians; Pocahontas lives more in American folklore than in history. As a young girl, she lived in the Powhatan Confederacy, a union of Indian people numbering at least 200 villages in what is now the state of Virginia. The legend about her rescue of Captain John Smith was first published in the General Historie of 1624; in writing about his own exploits in an earlier book, Smith did not mention the incident. According to the legend, in 1608 Smith, a captive of Powhatan, was about to be executed when the chief's daughter, Pocahontas, put herself between the white man and the ax to save his life.

Pocahontas would have been about 13 years old at the time. Her real name was Matowaka; her father used the word pakahantes, which meant "my favorite daughter," when speaking of her. Whether or not Pocahontas saved John Smith, it is known that she was a playful young girl who liked to spend time near the fort of the whites on Jamestown Island. In 1612 she was kidnapped by the English and held inside the fort while an exchange of prisoners was discussed with Powhatan. While living in the fort she fell in love with John Rolfe, "an honest gentleman," and soon converted to Christianity, taking the name Lady Rebecca. Her marriage to Rolfe was a fortunate one for the colonists, for despite many provocations, Powhatan kept the peace with them until his death. In 1616 Pocahontas sailed to England with her husband and was presented at the court of James I. As her ship prepared to return to America, she was stricken with smallpox and died at Gravesend, England, where she is buried today. She was only 22 years old. A son, Thomas Rolfe, had been born in England and returned to Virginia with his father, where he grew up to be one of the richest and most powerful men in the colony. Rolfe sired a dynasty that included some of the most prominent families in Virginia. The romantic legend of the "Indian princess" who married into a family prominent Euro-Americans continues today. This print, made in the 1820s, was copied from a portrait by R.M. Sully. The crumbling painting, now lost, is said to have been of Lady Rebecca when she arrived in England in 1616. A more famous portrait survives of Lady Rebecca wearing fashionable English clothing of the period.

west of the Mississippi was inhabited only by Indians, and since it would take many generations for Euro-American settlers to fill up the lands east of the river, why not move all unassimilated Indians to the west? To these policymakers, it made no difference that Indians who lived to the east of the Mississippi had different cultures and life ways from those to the west. After all, the thinking went, they were all Indians, and eventually they would all get along splendidly. An acre-for-acre exchange of lands in the East for those in the West would solve the problems of land-hungry whites and ease Indian acculturation by prolonging the process. The prospect of relocation could also be used as a threat or punishment, as evidenced by President Jefferson's thoughts in an 1803 letter to the governor of the Northwest Territory, William Henry Harrison: "Should any tribe be foolhardy enough to take up the hatchet at any time, the seizing of the whole country of that tribe, and driving them across the Mississippi, as the only condition of peace, would be an example to others, and a furtherance of our final consolidation."

It was the policy of relocation that would decide the fate of American Indians: During the mid-nineteenth century, U.S. government policy concentrated on the removal, at first voluntary and later by force, of Native Americans from their ancestral lands. Land was the key to American prosperity, and the happy yeoman farmer was thought to be the basis of true Jeffersonian democracy. Without land to provide to the growing populace, America would have faced an economic and social crisis. Land meant wealth, prosperity, and growth for nineteenth-century capitalists, for it could be exploited for precious metals, fur, timber, and agriculture.

Early in 1825, President James Monroe proposed to Congress that all the Indians who remained east of the Mississippi be relocated. Those living in New York, Ohio, Indiana, Illinois, and Michigan would be moved west of Lake Michigan and north of Illinois. The southern Indians would be moved west of the Mississippi. But Congress did not adopt Monroe's suggestions, and it

was not until the administration of Andrew Jackson, which began four years later, that the proposal became policy. Jackson believed that Indians should not continue to live in tribal groups as autonomous nations, and that they should be subject to the authority of the governments of the states in which they resided. While many commentators and policymakers felt that Indian people were not assimilating fast enough, Jackson felt that they were incapable of assimilation. He championed the Indian Relocation Bill, which he signed into law on May 28, 1830.

American Indians did not give in and vacate their lands as a result of the law. Some fought back with weapons, others challenged the law, and still others protested in the court of public opinion. But no approach availed the Indians, other than physically eluding the pursuers who would displace them. The tragic consequences of this law upon Indian people would be observed by Charles Bird King, George Catlin, and Karl Bodmer in the decade to come.

19 "Tah-Ro-Hon, An Ioway Warrior."

Tahrohon was one of many Indians interviewed by Thomas McKenney while he served as commissioner of Indian affairs during the 1820s. McKenney enjoyed Tahrohon's lively sense of humor. After a lengthy discussion of battles and horse raids, Tahrohon told him an anecdote about a raid on the Sioux. Game was unusually scarce on the Plains, he said, and the group had no food for the two days it took to reach the Sioux village. On an early morning scout, the hungry Tahrohon crawled through the grass and into the camp of the enemy. He spied what he thought to be two buckskin sacks filled with meal or corn, and in the dim light he picked them up, although they seemed very heavy. He quickly discovered that they were not sacks of food but the buckskin leggings of an old woman who was sleeping out of doors! This lithograph is taken from a portrait by Charles Bird King, painted in Washington, D.C. in 1837.

For King, Catlin, and Bodmer, the subject of the Indian people was fresh, new, and exciting. Yet, like most of their liberal-minded contemporaries, they romanticized American Indians as "noble savages." People of the early nineteenth century, schooled in the naturalistic philosophy of Jean-Jacques Rousseau, extolled the virtues of wilderness and deplored the filthy conditions of urban areas. Americans like Thomas Jefferson believed that the source of America's success lay in its land. A country composed of honest farmers, all living on land that they themselves owned, would constitute a stronger and healthier nation than any in Europe, according to Jefferson. The American Indian was the pure but raw manifestation of a life lived in concert with the earth—an icon that many white Americans venerated and emulated.

Authors such as James Fenimore Cooper, in his *Leatherstocking Tales*, applied this image of the natural human creature to the white man by romanticizing the frontiersman. Cooper's hero was a man who continually moved ahead of the wave of "civilization" to rediscover the purity of wilderness, only to be forced to move on when eastern settlers arrived to plant towns and farms on the frontier. For Cooper and figures like him, civilization was a corrupting influence. It stood to reason, at least for these philosophers and authors, that the people who had always lived in the unspoiled wilderness, the most wild and uncivilized people of all, the Indians, were the most pure and least corrupted people in the world. Most notably in *The Last of the Mohicans* (1826), Cooper's Indians were noble and stoic, acquiring the mythological status of ancient Greek gods.

Sculptors of the day portrayed Indian people in the classical poses of Greek and Roman statuary, and painters such as Thomas Cole depicted fanciful Greek temples in American forests. A certain level of the American intellectual community of the time admired Indian people for their childlike innocence and luck at escaping the bonds of civilization. George Catlin, after meeting and painting the Indians of the West, wrote that he had "for a long time been of the opinion, that the wilderness of our country afforded models equal to those from which the Grecian sculptors transferred to the marble such inimitable grace and beauty; and I now am more confirmed in this opinion, since I have immersed myself in the midst of thousands and tens of thousands of these knights of the forest; whose whole lives are lives of chivalry, and whose daily feats, with their naked limbs, might vie with those of the Grecian youths in the beautiful rivalry of the Olympian games."

Catlin, King, and Bodmer all brought their own cultural backgrounds and personal sensibilities to the creation of their Indian paintings. All saw their subjects as noble,

primitive people unaffected by Euro-American culture. All felt an urgency to record their cultures and lifestyles before they were lost forever. Although Indian cultures would ultimately survive the deprivations inflicted upon them, King, Catlin, and Bodmer were alarmed by the seemingly relentless march of *Euro-American* "civilization" across the continent. From the perspective of the 1820s and 1830s, the relentless push westward seemed to spell doom for the Indians. They would either assimilate or die.

Along with other chroniclers of the Indian, King, Catlin, and Bodmer were influenced by recent archeological discoveries that provided them a broader perspective on the development culture over time. According to this perspective, cultures became important and perhaps grew

20 BOTTOM *"Two Ball Players," Lithograph from a Catlin Original. George Catlin became fascinated with the Choctaw Indian game of ball, which he observed in Arkansas in 1834. He created many sweeping canvases of the ball play and made portrait sketches of the unique attire of ball players. The game, similar to lacrosse, was played with hundreds of participants upon a wide field, with very few rules and no referees.*

20-21 *"Buffalo Chase, A Surround By the Hidatsa," 1832-33. In this method of hunting buffalo, two columns of Hidatsa hunters on horseback approached the herd from two different directions, gradually getting closer. When the herd picked up the scent of their pursuers, they "fled in a mass in the greatest confusion." Catlin, who sketched the scene from a distance, recorded that "a cloud of dust was soon raised, which in parts obscured the throng where the hunters were galloping their horses around and driving the whizzing arrows or their long lances to the hearts of these noble animals; which in many instances, becoming infuriated with deadly wounds in their sides, erected their shaggy manes over their blood-shot eyes and furiously plunged forwards at the sides of their assailant's horses, sometimes goring them to death at a lunge, and putting their dismounted riders to flight for their lives."*

21

22 TOP *This engraving, dated 1875, depicts a scene common in spring: fur traders in a mackinw boat, loaded with bales of buffalo and other skins, are attacked by Indians while descending the Missouri River.*

22 BOTTOM *"The 1837 Rendezvous," by Alfred Jacob Miller.* This depiction of an important annual event was painted by an eyewitness, Alfred Jacob Miller, who chronicled the life of the mountain man. Even while Euro-Americans were moving into the Midwest on the eastern side of the Mississippi, entrepreneurial trappers and traders moving into the Far West to trap beaver. Some American Indians, especially those who had visited the East, realized that these entrepreneurs were but the spearhead of further western settlement. The mountain men explored and mapped the rivers and streams of the Rocky Mountains, noting the passes that would one day bring covered wagons and farmers to the Pacific Coast. As the pursuit of the dwindling stock of beaver moved farther and farther from any city or major transportation route like the Missouri River, the St. Louis fur companies maintained their trappers in the Rockies by holding a yearly Rendezvous in the mountains. The trappers brought their pelts to the Rendezvous and traded for supplies with the St. Louis entrepreneurs, who traveled to the assigned spot by wagon train along the Platte River Road. The Rendezvous was a time for serious trading, but it was also a boisterous, no-holds-barred party at which contests, races, and tests of strength alternated with the heavy consumption of liquor.

23 BOTTOM *"Approaching Chimney Rock," by William H. Jackson.* At the beginning of the 1840s, Euro-American settlers began to penetrate the Rocky Mountains and settle the Pacific Coast. In 1846-48 the United States fought a war with Mexico to gain territory, and in 1848 gold was discovered in California. These events stepped up the rate of transcontinental migrations, so that by 1866, when this painting was made, more than 300,000 Euro-Americans had moved into the Far West, disrupting the lives of countless tribes and tribal groups. During the 1850s, most of the Indians in California were exterminated through either conflict or disease.

22-23 *"Washinga Sahba's Grave on Blackbird Hills."* On May 7, 1833, Maximilian and Bodmer passed the grave of Washinga Sahba along the Missouri River. Maximilian quoted the explorer Stephen Long, who reported that Washinga Sahba had ruled his people, the Omaha, through false magic and the poisoning of his enemies. "An epidemical smallpox carried him off, with a great part of his nation, in the year 1800, and he was buried, sitting upright upon a live mule, at the top a green hill on Wakonda Creek. When dying, he gave orders that they should bury him on that hill, with his face turned to the country of the white men." Maximilian

also noted that "Washinga-Sahba was so feared by his own people, that nobody ventured to wake him when he slept." Maximilian and Bodmer received first-hand information from Indian people through interpreters as well as second-hand stories like this one, from fur traders who spoke French or English. Maximilian and Bodmer spoke English as a second language. As a result of the language barriers, the observations of all non-Indian reporters must be considered carefully, although it must be said that Maximilian and Bodmer were more sensitive to cultural differences than most of their contemporaries.

rich and powerful, but they did eventually die. All over the world in the early nineteenth century, the fossilized remains of ancient creatures were being unearthed, casting doubt upon literal interpretations of the biblical Book of Genesis and leading scientists to ponder the fact that an entire ecosystem of animals, all extinct, had lived on the earth before human beings. The term *dinosaur* was coined in the 1830s to refer to some of the lizard-like remains being found in England; King, Catlin, and Bodmer all saw a mastodon skeleton that was unearthed by Charles Willson Peale and displayed in his Philadelphia museum. If animals could thrive and become extinct, so could races and cultures. These discoveries gave a sense of mission to the three men—the urgent preservation through art and description of the lifeways of the original Americans, who were being overrun by Euro-American interlopers and seemed on the threshold of extinction.

Part of their mission was based on a fallacy, however. Not only would Indian cultures persist, but King, Catlin, and Bodmer did not, indeed could not, ever see Indians in a pristine state, unaffected by Euro-Americans. By the time King painted Indians in his Washington studio and Catlin and Bodmer traveled west, all American Indian tribes had had contact with Europeans. Although the tribes of the Upper Missouri

and Great Plains were less affected than other groups, the lives of all Indians were significantly different in 1830 from what they had been two hundred years earlier. Europeans had brought the horse, which freed Plains tribes from the confines of village life, enabling them to travel vast distances on hunts and raids. Some tribes became completely mobile, with no fixed village sites whatsoever. Iron implements, weapons, and cookware also changed Indian life, as did the advent of firearms. Many Indians procured these items by trade with other tribes, but by 1830 direct trade with whites was common throughout the West.

Although Catlin and Bodmer chronicled tribes that were relatively unaffected by European influences, life for Indian people was never static or isolated, either before or after European contact. It would be more accurate to say that Catlin and Bodmer recorded the lives not of culturally uncontaminated "noble savages" but of tribes as they existed in the early 1830s, freezing a single moment for us to behold and study nearly two hundred years later. That the societies they chronicled were forever changed by European contact cannot be denied. Only three years after the visits of the artists, several tribes, most notably the Mandan and Hidatsa, were struck so severely by disease that their lifeways were brought to

a virtual end. Although some traditions, customs, and religious elements survived, the village tribes never recreated the community that existed before 1837.

Although they romanticized the "noble savage," King, Bodmer, and Catlin were inevitably part of a Euro-American culture that believed itself superior to the cultures of everyone else. Not only did Euro-Americans feel themselves superior, but they also felt that their way of life was the only right way. This conviction was preached in the realm of

economics by proponents of the capitalist system, and in religion by Christian denominations. A good Christian was expected to spread the word of his or her faith to bring more believers into the fold. Heavenly rewards were not available to nonbelievers, according to most Christian sects. In general, Euro-American culture assumed and propagated its own supreme, received, and God-given worth; all nonbelievers, whether in economics, religion, democratic politics, agricultural methods, or land use,

24 TOP *"The Funeral Scaffold of a Sioux Chief."* Karl Bodmer, fascinated by the customs of the various Indian peoples he encountered, recorded many of them pictorially for Prince Maximilian and for posterity. This view shows the funeral custom of many Plains tribes of placing the dead on a scaffold with their earthly possessions. These burial sites were places of great power that were not to be disturbed.

24-25 *"The Scalp Dance of the Minatarees."* Adapted from a watercolor painting made by Karl Bodmer in the spring of 1834, this scene depicts a fascinating dance in which women of the Minatree (Hidatsa) tribe dress in men's clothing to celebrate male deeds on the field of battle.

25 TOP *"The Encampment of the Piegan Blackfeet."* Bodner created this panoramic view in Europe from several of the watercolors he had made in America in 1833. The groups of people in different parts of the scene were taken from individual portrait sketches. The lithograph brilliantly brings to life the immense and vibrant scene of the Blackfoot encampment, with its many and varied personalitites, its prized ponies, and ever-present dogs. Bodmer accurately shows the varying sizes and irregular spacing of the tepees.

had to change or be forever lost.

In contrast to the recent arrivals on the continent, American Indian people had very adaptable cultures. Indians were quite willing to assimilate those aspects of other cultures which they admired, while at the same time retaining their traditional ways. If new ways came into conflict with old ones, the better of the two might be adopted and the inferior one rejected. In the case of religion, American Indians saw nothing unusual about accepting the teachings of Christ and at the same time holding on to their ancient beliefs and religious systems.

That Indians would go to a Christian church and then attend a traditional religious ceremony devoted to "pagan" gods horrified Euro-American missionaries, who saw it as their duty to make the Indians give up their traditional religious beliefs completely. From differences in attitudes toward land use and different ideas of the role of culture, the cultural collision between Euro-Americans and Native Americans in the 1830s would cause untold strife and tragedy, both in individual encounters and through the broadest strokes of government.

*

The era's most far-ranging act of cultural superiority, Andrew Jackson's Indian Removal Act of 1830, had a profound and immediate effect on the Sac and Fox tribes, who inhabited Illinois, eastern Missouri, and Wisconsin. The effects of this act would define the environment in which King, Catlin, and Bodmer experienced the lives of the American Indians they painted.

In 1804 the Sac and Fox tribes had signed a treaty with the U.S. government that ceded a large portion of their land on the east side

of the Mississippi in exchange for an annuity of $1,000. The treaty stipulated that as long as the land continued to be a part of the public domain, the Indians could remain on it to live and hunt. However, squatters began to move into the area in the 1820s, going so far as to establish claims near the main Sac village, located near the confluence of the Rock and Mississippi rivers. Squatters even fenced the Sac cornfields, beating Indian women who tried to climb the fences and cultivate them. Boundaries were set by the whites, and if Sac children crossed them they were, whipped. Indians were accused of stealing, and the Euro-Americans burned their homes as retribution.

Around 1828 A Sac named Black Hawk was out hunting one day when he encountered three white men. "They accused me of killing their hogs," he wrote in his autobiography, "[and] I denied it, but they would not listen to me. One of them took my gun out of my hand and fired it off —then took out the flint, gave back my gun and commenced beating me with sticks and ordered me off. I was so much bruised that I could not sleep for several nights."

Black Hawk was a war leader of his people, a short, thin man about 65 years old, according to his own reckoning, who was looked upon as being wise and fair-minded. He and his tribe had sided with the British during the War of 1812 afterward and continued to resent Americans and the terms of the 1804 treaty. Neapope, a principal Sac chief, counseled war with the whites, as did the "Winnebago Prophet," a half-Sac, half-Winnebago who was thought to have mystic powers.

Being a prudent man, Black Hawk refrained from encouraging war, but in the summer of 1831, he became angry with whites who insisted on selling whiskey to his people. For the most part, distilled or fermented beverages had been unknown to the Indians of North America before the advent of the Europeans. It was soon discovered that many Indian people had little tolerance for liquor. Many whites took advantage of this situation, getting Indians drunk to make a profit through liquor sales, to coerce them into signing treaties that would strip them of their lands, or to make unfair trades for goods such as animal pelts. Breaking several barrels of the squatters' whiskey, Black Hawk reiterated his previous warnings and told the whites that if they would not leave his country, the Indians would have to force them to go.

Black Hawk's ultimatum caused panic among the homesteaders, who appealed to Illinois governor John Reynolds for protection. A proclamation calling for volunteers was distributed throughout the state, drawing a military force of 1,600 volunteers and nearly a thousand U.S. government troops. Making camp near the Sac village, the troops convinced Black Hawk that his cause was hopeless. That evening all his people slipped west across the Mississippi to Iowa. Black Hawk was forced to sign a peace treaty that contradicted the 1804 agreement, forbidding the Sac to return to the east side

of the river. Arriving in Iowa too late in the season to start a new crop of corn, the Indians nearly starved during the winter of 1832.

Cultural differences between whites and Indians became glaringly obvious in the spring of 1832, when a war party of Sac and Fox traveled up the Mississippi to Prairie du Chien to avenge the killing of some of their people by the Menominee. When the Sac and Fox killed twenty-eight Menominees in the raid, American authorities demanded that the killers be turned over to them for punishment. Black Hawk refused, and the U.S. government began putting together a force to make him comply.

The Sac chief Neapope had visited British authorities in Canada and reported to Black Hawk that several tribes, including the Ottawa, Ojibwa, Potawatomi, and Winnebago, would combine with British forces to assist Black Hawk in regaining Sac land. Neapope's scheme involved a consolidation of the Sac with the Prophet's Winnebago tribe, 30 miles up the Rock River in Illinois. During the summer they could grow corn and store enough food for an autumn campaign against the squatters. Black Hawk was convinced by Neapope's plan; he began to recruit volunteers, despite opposition from Keokuk, a chief who believed that the whites were too powerful to be overcome.

26 *"The Trapper's Bride," by Alfred Jacob Miller.* In 1837 Alfred Jacob Miller traveled to the Far West Iwith the Scottish nobleman William Drummond Stewart and lived the life of a mountain man. Miller's drawings and paintings depicting the lifestyle and customs of these hardy, lonely adventurers in the waning days of the fur trade are the best views ever made of this legendary era. Many trappers married American Indian women, paying the fathers of the women with horses and other trade goods. An Indian wife not only eased loneliness but was an important asset in preparing furs for market. Many of these Indian women were abandoned when trappers returned to Euro-American civilization at the end of the fur trade era.

27 TOP *"The Baptism of Pocahontas at Jamestown, Virginia, 1613."* In the rotunda of the U.S. Capitol in Washington, D.C., eight paintings representing American history are featured. Four portray incidents in America's revolutionary struggle with Great Britain; four depict scenes from America's exploration. The Baptism of Pocahontas is the only painting in which an Indian is the central figure. Here, in this 1840 canvas, the conversion of a "pagan" savage to Christianity is celebrated. On a deeper level the painting shows the submission of an Indian woman before white male conquerors as well as a seminal myth of American history. According to that myth, inferior Indian cultures melded with the culture of the Europeans, such that the Indians' lives were improved by the experience. The implied exchange of superior knowledge and religion for land was thought by European settlers to be more than a fair trade. It took Euro-Americans hundreds of years to understand that Indian people did not see this "exchange" in the same light.

27 CENTER RIGHT *"John Eliot among Native North Americans."* In 1646, Reverend John Eliot, the minister of the Puritan church of Roxbury, Massachusetts, began to work among the American Indians, converting them to Christianity. As he converted them, they were moved into special villages, where they were trained to live like Europeans. Eventually,

fourteen of these villages, so-called "praying towns," were established. Eliot's activities contain the seeds of all the future benevolent policies used by the U.S. government in Indian relations, including the encouragement of cultural assimilation, conversion to Christianity, and physical relocation to a controlled environment.

27 CENTER LEFT *"Mohawk Schoolmaster."* One of the chief goals of the U.S. government, following its independence from Great Britain, was to Christianize and "civilize" American Indian people, thus freeing them from dependence on the land and opening vast tracts to the growing Euro-American population. One of the best ways to reach this goal was to educate Indians, and with a "Civilization Fund" provided by the U.S. government, Indian schools were set up across the country. As one of the earliest woodland tribes to have extensive contact with whites, the Mohawk had many men who were trained in European ways, some with degrees from Euro-American schools. These men were able to educate the boys of the tribe in reading, writing, and arithmetic, allowing them to get along in a world increasingly overrun by whites.

27 BOTTOM *Frontispiece of Eliot's Bible.* To help Indians learn to read and write, Eliot, with the aid of several converted Indians, translated the Bible into the Massachusett tongue in 1663. It was printed at Harvard College under the auspices of the Corporation in England for the Propagation of the Gospel Amongst the Indians in New England. Eliot's was the first Bible in any language ever printed in the Western Hemisphere.

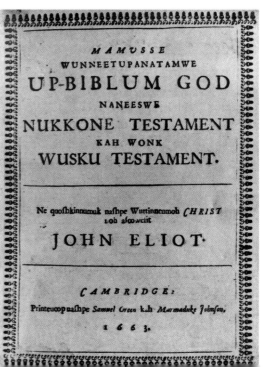

28 *Portrait of William Henry Harrison by Rembrandt Peale, c. 1814.* Harrison was a warrior who almost singlehandedly forced Indian people out of the Old Northwest, through treaties, coercion, or military force. Born into a wealthy Virginia family, he studied medicine but entered the army to fight on the frontier under Anthony Wayne. Active in territorial politics, he was appointed governor of the Indiana Territory in 1800, where his struggles with Tecumseh and the Prophet began. Although the efforts of Tecumseh and Tenskwatawa ended only in death and dissipation, Harrison's exploits against the Indians helped elect him President of the United States in 1840. Using the campaign slogan "Tippecanoe and Tyler Too," he and his running mate John Tyler won in a landslide over incumbent President Martin Van Buren. At age 68, however, Harrison was elderly and weak. After a lengthy inauguration speech he caught cold, and he died just one month after taking office, in April 1841.

29 *Lithograph by Catlin showing North American Indians.* This group of American Indian people, probably from the lower Missouri River Valley, is a composite of three separate portraits. The buffalo robe worn by the man on the left has pictographs extolling his prowess in battle. The portrait of the woman is a rare early view showing a woman full-length, depicting her modest dress, beautifully decorated robe, and the leggings covering her ankles.

Black Hawk did not realize that homesteaders in Illinois wanted an Indian war as much as he did. Through warfare they could take revenge on the Indians, while Indian resistance would ensure that they would be removed from Illinois permanently.

On April 6, 1832, Black Hawk, along with five hundred warriors and their wives and children, crossed the Mississippi and joined the Prophet in Illinois. Gen. Henry Atkinson of the U.S. Army, who was marching toward Iowa with a small force to confront Black Hawk about the Menominee murders, received word that Black Hawk was now east of the river. He appealed to Governor Reynolds for help, and once again a proclamation was issued calling for volunteers. Settlers panicked and fled, or moved into larger settlements for protection. Black Hawk made no hostile moves and in fact quickly discovered that Neapope's information had not been accurate; no coalition of Indians and British troops would aid him. He retreated farther north, planning to withdraw to the west side of the Mississippi if government troops pursued

him. Black Hawk sent out three Indians under a flag of truce to negotiate with a force of Illinois militia, but the amateur soldiers overreacted and shot one of them, causing Black Hawk to attack with a small force. Although outnumbered 340 to 40, the Indians chased the whites from the field in the Battle of Stillman's Run. Black Hawk moved northward into present-day Wisconsin, where he was joined by small numbers of Winnebago and Potawatomi, who set about burning farms and killing squatters. A full-scale Indian war threatened, whose echoes were heard in Washington.

President Jackson ordered that an example be made of Black Hawk, that his force be defeated, and that he be captured or killed. It was an election year, and Jackson's voice thundered in the dispatches. The army began a relentless pursuit of Black Hawk's band, which quickly turned toward the Mississippi. The Indians abandoned most of their equipment and soon ran out of food. Some were eating the bark off trees as they reached the threshold of starvation. Others, unable to keep up, were found in the woods

by the pursuing army troops and were summarily shot and scalped.

The army overtook the Sacs while they were crossing the Wisconsin River. Black Hawk fought a brilliant rearguard action to allow the women and children to escape. With the arrival of nightfall, many of the noncombatants were put on a raft and floated down the Wisconsin River to safety. But the army knew of this escape attempt and sent word to Fort Crawford to stop it. When soldiers from the fort spotted the raft coming down the river, they opened fire, killing many and capturing thirty-two women and children.

Meanwhile, Black Hawk's band continued toward the Mississippi. Soldiers found corpses in the woods of Indians who had died from their wounds or from starvation. On August 1, Black Hawk finally reached the river, but there were only three canoes to make the crossing. The Sacs began to ferry their force across the river, but in the afternoon a steamboat named the *Warrior* appeared. Black Hawk went to the shore with a flag of truce and announced

30 TOP *1827 Map of North America*.
This original map shows the United States
during the administration of President
John Quincy Adams. As the predominantly
Anglo-American population pushed
westward, lands formerly inhabited by
American Indians and later claimed
by France and Spain became
Louisiana Purchase lands. New
states entering the Union included
Louisiana in 1812, Indiana (1816),
Mississippi (1817), Illionois (1818),
Alabama (1819), and Missouri (1821).
A successful revolution in Mexico in 1821
expelled the Spanish and opened the new

nation of Mexico—which at that time included
Texas, New Mexico, Nevada, Colorado, Arizona,
and California—to trade with the United States.
In the Pacific Northwest, a treaty provided for
joint ownership of the Oregon Territory by the
United States and Great Britain. As the United
States became larger, it took on more problems.
Missouri wrote a constitution allowing slavery to
exist within its borders, but many abolitionists
did not want slavery to extend into the western
territories. A compromise in 1820 allowed Maine
to enter the Union as a free state, and Missouri to
enter as a slave state. This sectional strife would
continue without respite until the nation was
dissolved in Civil War from 1861 to 1865.

30 BOTTOM *Portrait of James Monroe.*
Monroe, the fifth President of the United States,
served between 1817 and 1825. He settled
boundary disputes with Spain over Florida and
Louisiana, and with Britain over the Oregon
question and the Canadian border, and he issued
his famous Monroe Doctrine, declaring that
European nations could not interfere with the
nations of the Americas. Caught in the midst of
all these changes were American Indian people.
During his administration, Monroe shifted away
from Jefferson's vision of Indian assimilation and
voluntary removal to lands west to the Mississippi,
to endorsing a policy of forced removal of all
eastern tribes. Monroe's removal policy was not
adopted by the United States until the Indian
Removal Act was passed in 1830 under Andrew
Jackson.

31 LEFT *William Clark Certificate of Peace
with the Indian Tribes, 1815.* Paper certificates
like this one, issued by William Clark as
superintendent of Indian affairs at St. Louis, were
awarded to chiefs along with peace medals. Lesser
members of a tribe might be issued silver arm or
wrist bands, gorgets, or military coats. Tribes were
also given special U.S. flags (with eagles rather
than stars) to fly above their villages. When U.S.
medals, flags, or uniforms were issued,
comparable gifts that had been given to the
Indians by other powers, such as Great Britain
and Spain, were confiscated by U.S. authorities.

that the Sacs wished to surrender. His reply was cannon fire from the boat. A fire fight developed between the two sides, and at nightfall the boat withdrew.

The following morning, as the Sacs continued to ferry their women and children across the river, the main force of the army attacked. The so-called Battle of Bad Axe quickly turned into a rout for the outnumbered Indians, and at least 150 were drowned as they tried to swim the river. Over 150 more were killed by the soldiers and guns on the steamboat *Warrior*. Only fifty Indians survived and were taken prisoner. The 300 who crossed the river were attacked and slaughtered by Sioux warriors who had been paid by the whites. Altogether, only 150 Indians out of the thousand who left Iowa on April 4 survived the so-called Black Hawk War.

For defying the Euro-Americans, Black Hawk's people were annihilated. They had been betrayed by the Winnebagoes, who led the army to them for a bribe of twenty horses and $100 cash. Jackson had succeeded in sending his clear message. No other tribe of the Midwest ever again rebelled against United States authority. Black Hawk was one of the survivors of the final battle; he was taken prisoner to be displayed to curious crowds in the East. He finally returned to live with Keokuk's Sacs on their reservation along the Des Moines River in Iowa, where he died on October 3, 1838. His skeleton was preserved and kept by the governor of the Iowa Territory on view in his office.

Black Hawk's story was but one of many that, for McKenney, Catlin, King, and Bodmer, demonstrated the ruthlessness of land-hungry Euro-Americans in the 1830s. Another was the story of the forced relocation of the "Five Civilized Tribes" of the southeastern United States. The Cherokee, Creek, Choctaw, Chickasaw, and Seminole tribes were called "civilized" because they had adopted, to a greater degree than most other nations, the clothing, culture, and technology of the Euro-Americans. In particular, the Cherokee had, over the course of a hundred years, become one of the most assimilated tribes in America. They dressed like white Americans, lived in homes like those of white Americans, farmed land in the European way, and even, in some cases, owned black slaves like their white neighbors. Numbering about 25,000 people living in sixty villages, the Cherokee established their own constitutional government with a senate, a house of representatives, and a democratically elected chief. The Cherokee had their own schools, and a brilliant young man named Sequoyah had even developed a written

31 RIGHT *Portrait of Andrew Jackson, by Ralph Earl. Born in 1767 on the border between the two Carolinas, Jackson had moved to Tennessee by 1788. A trained lawyer and politician, he gained his greatest fame as a soldier, leading troops against Indians and the British. On August 30, 1813, an Indian named William Weatherford led an attack on Fort Mims, Alabama, touching off the Creek War. Jackson responded by leading a militia force southward, where he experienced both victories and losses. On March 27, 1814, he gained a decisive victory over the Creeks at the Battle of Horseshoe Bend. A treaty was signed at Fort Jackson on August 1, 1814, where Jackson demanded that the Creek pay for the cost of the war. Payment was made in land, 23 million acres of it, encompassing large portions of Alabama and Georgia. During the War of 1812, Jackson won important victories over the British at Pensacola and New Orleans. In 1818, he led an attack on the Seminoles in Spanish-held Florida. His Seminole War enabled the purchase of Florida by the United States from Spain in 1819, but it also led to 40 years of sporadic guerrilla fighting with the Native Americans. Elected President of the United States in 1828, Jackson supported the Indian Removal Act of 1830 and believed that Indians and whites could never live side by side. It was with his administration that Thomas Jefferson's dream of a United States inhabited by whites and assimilated Indian people died. Jackson, known to Indian people as Sharp Knife, lived until 1845.*

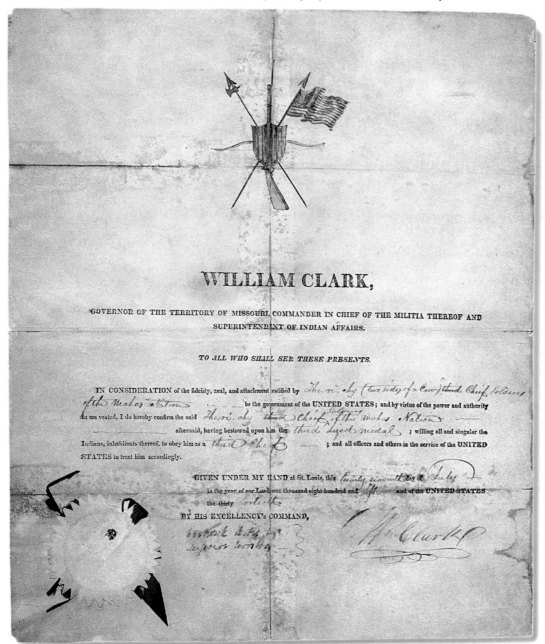

WILLIAM CLARK,

GOVERNOR OF THE TERRITORY OF MISSOURI, COMMANDER IN CHIEF OF THE MILITIA THEREOF AND SUPERINTENDENT OF INDIAN AFFAIRS.

TO ALL WHO SHALL SEE THESE PRESENTS.

IN CONSIDERATION of the fidelity, zeal, and attachment testified by *The mi chy (two sides of a Cow) third Chief Soldier* of the Mahas Nation to the government of the UNITED STATES; and by virtue of the power and authority in me vested, I do hereby confirm the said *The mi chy third Chief of the Mahas Nation* aforesaid, having bestowed upon him the *third sized medal*; willing all and singular the Indians, inhabitants thereof, to obey him as a *third Chief*; and all officers and others in the service of the UNITED STATES to treat him accordingly.

GIVEN UNDER MY HAND at St. Louis, this *twenty seventh* day of *July* in the year of our Lord, one thousand eight hundred and *17* and of the UNITED STATES the thirty *fortieth*

BY HIS EXCELLENCY'S COMMAND,

language for their native tongue.

But no matter how "civilized" the Cherokee became, the residents of Georgia wanted their tribal cornfields in order to plant cotton. Many white squatters moved onto Indian lands and set up farms there without permission, challenging the Indians in court for their right to the property. To add to the misery of the Indians, gold was discovered on Cherokee land in 1829. A general cry arose for Indian removal. The whites thought the law was on their side. The state of Georgia had made a deal with the federal government in 1802, which declared that after the state ceded its claims to western lands (which comprised the modern-day states of Alabama and Mississippi), the government would extinguish all Indian titles to land within the accepted boundaries of Georgia and move the Indians peaceably to the West.

Actually, a number of Cherokees had moved over the years, to be resettled in present-day Missouri, Arkansas, and Oklahoma. These "western Cherokees," numbering about 8,000, were unpopular both with white homesteaders and with the powerful Osage Indians

native to the area. Reports of their troubles in the new lands did nothing to convince tribal leaders in Georgia that a move west was in their best interest.

President Jackson backed the right of Georgia to remove the Indians, and the passage of the Indian Removal Act in 1830 made their removal inevitable. Each of the Five Civilized Tribes handled the impending removal in its own way, resisting for as long as possible. The first to move were the Choctaw, who signed the Treaty of Dancing Rabbit Creek in 1830. The Choctaw moved out of Mississippi in 1833 in a winter blizzard, barefoot and short on blankets and rations. By 1834, 12,800 Choctaw had been removed to Indian Territory in the modern-day state of Oklahoma. Next came the Creek from Alabama. Although they protested about the settlers who had come to squat on their lands, and the enforcement of Alabama laws upon them, their living conditions had become so bad that they were forced to sign a treaty on March 24, 1832. The government reneged on promises to protect their lands from white encroachment, and they were defrauded of most of their property. With resentment rising against the intruders, hostilities erupted in the spring of 1836 as the Creeks fought U.S. troops in a short-lived resistance effort. The Creeks were removed during 1836, with 2,500 "hostile" Indians in chains. An overloaded steamboat capsized along the way, drowning more than 300 Creeks. Altogether, 14,609 Creeks were moved to Indian Territory. Due to their small numbers, the Chickasaw of Arkansas and Mississippi were not able to mount an effective resistance; they signed a treaty on October 20, 1832, and were moved in 1837.

The Cherokee, however, were not about to leave quietly. They insisted upon staying on their ancestral lands, declaring that they had the force of law behind them.

As conditions worsened among the tribe, a minority faction of the Cherokee headed by subchief Maj. John Ridge decided to sign the Treaty of New Echota on December 29, 1835. The treaty agreed to the emigration of the entire nation and ceded their lands east of the Mississippi after a two-year period. The U.S. Senate, though aware that the treaty did not reflect the wishes of the majority of the Cherokee people, ratified it anyway by one vote.

The majority factions of the tribe, headed by John Ross, refused to give up or be moved. They had heard about the hardships and deaths encountered by other Indians trudging to Indian Territory. Their case was argued before the U.S. Supreme Court in *Cherokee Nation v. Georgia,* and surprisingly, the Indians won. Chief Justice John Marshall affirmed their sovereign status and that they had an "unquestioned right to the lands they occupy." But President Jackson had other ideas about the Cherokee. Although the

32 LEFT *"Ma-Ka-Tai-Me-She-Kia-Kiah, or Black Hawk, A Saukie Brave." After the capture of Black Hawk in 1832, the notorious Indian leader became an immediate celebrity. He spent the winter imprisoned at Jefferson Barracks, just south of St. Louis, where the author Washington Irving came to describe him in prose and the artist George Catlin to immortalize him on canvas. In the spring of 1833, Black Hawk was brought to the White House to meet President Jackson, then proceeded through Norfolk, Baltimore, Philadelphia, and New York, where he was greeted by cheering crowds. Far from being reviled, Black Hawk was greeted by friendly and curious crowds. This portrait of Black Hawk, by Charles Bird King, was completed in 1837.*

32 RIGHT *"Tens-Kwau-Ta-Waw, The Prophet."* Tenskwatawa was a Shawnee medicine man and mystic, the younger brother of the famous leader Tecumseh. Born about 1775, Tenskwatawa was witness to the dissipation, rejuvenation, and eventual removal of the Shawnee to the West. He lost an eye when still a child and wore a scarf over the empty socket. The Prophet's portrait was painted by James Otto Lewis in Detroit in 1823. This print, from McKenney and Hall's Indian Tribes, was made from an 1829 Charles Bird King copy of the Lewis painting. Tenskwatawa also had his portrait painted by George Catlin in 1832, after his removal to a Shawnee reservation on the south bank of the Kansas River. The Prophet died in November 1836 and is buried somewhere beneath modern Kansas City, Kansas.

33 *"Keokuk, Chief of the Sac and Fox."* Keokuk led the opposition within the Sac tribe to the policies of Black Hawk. Unlike Black Hawk, Keokuk was a distinguished diplomat, warrior, and chief—truly the headman of his tribe. He was born about 1783, the son of a half-French mother and a Sac father. He gained prominence in his tribe due to his skills as a warrior and a politician. Since Keokuk was amenable to removal, his goodwill was cultivated by U.S. authorities throughout the 1820s. After Black Hawk's defeat in 1832, Keokuk was appointed principal chief of his people. In 1837 he visited Washington, D.C., at the head of a delegation of

Sac and Fox, successfully arguing against the Dakota Sioux in favor of territorial claims in the state of Iowa. It was at this time that his portrait was painted by Charles Bird King. Arrayed in all his finery, Keokuk poses with his son Moses, who later became a Baptist minister. Both father and son wear unidentifiable peace medals, possibly from the Monroe administration. Keokuk holds a highly decorated spear, and his son sits on a shield. This is one of the rare full-length Indian portraits by King. He was also painted by George Catlin. Keokuk died in Kansas, to which his tribe had been removed, in 1848. In 1883, his remains were moved to Keokuk, Iowa.

highest court in the United States had granted the Cherokee the right to remain in Georgia, Jackson knew that Marshall's opinion was only print on a piece of paper and defied it. He sealed the fate of the Cherokee, allegedly stating that "Mr. Marshall has made his ruling, now let him enforce it."

By the May 1838 deadline of the Treaty of New Echota, only 2,000 Cherokee had departed west, leaving 15,000 in the South. Under President Van Buren's orders, the army rounded up the Cherokee and led them to detention camps. Often herded like cattle, the Indians were dragged off at the point of bayonets, without time to gather up their belongings. As soon as the army took away the Indians, their homes and fields were burned behind them by gleeful white settlers. Army Gen. John Ellis Wool, who took part in the round-up, noted that "the whole scene since I have been in this country has been nothing but a heart-rending one . . . I would remove every Indian tomorrow beyond the reach of the white men, who, like vultures, are watching, ready to pounce on their prey and strip them of everything they have."

Over the hot summer, dysentery, measles, and whooping cough spread through the ill-provisioned tribal camps, where at least 2,000 Cherokee died. Because the army had handled the relocation so badly, Principal Chief John Ross of the Cherokee negotiated with Gen. Winfield Scott to permit the Cherokee to conduct their own removal overland. As a result 15,000 Cherokee began moving 1,200 miles westward to Indian Territory during 1838 and 1839. Before the migration ended, at least 2,000 more Indians died and were buried in shallow graves along the route. The total death toll came to about 4,000, or one in four of the Cherokee who were relocated. Their journey came to be known as the "Trail of Tears."

The Seminole of Florida, the last of the five tribes to face removal, resisted the army so relentlessly for seven long years that their removal was never wholly accomplished. They fought so fiercely in part because their tribe was a mixture of Creek Indians and African-American slaves who had escaped bondage in the South to seek refuge in the Florida swamps. The slaves intermarried with the Seminole and rose to respected

positions within the tribe. If they were captured, these African-Indians could be returned to slavery under terms of U.S. law, although the government denied that any former slaves would be repatriated to their masters under the removal process. In order to retrieve the African-Americans, however, the government concocted a treaty stating the desire of the Seminole to move west, obtaining the signatures of chiefs who did not represent the entire tribe. Confronted with compulsory relocation, the Seminoles launched a guerrilla war.

A Seminole named Osceola rose to prominence in leading the Indian resistance. Osceola hated the whites and was a ruthless commander determined to stop their advance at all costs. When a Seminole chief surrendered to the whites and agreed to move west, Osceola murdered him. Osceola led a brilliant campaign against the whites, but he was captured and imprisoned. He died in shackles in 1838. Many Seminoles were moved to Indian Territory by 1841, but many others hid in the swamps, fighting on. The army had troops involved in fighting Seminoles until 1858, but the war was never

34 LEFT *"The Battle of Bad Axe," 1832.*
This lithograph shows the climactic portion of the battle, when Sac and Fox men, women, and children were driven by U.S. soldiers into the Mississippi and were caught in a crossfire by guns aboard the steamboat Warrior. *The raft was ferrying Sac and Fox refugees to the Iowa side of the Mississippi when the battle erupted.*

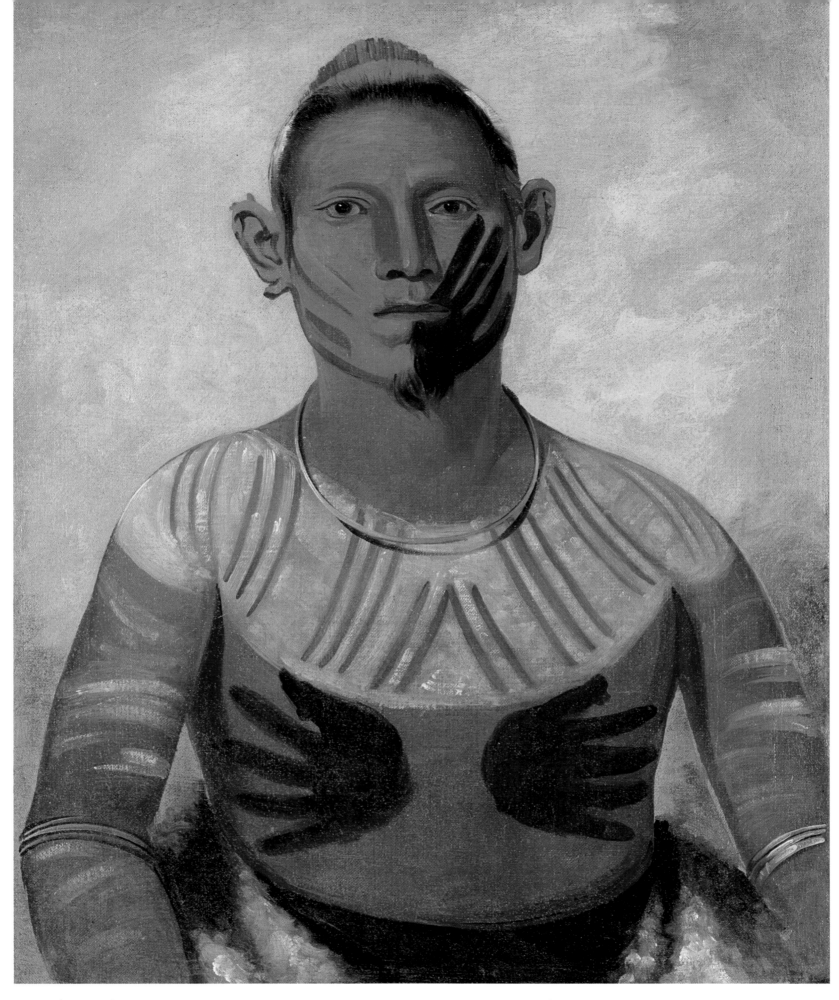

won, and Seminole people continue to live in Florida today.

The stories of the Black Hawk War and the Indian removals from the South show the determination of Euro-Americans to gain lands and move Indian people aside during the 1830s. Many of the tribes they moved were close to assimilating and finding a niche within the Euro-American culture, but the greed and racism of the early settlers quashed any hope of coexistence, as the government enforced the removal of the Indians. Their forced relocation tribes ranks as one of the most

tragic episodes in American history, although it is little known today.

This same pattern of land acquisition was repeated throughout the nineteenth century, with ever-greater horrors and consequences for American Indian people. As Americans pushed west of the Mississippi River in the 1840s and 1850s, the Indians of the Plains and of California sometimes became targets of the settlers. In contrast to the portrayal in Hollywood movies of marauding Indians attacking emigrant wagon trains, Indian people were actually helpful to the immigrants, and statistics prove that more

34 RIGHT *"Kai-Pol-E-Quah, White Nosed Fox."* *This print of a Charles Bird King portrait dated 1824 shows a chief of the Oshkosh band of the Sac and Fox; the other main band of the tribe was the Kishko, which was led by Keokuk. The European officer's sword carried by Kaipolequa may have been a sign of his rank.*

35 *"The Ioway, One of Black Hawk's principal Warriors, Sac and Fox,"* **1832.** *The Ioway was painted when he was a prisoner of the whites at Jefferson Barracks in 1832. The hand-print design in his war paint may signify the fact that he killed enemies in hand-to-hand combat.*

HARRISON & REFORM

36 TOP AND 36-37 *"The Battle of Tippecanoe," by P.S. Duval.* *Tenskwatawa was impetuous and often felt that the process of building the Indian confederacy was taking too long. Despite orders from Tecumseh not to fight the whites until the confederacy was together, in late 1811 he ordered an attack on the forces of Gen. William Henry Harrison. While Tecumseh was away organizing southern tribes, Tenskwatawa's attack was turned into a bloody rout by Harrison, in what became known as the Battle of Tippecanoe Creek.*

36 BOTTOM *"William Weatherford of the Creeks Submitting to Andrew Jackson After the Battle of Horseshoe Bend at the Talapoosa River, March 1814."* *William Weatherford, the Creek leader who sparked the Creek War in 1813, was defeated by Andrew Jackson on March 27, 1814, at the Battle of Horseshoe Bend. The defeat led to the treaty of Fort Jackson in August 1814, in which the Creek ceded over 23 million acres of their lands as "payment" for launching a war against the white intruders.*

Indians were killed by immigrants than immigrants by Indians. The Great Sioux War of 1876, the flight of the Nez Percé in 1877, and the Apache resistance of the 1880s are better known today because they happened closer to our own time and involved even larger numbers of Indian people than the events of the 1830s.

*

By 1890 the conquest was over. A young historian named Frederick Jackson Turner concluded from that year's census that settlement by Euro-Americans had reached all the formerly unsettled portions of the United States that had been called "frontier." The "frontier line"—beyond which the number of

inhabitants dwindled to less than two persons per square mile—no longer existed. Turner brought the end of the frontier to the attention of the American public in an 1893 essay he read at the World's Columbian Exposition in Chicago. Entitled "The Significance of the Frontier in American History," it was perhaps the most appropriate paper ever read to an assembled crowd; the Columbian Exposition itself was celebrating the four hundredth anniversary of the landing of Columbus in the Western Hemisphere.

Americans hadn't thought much about the frontier until it was gone. What would the country be like without a frontier? Would the lack of Jefferson's yeoman farmers erode the American spirit and its democratic politics? Would the nation's growth outstrip its food supplies? Would its character suffer, with no wilderness into which the adventurous could disappear and reinvent themselves? These questions provoked a crisis in American

thought. From the time the continent had first been settled by Europeans, America had been seen as a place of inexhaustible land and resources. Always, just beyond the fringe of civilization, there had been room to stretch out for a better life, with good, rich earth, free to anyone who was daring and hard-working enough to claim it and use it. Now, many thought that the adventure of American life was over. There were no more wild lands to flee to, and the future would consist of sprawling urban areas with citizens dutifully working in factories and turning their backs on nature.

The loss of the frontier also meant the disappearance of the American Indian from the consciousness of Euro-Americans. The Indian had always been synonymous with the frontier, but in the very year the frontier was declared to be nonexistent, 1890, the last battle of the Plains Indian wars was fought. A one-sided affair that many called

not a battle but a massacre, the clash at Wounded Knee Creek seemed to signal the end of the influence of the Indian on the development of America. The grisly photographs of Chief Bigfoot's frozen body in the snow graphically depicted the end of Indian ownership of the continent. The American Indian people, who are thought to have numbered some four and a half million at the time of European contact in 1492, had lost 95 percent of their aggregate population by 1890, when fewer than 240,000 survived. It was only a matter of time until the remainder either died off or assimilated into the more populous Euro-American culture.

The defeat, forced departure, and devastation of the Indians meant that fewer white Americans would interact with them, which in turn allowed Euro-American stereotypes of the Indians to prevail. Although most modern Americans genuinely want to learn about the American Indian

39 TOP AND CENTER RIGHT *"Se-Quo-Yah."*
One of the most famous Indians of all time, Sequoyah invented a syllabary composed of 86 characters representing the different sounds of the Cherokee language. In 1821 he produced his syllabary to refute the idea that only the whites could produce such a useful tool. On February 21, 1828, the first issue of the Cherokee Phoenix *was published in a log cabin, using the written language. The state of Oklahoma honored Sequoyah by placing a statue of him in the U.S. Capitol in Washington. The giant redwood trees of the California coast were named Sequoia in his honor. This portrait was painted by Charles Bird King in 1828.*

Cherokee Alphabet.

D a	R e	T i	Ꮼ o	O u	i v
S ga O ka	F ge	Y gi	A go	J gu	E gv
Ꮺ ha	P he	Ꭿ hi	F ho	Γ hu	Ꮛ hv
W la	C le	P li	G lo	M lu	Ꮮ lv
Ꮇ ma	O me	H mi	Ꭷ mo	Y mu	
Θ na Ꮛ hna G nah	Λ ne	h ni	Z no	Ꮔ nu	O nv
T qua	Ꮫ que	P qui	V quo	Ꮻ quu	E quv
U sa Ꮻ s	4 se	b si	Ꮪ so	Ᏹ su	R sv
L da W ta	S de T te	Ꮧ di Ꮨ ti	A do	S du	Ꮫ dv
Ꮝ dla L tla	L tle	C tli	Ꮩ tlo	Ꮨ tlu	P tlv
G tsa	V tse	Ꮱ tsi	K tso	J tsu	C tsv
G wa	Ꮻ we	O wi	O wo	Ꮢ wu	6 wv
Ꮿ ya	B ye	Ᏹ yi	Ꮒ yo	G yu	B yv

Sounds represented by Vowels

a, as *a* in *father*, or short as *a* in *rival*
e, as *a* in *hate*, or short as *e* in *met*
i, as *i* in *pique*, or short as *i* in *pit*

o, as *aw* in *law*, or short as *o* in *not*
u, as *oo* in *fool*, or short as *u* in *pull*
v, as *u* in *but*, nasalized.

Consonant Sounds

g nearly as in English, but approaching to k; d nearly as in English but approaching to t. h,k,l,m,n,q,s,t,w,y, as in English. Syllables beginning with g, except Ꮙ have sometimes the power of k,h,t,s; are sometimes sounded to, tu, tv; and Syllables written with tl except Ꮭ sometimes vary to dl.

37 CENTER LEFT *"McIntosh, A Creek Chief."*
McIntosh, a Creek war chief, distinguished himself in the battles of Atasi in 1813 and Horseshoe Bend in 1814. McIntosh's people, the Creek, were given their name by English traders because they built their villages along woodland creek and streams. In reality, the Creek were composed of several bands with similar cultural attributes. The Creeks, along with the Cherokee, Choctaw, Chickasaw, and Seminole, were known by the whites as the "Five Civilized Tribes" because their progress toward assimilation seemed more advanced than that of other Indians. At the end of the Creek War, pressure for the removal of the Creek to the West increased, and McIntosh gave in. On February 12, 1825, he signed the Treaty of Indian Springs, relinquishing Creek lands in the state of Georgia. Outraged, the Creeks sent out an execution squad to find him. On May 1, 1825, McIntosh was killed in retribution for signing away Creek lands to the whites. This portrait of McIntosh was painted by Charles Bird King, probably in 1825, when he was in Washington during Senate ratification of the Treaty of Indian Springs.

37 BOTTOM *"Me-Na-Wa, A Creek Warrior."*
McKenney called Menawa the Indian "Rob Roy" Thomas of the southern frontier. Like the hero of Sir Walter Scott's novel, Menawa did all he could for his people. At the Battle of Horseshoe Bend in 1814, he was wounded seven times and fought until he collapsed. Just 70 out of 1,000 warriors survived the battle. When the question of Indian removal split the Creek nation, Menawa sided against the Euro-Americans. After McIntosh signed the Treaty of Indian Springs in 1825, Menawa was given the task of executing him. Menawa traveled to Washington in 1826 to sign a treaty and was persuaded by McKenney to sit for this portrait. During the Seminole War, Menawa decided to help the whites in exchange for the promise that he could keep his lands. He tried to mediate the Seminole War, and when that failed, he led his warriors against the Seminole alongside U.S. soldiers. At the conclusion of the fighting, Menawa returned to his home to find that his lands had been confiscated. He had no choice but to follow his family west, but he told his neighbors that he wished "never again to see the face of a white man."

37

peoples, many myths and false notions remain to be overcome.

One of the biggest and most enduring misconceptions about Indians is that they are all one people. Nothing could be further from the truth. Indians cannot be one culture or one identity any more than Europeans can. To say that Navajos are like Lakotas is analogous to saying that Swedes are like Spaniards. Regional customs, religious beliefs, types of food and food preparation, crafts, folk tales, shelter, and social structures all continue to make individual Indian tribes singular.

White Americans tend view all Native Americans as being like the Plains Indians, when only a portion of Plains Indians actually lived in tepees and developed a semi-nomadic lifestyle of hunting buffalo. The Plains people were among the Indian people depicted by Charles Bird King, George Catlin, and Karl Bodmer. Thanks in part to their paintings, it was the Plains Indians who caught the imagination of the Euro-American public, with their seemingly free-spirited and adventurous mode of living. The average clerk or schoolboy in the nineteenth century could achieve vicarious thrills by imagining himself running off to join the Indians of the Plains. Because the Plains Indians were among the last of the Indian cultural groups to be forced to live on reservations, they were most often depicted as representing the "real Indians" of the frontier, long after the work of King, Catlin, and Bodmer was

copied and augmented by other western artists and photographers and, eventually, Hollywood moviemakers.

The more the real Indians disappeared from the American consciousness, the more the stereotype prevailed. The noble red man with a full headdress of eagle feathers, his long hooked nose reminding the viewer of his Indianness, his dark skin hinting at his savage past, became the way most Americans thought of their nation's first inhabitants. Since for most Americans the "real Indians" had disappeared with the frontier, Indian iconography was used to represent the vanished wilderness. The characteristics of the frontier so prized and coveted by Euro-Americans—characteristics that they themselves had destroyed by overpopulating and industrializing the landscape—seemed to be summed up by the faces of Indian chiefs used in advertising commercial products. Indian faces stared at the viewer from the pages of magazines, from gasoline pumps, from statues in front of cigar stores, from the sides of railroad engines and automobiles, and even from the jerseys of sports teams. In Hollywood movies, Indians became a favorite subject, although few roles were actually played by Native American actors. And on film, while Indians might at times be perceived as natural or noble, the movies taught Euro-Americans that Indians were savage, ruthless, primitive people who crept up on their victims at night and murdered them in their beds.

It remains difficult for contemporary Americans to envision Indian people separate from the stereotypes, particularly if their exposure to "real Indians" is limited. An Indian businessman in a suit, or Indian construction workers, schoolteachers, forest rangers, or U.S. Senators, continue to be difficult images for Euro-Americans to accept. The social cultural life of real Indians is elusive for the popular imagination.

In the late 1960s and early 1970s, protests by American Indian people called attention to the plight of neglected reservations, where malnutrition, alcohol abuse, unemployment, and high infant mortality were prevalent. Many Americans were not only shocked to learn of reservation conditions but surprised that there were so many American Indians still around. In fact, at the beginning of the twentieth century, for the first time since 1492, the population of Indian people began to rise. Indian people not only became more numerous, but they also successfully bridged the gap between the two worlds in which they were forced to live—the larger Euro-American world and the traditional world of their own cultures. Many became successful in business, others went into public office or managed tribal affairs, and still others won fame in the arts. Some continued to live on reservations, while others lived alongside Euro-Americans in towns and cities. In their success, American Indian people were particularly adept at holding on to their individual cultures. Most immigrants to America, be they from Europe, Africa, or

38 *"Trail of Tears," by Robert Lindneux.* *Painted in the twentieth century to give an idea of the bitter hardships encountered by the relocated Cherokee, this is one of the few illustrations in existence depicting this historic event.*

38-39 *Map of Indian Removal. After the Louisiana Purchase in 1803, President Jefferson championed a scheme whereby unassimilated American Indian people who lived east of the Mississippi River would be moved to the west side, thereby giving them time to assimilate and making room for land-hungry Euro-American farmers. During the successive administrations of James Madison and James Monroe, Indian tribal leaders were encouraged to move their people westward, but few were interested in leaving their ancestral lands for the unfamiliar, uncertain areas of the West. In addition, the small number of early removals created friction with tribes who already occupied the lands west of the Mississippi. In 1830, however, with the sanction of President Andrew Jackson, Congress passed the Indian Removal Act. The U.S. government would no longer give Indian people a choice; those who remained east of the Mississippi would be removed. Those living in New York, Ohio, Indiana, Illinois, and Michigan would be moved west of Lake Michigan and north of Illinois. The southern Indians would be moved west of the Mississippi. The massive disruptions in Indian life that took place between 1830 and 1840 as a result of the Indian Removal Act are chronicled on this map.*

STI REGIS 1796

TONAWANDA 1797

TUSCARORA 1797

ONEIDA 1788

OTTAWA AND OJIBWA 1836

ONONDAGA 1788

BUFFALO CREEK 1797

CATTARAUGUS 1797

OIL SPRING 1797

ALLEGANY 1797

SIOUX HALFBREEDS 1830

ONEIDA 1831

STOCKBRIDGE 1831

WYANDOT 1818

WYANDOT 1817

METOSINIA 1838

HALF BREEDS (OMAHAS. ETC.) 1830

IOWA 1836 / SAC AND FOX 1836

DELAWARE 1829

KICKAPOO 1832

KANSA 1825

OJIBWA 1836/OTTAWA 1831

KASKASKIA AND PEORIA 1832

SHAWNEE 1825

WEA AND PIANKASHAW 1832

POTTAWATOMIE 1837

MIAMI 1840

NEW YORK INDIANS 1838

CHEROKEE NEUTRAL LAND 1835

OSAGE 1825

QUAPAW 1833 SENECA 1831

SENECA AND SHAWNEE 1831

CHEROKEE OUTLET 1828

CHEROKEE 1828

CREEK 1833

CHEROKEE 1828

CHICKASAW 1837

CHOCTAW 1820

SEMINOLE 1833

39 TOP "John Ross, A Cherokee Chief."
John Ross was the articulate and brilliant leader
of the Cherokee faction who resisted relocation.
Born about 1790 along the Coosa River in
Georgia, his father was Scottish, his mother part
Cherokee and part Scottish. In 1809 Ross visited
the Arkansas Cherokee, thus seeing for himself the
western lands to which the whites were so eager
to move his people. In 1813, he married Quatie,
an almost full-blooded Cherokee, and established
Ross' Landing at present-day Chattanooga,
Tennessee. Ross helped establish a republican
form of government among the Cherokee and
moved to the new national capital—New Echota,
Georgia. The discovery of gold on Indian land
negated both the force of law and a Supreme
Court ruling, and the Cherokee were forced west
over the "Trail of Tears" in 1838. Quatie died
along the way. Although never implicated in the
murders of John Ridge, his son, and Elias
Boudinot, Ross never denounced them. He was
elected principal chief of the Cherokee in 1839.
He died in Washington, D.C., on August 1, 1866,
having supported the Confederacy during the
Civil War. The Charles Bird King portrait,
like the one of John Ridge, shows an assimilated
American Indian dressed in Euro-American
clothing.

**39 BOTTOM "Major Ridge, A Cherokee
Chief."** His Cherokee name was Nunnadihi, or
"He Who Slays the Enemy in the Path," and he
was born about 1771 in what is now Tennessee.
As a boy he fought the white settlers who came
over the mountains, until in 1793 a treaty was
signed with the Cherokee in Philadelphia. From
that point on, the man who became John Ridge
was obsessed with leading his people toward
adopting the ways of the Euro-Americans. He
built roads and was an important member of the
tribal council. When a tyrannical chief named
Doublehead emerged, Ridge was selected to
assassinate him—and carried out the task. Ridge
was a longtime opponent of removal, but over the
years he was worn down by the many pressures
that threatened to destroy his people if they did
not relocate. He signed the Treaty of New Echota
in 1835, which sold Cherokee lands in exchange
for territory in the West. In 1839, after Ridge
moved his people to the Indian Territory, he was
killed by the John Ross faction of the Cherokee,
along with his son and Elias Boudinot, the editor
of the Cherokee-language newspaper the Phoenix.
Ridge's portrait was painted by Charles Bird King
in 1835; his Euro-American clothing and the
ambience of the print yield no clue that he
is a Native American.

39

Asia, preserved their cultural heritage for two or three generations but soon became assimilated Americans. Although they remained proud of their background and heritage, few national or ethnic groups have been as successful at preserving their cultural and religious heritage as have American Indians.

Many Americans claim to have Indian ancestry—their numbers rise on census reports with each decade. The 1980 census listed about 1.5 million Indian people, while the 1990 census listed just under two million —a 40 percent increase in ten years! The U.S. Census Bureau says that a person who identifies himself or herself as an Indian is, at least in the eyes of the Census Bureau, an Indian. No official tribal affiliation is required to list oneself as an Indian. Granted, some tribes, like the Cherokee and Pequot, require that a tribal member have a lower percentage of Indian blood than other tribes do. But the suspicion exists that many Americans claim Indian heritage on the census who could never qualify as a member of an officially recognized Indian tribe. Many people may have been told by their grandparents that "there was an Indian who married into the family," usually an "Indian princess" in the mold of Pocahontas. Such images of Indian ancestor, are nonthreatening to Euro-Americans and gives them a sense of ownership of the American continent.

For most Euro-Americans, the image of the Indian continues to represent the primal loss of the frontier. A sense of guilt, a sort of

40 TOP LEFT *"Foke-Luste-Hajo, A Seminole."*
In 1835, when U.S. government agents were eager to have the Seminole sign the Treaty of Payne's Landing, they agreed to allow seven chiefs to travel westward to see the land the government was offering, then return to report to their people. Foke-Luste-Hajo was one of the seven, all of whom returned to sign the treaty. President Jackson sent a letter to the Seminole urging them to move, which was read at the treaty council. "Even if you had a right to stay," Jackson said, "how could you live where you now are? You have sold all your country. You have not a piece as large as a blanket to sit down upon." Because he supported removal, a price was put on the head of Foke-Luste-Hajo by his fellow Seminoles. He stayed within the walls of the U.S. Army's Fort Brooke for protection during the war. Foke-Luste-Hajo was painted by Charles Bird King in 1826.

40 TOP *"Chittee Yoholo, A Seminole Chief."*
Chittee Yoholo was an important war chief who opposed removal. In the early morning hours of March 29, 1836 ,he led an attack upon a large force of U.S. light cavalry and their Creek auxiliaries, killing them to the last man. In the end, however, he was forced to surrender at St. Augustine. In the summer of 1842, by the time the government announced that the eight-year Seminole War was finally over, it had spent $20 million dollars subduing the tribe, with the loss of 1,500 soldiers. In the end, many of the Seminoles stayed in Florida, but Chittee Yoholo gave up his lands and moved West. In this print, taken from Charles Bird King's 1826 portrait, Chittee Yoholo wears a caped hunting jacket, a white shirt and high collar with cravat, and an impressive series of five silver gorgets with a peace medal suspended around his neck. A large silver band covers a red bandana on his head.

40 BOTTOM *"Seminole Indians Attack a Blockhouse," 1840.* *Fort Brooke was established in 1824 on Tampa Bay and was a major staging area for the U.S. Army during the Seminole wars. The first Seminole War lasted from 1816 to 1821, the second from 1835 to 1842, and the third from 1856 to 1858. The bloodiest of the wars was the second, during which Seminole warriors resisted forced relocation. Fort Brooke was one of three Florida forts (the others being Fort Scott and Fort Clinch) used as supply areas during the second Seminole War.*

"original sin," pervades American thought about their conquest of the continent. Although many Americans continue to justify the struggles of the nineteenth century, saying that "might makes right" and "to the victor belong the spoils," others are amazed and sickened by what their ancestors did to Indian people.

Some twentieth-century Euro-Americans have gone to extremes in their obsession with Indians and in their wish to remedy their own cultural and religious barrenness. Hobbyist groups take on the dress, crafts, traditions, and even language of some tribes, holding powwows and "becoming" Indian. Practitioners of New Age religions conduct vision quests, naming ceremonies, and sweat lodge rituals for a fee, using active Native

41 *"Asseola, A Seminole Leader."* Osceola inspired his people to fight the Euro-Americans and never surrender their lands. He was born about 1803 near the Alabama-Georgia border, and although many sources claim he was part European, he claimed to be a full-blood Seminole. He moved to Florida with his mother about 1815 and fought Gen. Andrew Jackson in the first Seminole War of 1816-21. On May 9, 1832, a group of the Seminoles signed the Payne's Landing treaty, which surrendered Seminole lands, required evacuation to western lands within three years, and decreed that any Seminoles with African blood be treated as runaway slaves. Osceola soon emerged as an implacable foe of removal, swearing to kill any Seminole who would sell out his people. In April 1835, one group of Seminoles was preparing to move West, while Osceola dug in for a fight, traveling from band to band and urging resistance. Indian agent Wiley Thompson forced many Seminole leaders to sign a new treaty at Fort King, including Osceola, who was held in irons until he was forced to sign, but then he escaped into the wilderness. In November Osceola's men killed Charley Amathla, a leader of the Seminoles who were willing to move West; the money Amathla had received in payment for supporting the whites was left scattered over his dead body. On December 28, 1835, while one group of Seminoles killed more than 100 U.S. soldiers in the "Dade Massacre," Osceola led a party that ambushed Thompson, killing him and six others. For two years Osceola led his people in a guerrilla war, opposed by four U.S. Army generals in succession. It was only when Gen. Thomas Jesup took the field, leading 8,000 soldiers in a vicious campaign that borrowed the Indians' own guerrilla tactics, that the tide started to turn against the Seminoles. Jesup could not defeat or capture the wily Osceola, however. It was only through treachery that Osceola was taken. In October 1837, Osceola agreed to attend a peace council at St. Augustine under a flag of truce. When he arrived, Jesup ordered Osceola's arrest, and the Indian leader was immediately struck on the head and chained, along with members of his band. They were taken to Fort Moultrie, South Carolina, where Osceola painted himself for war and welcomed death, which came on January 30, 1838. The post surgeon displayed the remains of Osceola in a medical museum in the fort, until it was destroyed by fire. This portrait of Osceola is from a painting by an unknown artist. One of the few full-length portraits in the McKenney and Hall Indian Tribes *portfolio, it shows Osceola in a calico hunting shirt with woven sashes and red leggings. A series of three gorgets are worn around his neck. Incongruously, tepees are shown behind Osceola, despite the fact that none of the southeastern tribes lived in them. A beautiful portrait of Osceola was painted by George Catlin, just days before his death in 1838.*

42 TOP *"Old Bear, A Medicine Man," 1832.*
Catlin had a problem when Mahtoheha, a medicine man of the Mandan tribe, objected to his portrait painting. Mahtoheha told those waiting outside Catlin's venue that if their image was painted, they would soon die. The number of Mandans waiting to be painted began to dwindle, and Catlin had to think quickly. He told Mahtoheha that he had been looking at the

medicine man for several days and was pleased with his appearance. The portraits he had been making on the previous days, he said, were but practice runs so that he might do a portrait of the Old Bear justice. The artist's flattery did its work, for Mahtoheha sat down, the two smoked a ceremonial pipe together, and then the medicine man left for his lodge to prepare. After several hours, Mahtoheha reappeared, "bedaubed and streaked with paints of various colours," Catlin recalled, "with bear's grease and charcoal, with medicine-pipes in his hands and foxes' tails attached to his heels... He took his position in the middle of the room, waving his eagle calumets in each hand, and singing his medicine song... looking me full in the face until I completed his picture." After this, Mahtoheha was Catlin's strongest supporter.

42 BOTTOM *"Snowshoe Dance at First Snowfall," 1835-37. Along with the Sioux, Catlin also encountered the Chippewa or Ojibwa people in the North. This Ojibwa dance was an occasion when "they sing a song of thanksgiving to the Great Spirit for sending them a return of snow, when they can run on their snow shoes in their valued hunts, and easily take the game for their food." Catlin never actually saw this dance performed during the winter months; perhaps the Ojibwa recreated the scene for him, or perhaps he invented it based on the information he had been told by the Indians.*

42-43 *"Ojibwa Portaging Around the Falls of St. Anthony." The Falls of St. Anthony are located within the modern-day boundaries of Minneapolis, along the Mississippi River.*

American religious sites against the wishes of tribal leaders. Many Indian people are uncomfortable with the new-found popularity of their cultural and religious beliefs. They are offended by mimicry of their customs, and by aggressive attempts to obtain information about their most sacred and private rituals. Being an Indian was not always so popular or healthy in America; one wonders if the Americans who today wish so fervently that they were Indians would be so excited if they had to march along the "Trail of Tears" in 1838, stand on the gibbet at Mankato in 1862, or withstand the gunfire of Hotchkiss guns at Wounded Knee in 1890.

*

When the three artists in this book were meeting American Indian people, the Black Hawk War and Indian removals were making national headlines. Catlin, King, and Bodmer painted the Indian celebrities of their day: Black Hawk, Osceola, Keokuk, John Ross, and others who either resisted removal or sided with the whites. The stories of the Sac and Fox, the Seminole, and the Cherokee particularly disturbed Catlin as he traveled the West, for he knew that it was only a matter of time before the Indians of the Far West—the Sioux, Blackfeet, Comanche, Mandan, and others he befriended—would be similarly threatened with removal or annihilation. When Bodmer wintered with the Mandan, he too realized that the way of life he was witnessing would not last long. The story is indeed depressing, but we are fortunate today that a few individuals had the foresight, nearly 150 years ago, to

44 *"Tel-Maz-Ha-Za, Creek," 1834.*
Catlin painted this portrait in 1834 in the vicinity of Fort Gibson. Tensions were high on the Arkansas frontier, due to the number of Indians from eastern tribes who were moving onto lands traditionally the hunting grounds of

the Osage. The Creek built their homes near the fort, where they could not only receive protection from the Delaware and Osage but also make a living by providing the army with meat and produce from their farms.

chronicle the cultures of Indian people that were rapidly slipping away. In hindsight, it is amazing that so few Euro-Americans saw what was happening, and that so few cared.

Foremost among the persons responsible for chronicling the Indians of America at this crucial point in their history was Thomas L. McKenney, superintendent of the Indian trade and later commissioner of Indian affairs. McKenney took advantage of the official visits of Indian delegations to Washington, D.C., by arranging to have portraits painted of each visiting chief and dignitary. Most of these portraits were painted by Charles Bird King (1785–1872). McKenney championed government sponsorship of the largest artistic project of his time, in order to preserve the customs and appearance of American Indian people. Upon his removal from office, McKenney spearheaded a project to publish lithographs of King's Indian portraits, in a book entitled *The Indian Tribes of North America.* The importance of this book in disseminating information about the history and appearance of American Indian people cannot be underestimated.

At about the time that McKenney's book was being readied for publication, a young artist named George Catlin (1796–1872) became fascinated with the idea of preserving the cultures of American Indian people through works of art. Much as John James Audubon recorded the bird and animal life of the continent for posterity, Catlin wanted to do the same for the Indian. While King painted Indian portraits in Washington, Catlin wanted to go a step further and paint Indian lifeways in the field. It is estimated that he painted scenes of 48 tribes, completing at least 310 unique portraits and 200 genre scenes. He took his paintings on a tour of eastern cities, giving most Euro-Americans their first real idea of how the Indians of the plains lived. Sailing to Europe, he put on "Wild West Shows" with real Indian dancers, thirty-five years before Buffalo Bill did the same.

At the same time Catlin traveled up the Missouri River in 1832, a German prince named Alexander Maximilian of Wied-Neuwied arrived in Boston, accompanied by a Swiss painter named Karl Bodmer (1809-1893). Maximilian saw himself as a serious man of science; he patterned his trip after the voyages of the naturalist Alexander von

45 *"He Who Ties His Hair Before, Crow," 1832.*
Catlin realized this painting during his visit to the Hidatsa. Eeheaduckcheea, a chief in his tribe, stood six feet tall, and his natural hair flowed all the way to the ground. He wears a necklace and earrings with a large peace medal of unknown origin suspended from the necklace.

His eagle-feather headdress has an attached tail nearly reaching to the ground, visually signifying the great number of coups he has counted in battle. His buffalo robe is painted with personal symbols recounting his exploits, while his lance, shield, and bow are propped up in front of him.

Humboldt, whom he admired. Although other European men of science, most notably Thomas Nuttal and the Duke of Württemberg, had already traveled the American West on similar quests, the work of Maximilian's artist made his journey distinctive, for Bodmer's beautiful portraits preserved forever a turning point in Indian life. The prince's book describing their travels, illustrated with Bodmer's scenes, opened a new body of knowledge to the world at large.

Curiously, all four men had a profound effect on the cultures of the very people in whose welfare they were so interested. Their work created a lasting image in the public mind of Indians as savage and primitive but nevertheless colorful people. Their draftsmanship, especially Bodmer's, influenced American Indian artists, to give their work a new, three-dimensional quality. George Catlin's investigations of the Minnesota quarry where Indians procured a unique red stone used for ceremonial pipes popularized the area and gave the name "Catlinite" to the stone itself.

The artists' later promotions—exhibits of their paintings, as well as books containing lithographs and engravings of them—disseminated their knowledge to a broad audience. They also influenced a new generation of artists, including Paul Kane and John Mix Stanley, who in a sense continued their work by chronicling other Indian tribes and lifeways in the homelands of the Indians themselves.

By the 1840s, they had created a new awareness of who Indian people were and how they lived. McKenney, Catlin, and Bodmer were at their best in their own younger years; when their ambitions shifted to other pursuits late in their lives, all three became embittered and lonely old men. Moreover, all three artists had to accept that their work did little to halt the tide of westward expansion and the disruption of Indian cultures.

Most of the priceless King portraits were lost in a fire in 1865. But the survival of many originals, as well as the lithographs and engravings based upon them, and the artifacts collected by all four men (which would establish several museum collections of Indian items) constitute a priceless resource documenting a vanished world. As Catlin phrased it, "Art may mourn when these people are swept from their earth, and the artists of future ages may look in vain for another race so picturesque in their costumes, their weapons, their colors, their manly games, and their chase."

Ironically, in trying to capture the primitive lifestyles of Indian people, Catlin, Bodmer, and King actually depicted the encroachment of white culture and the change it wrought. The artists also captured that unique dichotomy of the American psyche, its love-hate relationship with its native peoples. While they were fascinated with Indians and often aspired to live like them, Americans also rejected them as too primitive to live alongside, banishing them to reservations and killing them with diseases and bullets. In a strange twist of popular taste, the same people who were appalled by stories of Indian uprisings and supported Indian removals were fascinated by the skillful artistic representations of Indian people by Catlin, Bodmer, and King. If not for the vision of these three artists, and the man who influenced them all, Thomas McKenney, our modern knowledge of American Indian people and their original cultures would be far poorer than it is.

CHARLES BIRD KING AND THOMAS MCKENNEY: PORTRAITS FOR THE RECORD

50 Self-Portrait, by Charles Bird King.
This self-portrait, painted in 1815, provides an early look at the man who helped create the Indian Gallery displayed at the War Department in the 1820s. A classically trained artist who was highly respected in his time, King is best remembered today for his portraits of American Indians, despite the fact that so few originals survive.

In the spring of 1828, a congressional committee investigating wasteful spending in the U.S. government uncovered the fact that Thomas L. McKenney, the commissioner of Indian affairs, had spent at least $3,000 to have portraits painted of American Indian visitors to Washington. The completed pictures, executed over a period of eight years, were hanging in his office at the War Department. Although they were open to public view, the congressional committee considered these oil paintings, depicting individual chiefs and warriors, to be evidence of corruption. When the facts were revealed to the press, McKenney was publicly ridiculed for undertaking the venture and reviled for misappropriating government funds.

In an attempt to vindicate himself, McKenney responded in the pages of local newspapers: "Apart from the great object of preserving in some form the resemblance of an interesting People," he wrote in the *Alexandria Gazette* of May 22, 1828, "it is the policy of the thing. Indians are like other people in many respects—and are not less sensible than we are, to marks of respect and attention. They see this mark of respect to their people, and respect it. Its effects, as is known to me, are, in this view of the subject, highly valuable." The public was not convinced, however, and the use of public money to finance Indian portraits all but ceased. This incident marked the unfortunate end of one of the most innovative and important public works projects ever undertaken by an official of the U.S. government.

The story of how more than one hundred Indian portraits came to be painted with government funds involves two men, McKenney and the artist he hired, Charles Bird King. Although the lives of these two men involved far more than the Indian Gallery they fathered, it was the Indian portraits that ensured their place in American history and culture.

Charles Bird King was an academically trained artist who, in his time, was respected as a talented painter. King's life was rather uneventful, and little is known about him. He speaks to us today primarily through the paintings he completed, although just a small fragment of his total output survives. He left no autobiographical works. The few contemporary sources of information about him include a study in the 1834 book *History of the Rise and Progress of the Arts of Design in the United States,* by William Dunlop, and letters by King and King's friends, most notably the famous American portraitist Thomas Sully. In our own time, John C. Ewers and Andrew Cosentino have pieced together King's life story from the fragments of information and art he left behind.

Thomas McKenney also remains a little-known figure, although far more documentary evidence survives about him. As superintendent of Indian trade and later as commissioner of Indian affairs, McKenney shaped government Indian policy between 1816 and 1830. In addition, he was a pioneer in American ethnology, amassing a collection of Indian artifacts, buying books about native people, and commissioning portraits of visiting delegates from Indian nations. It was McKenney who established the Indian Gallery and, in large measure, the fame of Charles Bird King as an artist. Luckily, McKenney left behind copious correspondence, an autobiography, and even a book documenting the Indian portraits for which he was the patron.

Charles Bird King was born on September 26, 1785, in Newport, Rhode Island, which at that time was an important seaport and center of crafts like furniture-making. An only child, King's parents were Captain Zebulon King and his wife, Deborah Bird. Awarded lands for his faithful service during the American Revolutionary War, Zebulon set out alone for Ohio to begin farming them in 1789. Like many Americans, Zebulon was aware that the original Indian owners of the land had been pushed aside to make way for the influx of Euro-American settlers. The Ohio Indians, including the Miami and Shawnee, unused to the ways of Euro-Americans and angry over the loss of their

51 *"Black Hawk."* This beautiful portrait of the Sac brave Black Hawk was painted in 1837. Although Black Hawk was near the end of his life, and was often described at this time as dressing in shabby European-style clothing. King depicted the proud warrior as a vigorous man in traditional attire. This portrait is significantly different from a lithograph in McKenney and Hall that shows Black Hawk as an old man in a different pose. In this excellent portrait, perhaps more than in the many others done of Black Hawk, we can see the determined man who led a futile gambit to recover his tribe's lost lands. Black Hawk was also painted by George Catlin in 1832.

King did not remain in London for the ten-year course of instruction but returned to America in 1812, shortly after the outbreak of war between the United States and Great Britain. After a short stay at home in Newport, he set up a studio in Philadelphia, then the largest and most elegant city in the United States. America's finest artists lived in Philadelphia; King's friends included two of the sons of Charles Willson Peale (named for the artists Raphael and Rembrandt), Thomas Birch, and Bass Otis, as well as his closest companion Thomas Sully. Although King received few commissions during this period, his paintings were praised by critics when they were shown at the Pennsylvania Academy.

In 1814 King tried to obtain commissions for portrait work in Richmond, Virginia, and in Washington. His break came when a Baltimore publisher-bookseller-art dealer named Joseph Delaplaine printed a serial publication called *Delaplaine's Repository of the Portraits and Lives of the Heroes, Philosophers, and Statesmen of America.* Each edition of this serial was composed of six short biographies, accompanied by six engravings of the Americans profiled within. Each engraving was made from an original painting commissioned by Delaplaine. Art historian Andrew F. Cosentino theorizes that King lived in Baltimore between 1815 and 1818 and received important commissions

hunting grounds and religious sites, were striking back against the settlers during this period. Zebulon King was an unfortunate victim of the tensions caused by this fight, and in April 1789 he was shot in the chest, tomahawked, and then scalped by Indians.

It must have been a lonely death, far from his wife and son in Rhode Island. It also marked an ironic beginning for King's four-year-old son, who would be so closely identified with preserving the appearance of American Indian people for posterity. Upon Zebulon's death, young Charles inherited so much money that he was never in want for the rest of his life. In addition, later bequests from his mother's side of the family included a home and studio in Newport and funds that allowed him to study in England and live in high style in Washington, D.C.

Little is known of King's early education, except that he was raised in the Moravian faith. His early interest in art may have stemmed from his grandfather, the merchant Nathaniel Bird, who was an amateur artist. It helped that Charles grew up in a community notable for its influence on and promotion of such important early American painters as John Singleton Copley, Gilbert Stuart, and Washington Allston. Showing real promise in art, Charles was sent to New York City in 1800, where he received instruction from one of the foremost American artists of the

day, Edward Savage. At the end of his apprenticeship in 1806, King set sail for England, where a far more advanced training was possible. In London, King was taught by the legendary Benjamin West, a Pennsylvania Quaker who himself had traveled to England in the 1760s to refine his raw artistic talent. West never returned to America, but instead became a successful British artist, rising to the presidency of the Royal Academy of Art.

A normal program of instruction at the Royal Academy lasted ten years. Admission was based upon the presentation of one drawing of a plaster cast or still-life subject. This drawing, chosen by the student from his best work, was submitted to a jury after the completion of his first year. Evidence suggests that King was admitted to the Academy through this procedure. Most young students at the Academy were quite poor, but King's fellow students never knew that he was wealthy. During his Academy years, he made a great show of asceticism, eating inexpensive foods and sleeping on a mattress on the floor. Personable and amiable, he made many friends, particularly with American art students Thomas Sully, Washington Allston, Samuel F. B. Morse, and Charles Robert Leslie. Each of the young students had access to statuary and paintings by the great masters to copy and emulate, and to be inspired to develop styles of their own.

52 LEFT *"No Tin (Wind), Ojibwa."* In 1974, a descendant of one of King's first cousins, Bayard LeRoy King, discovered sixteen charcoal sketches among his family papers. The sketches had been made by King nearly 150 years earlier as preliminary drawings for sixteen of his American Indian portraits. All but two of the sixteen could be matched to known King portraits or McKenney and Hall lithographs.

52 RIGHT *"Peechekir (Buffalo), Ojibwa."* A second charcoal sketch by King, one of the discovered sixteen. In addition to the Indian portrait sketches, a seventeenth drawing of the Marquis de Lafayette, made from life in 1825, was also found among the King papers. Each of the sketches is made on rough gray paper.

53 *"Mon-Chonsia, A Kansas Chief."* One of the sixteen Indians who composed the O'Fallon delegation was Monchonsia, from a small tribe called the Kansa. By 1821, warfare with the Sac and Fox and the Iowa had reduced the Kansa to just 1,500 people. This portrait by King is accentuated by the beautiful jewelry, the turban, and peace medal he wears. In later years, Monchonsia became the principal chief of the Kansa, pursued a friendly policy toward the United States, and became very corpulent.

from Delaplaine for the *Repository*. Several fine pictures by King have survived from this period, including a handsome self-portrait and portraits of jurist-politician William Pinckney, Gen. John Stricker, and a Maryland signer of the Declaration of Independence, Charles Carroll of Carrollton.

King employed a distinctive style, which placed the subjects of his portraits in the foreground, contrasting the human figure against a very plain background with few details or objects to indicate depth. The subject of a King portrait was undeniably the sitter, and not peripheral subject matter, although King often included details of clothing or ornament that told the viewer about the occupation, and sometimes the deeds, of the sitter. King was also adept, in most cases, at capturing the personality of his subject, a power that often eluded many otherwise talented artists.

By 1818 King had permanently settled in Washington, in a home built to his design at the corner of 12th and F streets. Just three blocks to the east of the White House, the house was described by Thomas Sully as having an exhibition room with a large skylight and two painting studios, plus a fine garden at the back. King was busy now, painting away at portraits that had been ordered in a flood of commissions. These included two of the nation's most prominent men, President James Monroe and Senator Daniel Webster. King's mother died suddenly in 1819, leaving him money that enabled him to carry on through a national financial depression. King had also purchased real estate in the capital, successfully investing revenues from rents in stocks, which, together with his portrait commissions, ensured that he would live comfortably his entire life.

In 1818, Washington was little more than twenty years old, a seat for the U.S. government that had been carved out of a swamp. With very few year-round residents, most of Washington's populace worked for the government or in such service enterprises as hotels, boarding houses, and restaurants. The massive edifices of major public buildings were still being erected, while two of the earliest, the President's House and the Capitol, were being rebuilt after having been burned by British troops during the War of 1812. There were no paved roads, and whenever it rained, the carriages of foreign ministers, congressmen, and even the President himself were bogged down in mud. Mosquitoes were the bane of the inhabitants, breeding in unimaginable numbers in the nearby marshes, while hogs rooted through the garbage thrown in the streets. It was left to the already established nearby communities of Georgetown and Alexandria to provide the merchant, trade, and support services needed to keep the new capital going.

Although far from a paradise, Washington was nevertheless where the important and wealthy people of the United States came when

54 *"Shau-Hau-Napo-Tinia, An Ioway Chief."*
Shauhaunapotinia means "The Man Who Killed Three Sioux," and that is just what this warrior did. As a young man, when his best friend was killed and scalped by the Sioux, Shauhaunapotinia made a solo raid into a *Sioux camp, killing and scalping three of the enemy and living to tell the tale. Shauhaunapotinia was a member of the Iowa delegation that visited Washington in 1836, and he had his portrait painted at that time by Charles Bird King.*

55 *"Chon-Mon-I-Case, An Otto Half Chief."*

With a culture similar to that of the Iowa and Missouri tribes, the Oto were dwindling rapidly during the early nineteenth century as a result of disease. In 1820, they had merged with the Missouri, together numbering fewer than 800 individuals. Both tribes had moved to the Platte River in Nebraska, where they were protected by the more numerous Pawnee. Contrary to popular depictions of the Indians of the Plains, the Oto lived most of the year in earthen lodges, not tepees, and as evidenced by Shaumonekusse, they wore a variety of headdresses, not just eagle-feather war bonnets. His daring feats had earned him the nickname Ietan (Comanche) among his people. Ten years after this portrait was painted, Shaumonekusse got into an argument with his brother over some horses. During a scuffle, his brother bit the end of Shaumonekusse's nose off. Swearing revenge, Shaumonekusse trailed his fearful brother out onto the prairie, where he killed him.

Congress was in session, and Charles Bird King became a fixture in the city. William Dunlop noted in 1824 that King was "full of business and a great favorite, assiduously employed in his painting room through the day, and in the evening attending the soirees, parties, and balls of ambassadors, secretaries of the cabinet, [the] president or other representatives and servants of the people, and justly esteemed everywhere." King continued to make many portraits of the famous and powerful who congregated in Washington, his most successful being those of John C. Calhoun, Henry Clay, and John Quincy Adams. In addition to portrait work, King also painted still lifes, genre works, and landscapes. He was not only a painter, but an inventor, architect, horticulturist, and art instructor. His connections in the artistic and political world were far reaching, and he was much admired for his steadfast and hearty personality. However, King joined few artistic societies and was not known for his gregariousness. He was a lifelong bachelor.

Despite his successes in portraiture and Washington society, King's most famous works of art remain those of American Indian people. He was the first artist to be officially commissioned by the U.S. government to create Indian portraits. His participation in this project began late in 1821, when a delegation of Indian chiefs from the Upper Missouri River area came to Washington to negotiate with the government. The motivating force behind the creation of these portraits was Thomas McKenney, the superintendent of Indian trade.

McKenney was born in Somerset County, Maryland, on March 21, 1785. He was the same age as Charles Bird King, and like King, he grew up in a wealthy environment.

Unlike King, he came from a large family of six full brothers and sisters and seven half-brothers and half-sisters. McKenney's mother died when he was ten years old, but her Quaker religion influenced him profoundly. He stated that he remained a Quaker throughout his life, in spirit if not in dress or demeanor. Raised on a plantation called Hopewell, he went to Washington College, where well-to-do young men of Maryland's eastern shore were educated. His ambition was to be a physician, but "the delicate appearance of my physical powers led my Father to change This purpose," recalled McKenney in his memoirs. Fearing that his son would be worn out in making the rounds to see patients in foul or hot weather, the elder McKenney took young

56 *"Chippeway Squaw & Child."*
James Otto Lewis, at the Fond du Lac council, painted several Ojibwa women, paintings that were later copied by Charles Bird King and made into lithographs for Indian Tribes of North America. *In this print, a Ojibwa woman is shown carrying her baby swaddled in a cradleboard. A cradleboard freed a woman to perform her work while knowing at all times where her child was. The term* squaw, *derived from the Algonkian word for* woman, *was used by the Narrangansett people studied by Roger Williams in the 1600s. It was later applied to all Indian women by the whites with such frequency and derision that modern Indian people consider it an extremely insulting term.*

57 *"Tshusick, An Ojibway Woman."* Thomas McKenney told the story of Tshusick, one of the greatest impostors ever known, an Ojibwa woman who became assimilated to Euro-American culture. Tshusick arrived in Washington on a bitterly cold night in the late 1820s and was brought to McKenney's residence. She told him that her husband had recently died, and that she had walked from upper Michigan to the nation's capital, begging food and sleeping in the woods along the way. She claimed she had worked in the household of Michigan governor Lewis Cass, and she related details about the sister of the First Lady, Louisa Adams, who was married to the Indian agent at Mackinac, George Boyd. She knew all about life at Mackinac. McKenney took her in, and she was invited to the White House, where she quickly charmed everyone, including President Adams and the First Lady, who was eager to hear about how her sister was faring on the frontier. Tshusick spoke fluent English and French as well as Ojibwa. She was wined and dined in Washington society—until McKenney mentioned that he had written to Lewis Cass about her virtues. It was at that point that Tshusick announced that she had to return to Mackinac. Laden with gifts, including a money belt full of cash, she was seen off by the wealthy and powerful of Washington society and never heard from again. Governor Cass revealed that Tshusick was the wife of a Frenchman who worked in the kitchen of the Boyd residence, but that she had run away and gone from city to city, perpetrating the same artful charade as she had pulled on Washington society. McKenney called her trip to Washington "a masterpiece of daring and successful enterprise," which would "compare well with the most finished efforts of the ablest impostors of modern times." Tshusick sat for her portrait by Charles Bird King in 1827, wearing a lovely native outfit of calicoes decorated with rickrack and ribbons, holding a sweetheart rose in her hand.

58 *"Pow-A-Sheek, A Fox Chief."* *Powasheek was one of the most influential chiefs in his tribe, along with Keokuk and Wapella. Thomas McKenney called Powasheek "a daring warrior [who] held a respectable standing in council, as a man of prudence and capacity." Powasheek visited Washington in 1833 and 1837 as a member of large Sac and Fox delegations, and his portrait was painted by George Cooke. In 1836, he met the Mormon leader Joseph Smith at Nauvoo, Illinois, but did not convert to the Mormon faith. Powasheek signed one last treaty in 1842 and died that same year in Kansas, aged just 30.*

Thomas into the family's prosperous Chestertown merchant house. By 1804, when McKenney was only nineteen, he was in charge of the business, and the prospect of a prosperous merchant's life stretched out before him. He married well, taking as his bride Editha Gleaves, with whom he had two children, Maria, who died in infancy, and William.

Thomas McKenney's life was shaken when his father abruptly died, leaving no will and many debts. McKenney watched helplessly as his fortune melted away. The little that remained, including the family plantation, he gave to his stepmother and his underage half-brothers and half-sisters for their continuing financial support. He moved from the eastern shore to Georgetown in the new District of Columbia, joining the mercantile firm of his brother-in-law, Samuel Osborne.

During the War of 1812, despite his Quaker

background, McKenney served as an aide-de-camp, rising to the rank of major. Military service brought McKenney into contact with many prominent people, including President James Madison. After the war, however, McKenney had trouble adjusting to civilian life. Dissatisfied with the merchant jobs he held, he tried to obtain an appointment to a government position but was frustrated until 1816, when President Madison appointed him superintendent of Indian trade. The job would be a turning point in his life.

McKenney, who had no prior experience with either Indians or the fur trade, launched into his new job with great enthusiasm. He brought to the job the one thing he knew well—the complexities of the merchant's occupation. However, few men could have been prepared for the position's enormous responsibilities. McKenney had been named to oversee a system of official government trading houses called "factories." The system had evolved after the Revolutionary War, during which the Americans had alienated the Indians and sent them to the side of the British. The British had promised the Indians that they would not take their lands; the American rebels made no such assurances and in fact were eager to expand, settle and exploit the West. Once the war was won, the United States was left with a dilemma on the frontier. The Indians had to be placated so that negotiation and not warfare might win their lands. To launch a policy of fair trade and goodwill with the Indians, and to woo them from the British by providing better bargains, the United States established official government "factories," run by government agents called "factors," in 1795. All private trade with Indians was discouraged; instead, the Indian trade would take place in these "factories." Once the Indians were dependent upon American trade goods, the government could control and coerce the tribes with an eye to acquiring their land. All this could be accomplished without costly military posts or a large standing army. Of course, the scheme depended entirely upon the goodwill and expertise of the factors in the field, all of whom would now be under the direct control of Thomas McKenney.

59 *"Pow A Sheek."* This is one of several paintings by Charles Bird King that do not match up with corresponding lithographs in Indian Tribes of North America. *The pose and attire of Powasheek in this painting are different from those of the lithograph. The Fox warrior is shown here wearing a peace medal and fitting an arrow to his bow.*

60 *"Peah Mas Ka."* The model for the McKenney and Hall print, this King original is far more detailed and shows greater realism and depth than the lithograph. Painted in Washington in 1824, King hinted at the woodland forest home of the Fox tribe with his lush (if flat) background. Peahmaska was a peaceful man who walked into an ambush with a party of hunters in 1830. Attacked by Santee Sioux and Menominee warriors fifteen miles from Prairie du Chien, his death resulted in an intertribal war. In reprisal, Sac and Fox warriors slaughtered more than thirty Menominees a few months later.

The factory system was a sound scheme and should have worked. In practice, Congress authorized money for it in fits and starts. The very legislation that authorized the Indian factories lasted for periods of only two or three years, occasionally lapsing before being renewed by Congressional vote. Control of the factory system was divided between the secretary of war and the secretary of the treasury, making its administration complex. However, the most devastating enemy of the factory system was the fur trade barons, who wished to deal directly with the Indian people who supplied them with animal pelts. They lobbied incessantly in Congress for the abolition of the factory system.

Despite the politics and the potential pitfalls, McKenney thrived in his new post. It was, after all, a business like the many he had run in the past. Furs, shipped from factories ranging from Canada to the Gulf of Mexico, came into the Georgetown headquarters of the Indian trade, where they were sold; the money they brought in was used to buy the trade goods that Indians wished. Such items as cloth, trade guns, pipe tomahawks, knives, jewelry, beads, blankets, and toys were then distributed from Georgetown to the factories. McKenney improved the quality of the goods sent out, finding the very best values and improving the reputation of the factories among Indian people. At the start of 1816 he was responsible for eight separate factories in Green Bay, Chicago, Prairie du Chien, Fort Osage, Chickasaw Bluffs, Natchitoches, Fort St. Stephens, and Fort Hawkins. Trade goods were delivered to these factories over three different routes. Added to the complexity of the system were the varied hazards of delivery, which included shipwreck, pirates, lazy boatmen, and low water on the rivers.

McKenney was equal to all of these challenges, however, retaining his post when the new President, James Monroe, was inaugurated in 1817. Along with the change in administrations came a new secretary of war, John C. Calhoun of South Carolina. Calhoun relied upon McKenney's expertise as a trader and administrator—and his wise instincts in the realm of Indian affairs. McKenney, in fact,

61 *"Push-Ma-Ta-Ha."* A Choctaw born about 1764 in present-day Mississippi, Pushmataha was a respected warrior in fights with the Osage and Caddo. He became a chief in 1805. Pushmataha supported the United States against Tecumseh's efforts to have the Choctaw join his confederacy, and he later opposed the Creek Red Sticks under William Weatherford. A member of the 1824 delegation of his people to Washington, Pushmataha met Gen. Lafayette during his triumphal return to America, and had his portrait painted by Charles Bird King. He wears the U.S. Army officer's uniform coat given to him during his army service, when he was known as the Indian general. Staying at Tennison's Hotel on Pennsylvania Avenue, he died suddenly of a throat infection in December 1824. His eulogy was given in the U.S. Senate by John Randolph of Roanoke, and he was buried in the Congressional Cemetery. The painting differs in some of its details from the McKenney and Hall print; most notably, the plumed hat is absent from the litographic version.

62 "Keokuk." *A completely different painting from the full-lenght view of Keokuk and his son used in the McKenney and Hall lithograph, this handsome portrait depicts the chief as a warrior rather than as the leader of his people. Stripped to the waist, his head bound in a turban and holding a "gunstock"-style war club, Keokuk appears ready to lead men into battle. This portrait was probably painted in 1837, when Keokuk visited Washington at the head of a delegation of Sac and Fox.*

had begun to see the concept of land ownership from the Indian perspective. As a result, Indians, reformers, and those with benevolent feelings toward Native American people began to approach the government through the sympathetic McKenney.

One of the most controversial events of this period was the attempt by Euro-Americans in Georgia to appropriate the lands of the Cherokee people. In their fight to retain their ancestral lands, Thomas McKenney sided with the Indians, who sent delegates to Washington to lobby for their cause in Congress. Cherokee leaders like John Ross took up virtual residence in the nation's capital. Indian lobbyists from the Six Nations of the Iroquois and the Stockbridge Indians of Massachusetts also lived for long periods in Washington, developing firmer ties with the superintendent of the Indian trade.

Despite his sympathy for Indians' claims to their lands, McKenney was an advocate of Indian assimilation. He promoted Euro-American schools and Christian missionaries at the factories to encourage Indians to give up their "uncivilized" ways. As he wrote Isaac Thomas in December 1816, he felt that "all cases of advancement" of Indian people "may be traced to their . . . intercourse with the whites." As a result, McKenney's concept of Indian reform was to expand the factory system to promote a faster assimilation of Indian people. He deplored the idea of forcibly removing Indians from the East and resettling them west of the Mississippi, saying that Indians would never assimilate if not kept in close proximity to whites. In promoting the expansion of the factory system, McKenney took his case to Congress and to the people, drafting a bill that allowed missionary schools at the factories.

McKenney's bill enjoyed wide public

63 *"Ma-Has-Kah, Chief of the Ioways."*

Mahaskah was a man who learned that having more than one wife is not always advantageous. While traveling to a conference in Washington, in 1824, he was accosted on the prairie by his youngest, newest wife, Flying Pigeon, who wished to accompany him to the East. Realizing that if he took just one wife the others would be jealous, he returned to his village and brought all seven. Jealousy existed between the women, however, whether he brought them or not, and their violent arguments escalated as the family group traveled eastward. By the time

Mahaskah reached Washington, tensions were high. While they were staying on the second floor of Tennison's Hotel, a fight erupted, with Mahaskah attempting to beat his bickering wives with the broken leg of a chair. Called to the hotel to help break up the fight, Maj. Benjamin O'Fallon walked into the room, and an embarrassed Mahaskah walked out—of the second-story window! The chief broke his arm in the fall and grimaced during the sitting for this Charles Bird King portrait. In 1834, Mahaskah was killed by a warrior he had turned over to the authorities for committing murder.

support, but the factory system he headed was doomed. Congress wondered why the factories continually lost money, and why items were supplied to the Indians on credit. The final breakdown came because of the opposition of private traders, led by John Jacob Astor, the rich and powerful director of the Bank of the United States, who owned the American Fur Company and had direct ties to President Monroe. Astor wanted a monopoly of the American fur trade and viewed Thomas McKenney and the factory system as the chief impediment to his goal. Astor's agents spread antifactory propaganda by word of mouth among the western tribes. Thanks to Astor's political influence, McKenney was unable to prevent private traders from obtaining congressional permission to trade with the Indians, which allowed his rivals to move in on the trade. By 1821, powerful forces led by John B. Floyd in the House of Representatives and Thomas Hart Benton in the Senate succeeded in abolishing the factory system, in a bill signed into law on May 6, 1822, by President Monroe. McKenney's political foes had won, and he was temporarily out of a job.

One of McKenney's lasting accomplishments during his six years in office was his creation of an Indian museum. In November 1820 he wrote to T. Lewis that he had "often regretted that no Archive exists in which might have been enrolled the progress of things relating to our aborigines." Convinced that the process of assimilation, of which he so strongly approved, would soon erase all the unique cultural aspects of Indian people, in 1817 McKenney began to gather artifacts, books, and manuscripts about Indians, with limited funds but great optimism. In a July 22, 1817 letter he asked his agents in the field to offer as much as $100 worth of factory goods in return for bows, arrows, clothing, or any "natural curiosity whether of minerals, or animals, or plants." He asked that these specimens be sent to the Indian office and that they be properly identified.

Even more important was McKenney's idea that portraits of Indians who made official visits to Washington should be painted for his museum. It is not known what previous connection McKenney may have had with Charles Bird King, other than the fact that King was a well-known painter and social figure in Washington. In any event, King was asked to paint the first portraits for the Indian Gallery in 1821, and he continued to receive commissions from the government until 1842. Over twenty years, King completed 143 portraits of Indian leaders, for which he received more than $3,500. Most of these paintings were executed before 1830.

The portraits were created in conjunction with the official visits of Indian delegations to Washington. These visits took place within a prescribed ritual described in Herman J. Viola's brilliant study, *Diplomats in Buckskins*. When ever a treaty was negotiated or signed, whether in the Indians' homeland or in Washington, established protocols were followed. These included the distribution of presents, such as peace medals, flags, and military uniforms, and the delivery of flowery speeches, followed by colorful ceremonies. Peace medals, produced in silver for the principal chiefs and subchiefs of a tribe, were created with great care, and skilled sculptors were commissioned to ensure that they were items of artistic merit. Thomas McKenney remarked that the medals were "intended, not for the Indians, only, but for posterity." For Native Americans, the medals were cherished possessions to be worn on important occasions, including the creation of a portrait.

In addition to the distribution of peace medals and other presents in the field, Indian delegations were invited to the nation's capital, most notably during the Lewis and Clark expedition of 1804-1806, to visit with the new "Great Father," the President of the United States. Although few treaties were ever negotiated in the nation's capital, visits from Indian delegations were encouraged. It was in this tradition that Maj. Benjamin O'Fallon, Indian agent for the Missouri River tribes, persuaded leaders of seven major Plains tribes to come to Washington in 1821. With this visit Secretary of War Calhoun wished to put off hostilities with tribes who were anxious about the encroachments of Euro-American fur traders and to establish the right to locate two forts in their territory; one at the confluence of the Missouri and Yellowstone rivers, the other at the mouth of the Minnesota along the Mississippi.

O'Fallon, who accompanied the delegation to Washington, realized that all these Indians knew of Euro-Americans stemmed from the limited contact they had had with trappers and traders in the Northwest. Their estimate of American strength and resolve was consequently low. Calhoun, McKenney, and O'Fallon reasoned that if the Indian leaders were given the opportunity to see the power and might of the United States during a visit to the East, they would be less eager to start a war.

In addition, government officials and others hoped that the visit would encourage Indian people to assimilate into the "superior" lifestyle of Euro-Americans. According to the white Americans now coming to dominate the continent, Indians should have their children educated in

Mak·we·hah·mak, Goway Chief.
(Great Walker.)

64 *"Moa-Na-Hon-Ga, An Ioway Chief."*
In an 1824 conference at Washington, Moanahonga (Great Walker) unwittingly signed away the lands of his people in the new state of Missouri for an annuity of $500. While in the capital Moanahonga's portrait was painted by Charles Bird King. By the time he returned to his village, Euro-Americans had begun their invasion, moving in to settle on Iowa land. Moanahonga traveled to St. Louis to plead his case before William Clark, the Indian agent for the West, but it was no use. He had signed away the lands of his people. Soon the attacks on his tribe came. In 1829 a militia group composed of squatters shot down many Iowas in cold blood, including Moanahonga's brother and sister. A brief war with the whites flared up, and Moanahonga was asked by William Clark to surrender himself. Moanahonga was tried for murder in Randolph County and found not guilty. Thomas McKenney wrote that Moanahonga was a man "sound in council and brave in battle."

65 *"Petalesharro, A Pawnee Brave."* Petalesharro visited Washington in 1821, and in the winter of 1821 his story was printed in East Coast newspapers, a poem was written entitled "The Pawnee Brave," and a girls' school presented him with a silver medal with the inscription "The Bravest of the Brave." The uproar was started by Petalesharro's objections to a yearly ritual Pawnee called the Morning Star ceremony, in which a captive virgin girl was sacrificed to the Morning Star. The captive girl was tied to a scaffold with her arms outstretched in the attitude of a crucifixion, and a warrior shot an arrow through the girl's heart. Her blood was used to ensure fertility for the coming season. Opposed to the concept of human sacrifice, Petalesharro saved a Comanche girl from the ritual in 1817. Why was Petalesharro, or more properly Pita-risaru (Man Chief) so opposed to the centuries-old practice of his own people? In 1811 Petalesharro traveled to St. Louis with his father, Lachelesharo. They visited with Superintendent of Indian Affairs William Clark, who oversaw native relations in the area encompassing the Louisiana Purchase and the Pacific Northwest. Clark impressed one thought upon father and son: the white people were coming in ever-increasing numbers, "like the waves of an ocean," and the Pawnees must adapt themselves before the whites reached their earthen lodges on the Plains. From the point of view of Petalesharro, in saving the Comanche girl he was sacrificing himself, since in the Pawnee belief system anyone who touched her would soon die. But Petalesharro did not die. He continued to save those who were to be sacrificed to the Morning Star, including a young Mexican boy in 1820. The tale of Petalesharro provoked admiration and hero-worship among Euro-Americans, but few realized that a Euro-American, William Clark, had set the events in motion that saved the Comanche girl.

eastern schools, till the soil if they were not already farmers, convert to Christianity, and give up the "pagan" religions of their ancestors. However, in the years that followed, these wishes were rarely met. Many top officials puzzled over why Indians were not eager to change their ways and bow to the superior culture they saw laid out before them on visits to the nation's capital.

The O'Fallon delegation consisted of seventeen Kansa, Missouri, Omaha, Oto, and Pawnee people. It was the first large contingent of Indians to come to Washington. The Indians were an instant social success, becoming very popular with the city's residents. They were treated to a round of parties and balls and were the highlight of the 1822 New Year's reception at the White House, arriving in full ceremonial regalia, their faces painted in bright reds and blues. One Pawnee delegate wore the first eagle-feather headdress ever seen in the East, while three others were wrapped in brightly painted buffalo robes. That winter, dressed only in breechclouts, the Indians presented an outdoor demonstration of traditional dancing. With their nearly nude bodies painted in wild colors, they jumped and leaped to the beat of drums before a crowd of more than six thousand fascinated spectators. The Indians were so much the hit of the social season that they became objects of curiosity and had to be isolated in their hotel rooms and whisked about in fast, closed carriages to prevent the horrible crush of the eager crowds.

Superintendent McKenney met with the Indians almost daily and supervised their activities in Washington. He arranged for the creation of their portraits by Charles Bird King, perhaps at King's home and studio on 12th and F streets. One wonders if King, as he worked on the individual portraits, ever reflected upon the fact that his father had been killed by Indians in Ohio so many years earlier. If he did, the thought never diminished the skill with which he rendered the people who sat before him. King's portraits were nearly all busts, showing the face and upper body. All were painted on

67 LEFT *"Shaumonekusse, An Otto Half Chief."* Shaumonekusse (Prairie Wolf) was a renowned warrior who fought five enemy tribes and the Spanish. He was part of the famous 1821 delegation to Washington led by Maj. Benjamin O'Fallon, which included Petalesharro and Shaumonekusse's wife Eagle of Delight. Shaumonekusse died in a fight at a trading post in 1837.

67 RIGHT *"Ne Sou A Quoit, A Fox Chief."* Nesouaquoit, famous for his objections to liquor and tobacco, was a member of a Fox tribe called the Mesquakie. In the summer the Mesquakie lived as farmers; in the winter they became seminomadic hunters. They lived in the region to the west of the Great Lakes. In 1734 the Fox entered into a permanent alliance with the Sac. The chief Nesouaquoit came to Washington in 1837 to remind the government that the Sac and Fox had been promised an annuity in 1815, but they had not seen a penny for over twenty years. Despite promises made in 1837, they never did.

wood panels about 18 inches high by 14 inches wide. The one major criticism of King's portraits was that he often gave the Indians Caucasian features. Because King never lived with Indians in the field, learned their customs, or got to know them as individuals, his work retains a romanticized and uninformed detachment, particularly compared with later portraits executed by George Catlin and Karl Bodmer. However, King's work was by far the most accurate, most advanced representation of Indian people made up to that time. Altogether, King painted 25 portraits of the 1821 delegation, eight for McKenney's archives and 17 others that were sent home with the Indians as keepsakes.

King's portraits included a represenation of the only woman in the O'Fallon delegation, a 14-year-old Oto girl named Eagle of Delight, who accompanied her husband Shaumonekusse to Washington. Much was made of the young woman in Washington society, and she was even invited to dance at a cotillion ball, although she politely refused. Unfortunately, Eagle of Delight suffered the same fate as far too many members of Indian delegations during the next decades; she died of disease soon after leaving Washington.

The highlight of any visit to the capital was an official audience with the President of the United States. When the O'Fallon delegation met with President James Monroe, they were escorted by Thomas McKenney and John C. Calhoun. The Indian leaders were dressed in new clothes they had been given, consisting of military uniforms with plenty of silver lace and epaulets. They also wore European-style hats and black boots. President Monroe made the delegates wait before entering the room where they were gathered, and he read to them from a prepared speech. He said he hoped that after seeing the advantages of the "civilized" world, the Indians would want to adopt them for themselves. The speech was translated for the Indians line by line as Monroe droned on. Finally, he invited the Indians to speak. Each in turn told the President that they had been pleased to see the land of the whites, but that they were not ready to give up their own way of life. After they finished their orations, they brought presents forward and placed them at Monroe's feet. These included buffalo robes, ceremonial pipes, moccasins, and feathered headdresses. Sharitarish, a Pawnee leader, told Monroe that he hoped he would keep the gifts "in some conspicuous part of your lodge, so that when we are gone . . . [and] our children should visit this place, as we do now, they may see and recognize with pleasure the deposits of their fathers, and reflect on the times that are past." After withdrawing to another room for cake and wine, the Indians passed a ceremonial pipe to all present, with each dignitary taking a solemn pull or two, including the President and Chief Justice John Marshall.

Altogether, the Indians with the O'Fallon delegation were away from home for about a year. Thomas McKenney was pleased with their progress in understanding the new nation's customs, mores, government, and military might. Before returning west, the delegation saw several forts, arsenals, and

"Hayne-Hudjihini, The Eagle of Delight." *This was the young woman who caused such a stir when she was presented in Washington society in 1821. One of five wives of the Oto chief Shaumonekusse, she was only fourteen years old when she made the trip. She was the only woman with the O'Fallon delegation of 1821. Tragically, she died of measles on the return journey. Her portrait was painted by King.*

naval yards, as well as the cities of Baltimore, Philadelphia, and New York.

The O'Fallon delegation set a precedent for future groups who visited Washington. Each year brought more Indian delegations to the capital, many of whom came to complain about increasing encroachments upon their land. The expense and time involved in transporting and entertaining these delegations prompted many officials, including several Presidents, to ask their

agents in the field to discourage the practice. Some Indians came to Washington on their own, with no permission and no schedule; most were entertained by the government anyway and were sent home with the same presents, speeches, meetings, and promises as those received by the invited delegations. At least one official delegation came to the city each year, which gave Thomas McKenney's artist, Charles Bird King, plenty of subjects to paint and immortalize.

Although he was forced from office in 1822 by the abolition of the factory system, McKenney was not out of government service or Indian affairs for long. With the aid of his benefactor, Secretary of War John C. Calhoun, he was given a minor position in the war office in 1824. Meanwhile, Calhoun proposed a new "department of Indian affairs" to oversee government relations with Indian people throughout the United States.

As soon as the department was approved by Congress, Calhoun named McKenney the first commissioner of Indian affairs. McKenney's responsibilities included protecting Indian lands from illegal settlement, regulating the fur trade, controlling liquor in Indian country, enforcing the law in areas where Indians and whites lived in close proximity, and encouraging the acceptance by the Indians of Euro-American civilization, religion, and education.

McKenney also continued building his Indian Gallery. Recovering the Indian artifacts he had collected as superintendent of Indian trade, he began to expand the collection, now housed in his second-floor office in the War Department building near the White House. King's portraits hung on McKenney's walls, and a full-size canoe hung over the door. Bows, arrows, ceremonial pipes, buffalo hides, and other Indian-made

68 RIGHT *"Ong Pa Ton Ga, Chief of the Omahas."* *This chief, whose name means "Big Elk," wears a buffalo robe, fur side in, and a peace medal. His tribe, the Omaha, were related to the Kaw, Osage, Ponca, and Quapaw, and lived southeast of the mouth of the Niobrara River in what is now northeastern Nebraska. As farmers, they lived in earth lodge villages and hunted*

buffalo seasonally. In 1802 a smallpox epidemic greatly reduced their numbers. Ongpatonga was perhaps the most distinguished member of the 1821 O'Fallon delegation. He claimed that no member of his tribe had ever harmed a white man, and that he liked the Euro-Americans so much that "he should, at a future day, be a white man himself." He was painted by Charles Bird King in 1821.

objects were displayed throughout. McKenney's office became a museum of the American Indian people; visiting it was a central event for any traveler to Washington, and it was praised by such noteworthies as British traveler Frances Trollope. An 1830 Washington guidebook written by Jonathan Elliot described McKenney's collection: "But for this gallery, our posterity would ask in vain—'what sort of a looking being was the red man of this country?' In vain would the inquirers be told to read descriptions of him—These could never satisfy. He must be seen to be known. Here then is a gift to posterity."

The paintings in McKenney's War Department gallery were not all originals by King. Some were King's interpretations of portrait sketches done by other artists who had observed Indian lifeways in the field. In 1826 and 1827, for instance, King copied more than thirty portraits by James Otto Lewis of Detroit, which had been made among the Great Lakes Indians. In many ways Lewis was the unsung hero of the gallery, for his paintings—created in the field and at treaty ceremonies—presented another dimension when compared with the static portraits completed by King exclusively in Washington. Other paintings were copied by a Washington artist named Athanasius Ford. The practice of commissioning original portraits and copying others continued until 1828, when the use of public funds to create these works of art was criticized in Congress and denounced in the press. For a time, Congress even threatened to take McKenney's museum away from him. Although the museum stayed, the portrait painting was brought to an untimely end.

There were exceptions, however. After touring the gallery in 1828, a Winnebago contingent from Wisconsin demanded that their portraits be added to those on McKenney's walls, saying, "We see no Winnebago here." Congress gave McKenney special permission to have King paint the Wisconsin tribespeople. The Winnebago seemed to intimidate everyone in Washington on their visit. In their home country, they were on the verge of war with white farmers who had illegally settled on their land. The Washington trip had been arranged by McKenney on the hope that the Winnebago would sell their land, much of which was thought to be rich in mineral deposits. When the Winnebagoes met President John Quincy Adams, their principal chief, Nawkaw, made a speech in which he described a thick, black cloud existing between his people and the whites. Nawkaw passed a ceremonial pipe around the room. President Adams, asking that his words be translated for Nawkaw, told the chief that he hoped that like the smoke from the pipe, the black cloud between the two peoples would dissipate as a result of their conference. Adams also granted the Indians a wish they had not thought possible —the release of Winnebago warriors who had attacked and killed white trespassers. Although the Indians had been condemned to death, Adams commuted their sentences.

When he followed up this act of benevolence by asking the Winnebagoes to sell their land, they replied that they hoped they would be asked for only a small portion.

The Winnebago delegation of 1828 illustrated one of the worst aspects of bringing Indian delegations to Washington: white "entrepreneurs" often took advantage of them. The Indians, sadly, were often plied with liquor and taken to houses of prostitution, all at government expense. The

69 *"Rant Che Wai Me, Female Flying Pigeon."* This is a portrait of Mahaskah's youngest wife, Female Flying Pigeon. Much beloved by Mahaskah, she died in a fall from her pony a year after her visit to Washington.

70 LEFT *"Joseph Polis."* Joseph Polis was a Penobscot Indian from the state of Maine. During the colonial era, the Penobscots had been part of the powerful Abnaki Confederacy. By the time this portrait was made in 1842, the Penobscots had dwindled to a few hundred survivors—so few that they were not even considered when most eastern Indians were moved westward during the relocation era. Polis was given a peace medal by the commissioner of Indian affairs, and Charles Bird King was commissioned by the government to make this portrait, one of the last Indian pictures to be made by King.

70 TOP RIGHT *"David Vann."* A Cherokee leader who thought that western resettlement would be best for his people, Vann came to Washington to work with government officials. During an 1825 visit, his portrait was painted by Charles Bird King. This beautiful original, one of King's best surviving paintings, features a careful rendering of Vann's woven belt and sash, and the fine light blue color of his hunting frock.

padded account books were then used to the advantage of unscrupulous hotel proprietors and other shady figures who received monetary kickbacks. Strangely, although liquor was forbidden in Indian country because of their notable susceptibility to it, it seemed to be a staple of a Washington visit, and the government often paid bills representing prodigious feats of consumption without blinking. The Winnebagoes became drunk on several occasions, fighting among themselves and causing a great deal of property damage. They also chased young women on the streets, kissing them and causing a general uproar in the city. Thomas McKenney was probably relieved when the group left Washington, but their portraits joined the others on the walls of his office.

When the government project seemed at an end, Charles Bird King kept painting Indian people. In addition to creating the individual portraits for McKenney, he used them as the basis for his own independent works of art, including a group portrait of the

heads of five Indian men, which he titled *Young Omaha, War Eagle, Little Missouri and Pawnees*. King also showed his romantic view of Indians when he depicted a full-length, bare-breasted Indian maiden in the forest, examining her reflection in a hand mirror. This painting, far more than any of King's infrequent portraits of real Indian women, reflected a romantically lustful vision of Indian women as foreign, exotic, and erotic woodland sprites ripe for vicarious conquest by white males. King displayed these paintings, along with his copies of individual portraits, in his studio on 12th and F streets.

As commissioner of Indian affairs, Thomas McKenney worked to root out corruption in his department, to stop the illegal sale of whiskey to Indians in the West, and to promote the assimilation of Indian people. However, he spent some of his time on a project that took fifteen years to complete: the publication of King's Indian Gallery portraits. As he sat behind his desk in his War Department office, McKenney must have gazed upon the paintings surrounding him and aspired to find a way to allow people who might never come to Washington to see what Indian people looked like. The project began in earnest in 1830, when McKenney was able to interest the firm of Childs and Inman, lithographers in Philadelphia.

Since the science of photography was not perfected until 1839, the only way paintings and other works of art could be published before that time was to have an artist copy the original work by drawing it out on a wood block, a steel or copper plate, or a lithographic stone. When ink was rolled over a wood or metal carving and the excess wiped off with a cloth, it stayed in the carved grooves and could be printed on paper. This process was known as intaglio printing. The newer process of lithography, first used in the United States in 1818, was faster and easier than previous methods of printing illustrations and was chosen by McKenney as the method for printing the Indian portraits. Lithographs were made with a special porous calcium carbonate stone imported from Bavaria. An original picture was made on the stone, using a greasy crayon. When the stone was dampened, oily printing ink was applied that adhered only to the crayon drawing; the damp part of the stone repelled the ink. The inked stone could then be used to print the image. Not only could the Childs and Inman firm print the one hundred or more

lithographs that would be needed; but they also had a gifted craftsman named Albert Newsam, a deaf-mute who was a master of the lithographic art and could accurately copy the King paintings, converting them from one medium to the other.

In completing the book of lithographs, however, Thomas McKenney's burden would be heavy. One obstruction after another would delay his ambition year after year. His first setback came with a change in the political administration. As an advocate of the gradual relocation of Indian people, McKenney opposed the stated policies of Andrew Jackson, who was elected President in 1828. Because Jackson knew that

McKenney was a political and ideological opponent of his plan to force the Indians to relocate west of the Mississippi, McKenney's days were numbered. He did his best to stay in office, so that he could protect the Indian people from Jackson's harsh policies. But many political enemies were ranged against him, and even though he began to implement Jackson's policy of forced removal, he was forced to resign in 1830. His dismissal saddened him, for loved his job and believed he had improved the lives of Indians.

After his dismissal McKenney moved to Philadelphia, where he could be closer to Childs and Inman He took a job as a newspaper editor to pay his bills. Because he

70 BOTTOM RIGHT *"John W. Quinney."*
Quinney was a member of another once-powerful tribe, the Stockbridges. Part of the Mohican Confederacy in Massachusetts, the Stockbridges had been allies of the British during the colonial wars and of the United States during the Revolutionary War. Homeless by 1785, 200 surviving Stockbridges moved to New York State and later to Green Bay, Wisconsin, where they shared a reservation with the Munsees. Bitter at their treatment over the years by the whites, in 1841 the Stockbridges sent John Quinney and John W. Chicks, the two principal chiefs of the tribe, to Washington to present their grievances. They appealed to President John Tyler to honor a treaty obligation of a $350 annuity, which the government had suddenly stopped paying in 1838. Tyler granted this request, but other problems involving land sales to whites in Wisconsin were not worked out until many years later. Chicks and Quinney were able negotiators and represented their people well. The government rewarded Chicks with a peace medal and the urbane Quinney with this portrait, completed in 1842.

71 *"The Prophet."* *In this beautiful King portait of the one-eyed Prophet, the reflections from highly-polished metal jewelry and decorations frame the face of this once-feared Indian leader.*

was no longer commissioner of Indian affairs, he found the task of converting the Indian portraits to lithographs increasingly complicated. Some lithographs had been made from the original portraits before he left the government, but now the contents of the Indian Gallery were no longer under his control. Consequently, McKenney had to cajole his former co-workers into sending the King paintings to him in Philadelphia, a few at a time. McKenney took precautions by commissioning the well-known portrait and genre painter Henry Inman of New York to copy all of the King portraits in oils. Inman was faithful to the originals, except for minor changes in the backgrounds. The Inman copies were then copied once more by Newsam and Childs onto lithographic stones, to become handsome 14-by-18-inch lithographic prints. The eye-popping colors and strong, clear images of the lithographs, combined with McKenney's romanticized descriptive texts of Indians and tribes, gave an entire generation of Americans a vision of who American Indian people were.

McKenney based his text on his travels in the Great Lakes region and the South, his observations of Indian people at tribal ceremonies and treaty councils, and stories he heard from frontiersmen and Indians. Concerned about his prose style and the readability of the narrative, McKenney submitted his drafts to former President John Quincy Adams for review. On September 12, 1831, Adams wrote that he hoped that McKenney's words would "survive the unfortunate race of men whom we are extinguishing with merciless rapidity." Albert Gallatin, a former secretary of the treasury who had studied Indian people, and Governor Lewis Cass of Michigan, by now secretary of war and a veteran of many tough negotiations with Indian tribes, also offered criticisms and suggestions. In addition to

72 TOP *"Rant Che Wai Me, Female Flying Pigeon."* *Female Flying Pigeon was the mother of the famous chief Young Mahaskah.*

72 BOTTOM *"Young Ma-Has-Kah, Chief of the Ioways."* *Young Mahaskah was elected chief of his tribe after his father's death, and he worked to gain the annuities the Iowa had been promised for the lands they had vacated in the East. This portrait was painted by King in Washington in 1837. In 1843-44 Young Mahaskah was in London and Paris with a group of Iowa dancers, who performed in George Catlin's Indian Gallery, drawing huge audiences.*

these sources, McKenney was able to interview Indian leaders such as John Ridge, John Ross, and Elias Boudinot of the Cherokee, as well as Black Hawk, the Sac chief captured after his violent encounters with government forces in 1832.

Bad luck dogged the project, however. McKenney's printer went bankrupt, and his hopes for large subscriptions (advance copies bought on speculation) were not fulfilled. McKenney convinced two young Philadelphia printers, Edward C. Biddle and John Key, to buy out the bankrupt printer and save the project. But then lithographers Childs and Inman went out of business, halting work on the portrait reproductions. McKenney, disgusted, quit the project and spent two years working for the Whig political party in Pennsylvania. During this

73 *"Naw-Kaw, A Winnebago Chief."*
Nawkaw's village was at Big Green Lake in Wisconsin. He was born in 1735. A follower of Tecumseh, he was reported to have been by his leader's side when Tecumseh fell at the Battle of the Thames in 1813. When Nawkaw visited Washington in 1828 as part of the wild Winnebago delegation, he told Thomas McKenney that he was 94 years old. He stood six feet tall and was still muscular and vigorous. The original of this painting was made by James Otto Lewis at the Butte des Morts council in 1827 and was later copied by King. Nawkaw is shown wearing a striped flannel shirt with a trade blanket wrapped around his waist. He sports two silver armbands and three peace medals with the likenesses of different presidents. He carries a ceremonial pipe with a wooden stem and a red stone bowl, decorated with feathers, beads, and human hair. Nawkaw died in 1833, aged 98.

period, McKenney occasionally grasped at straws. He unsuccessfully tried to lure the artist George Catlin, who was just then rising to prominence, into the projecct. Catlin was not interested in displaying his work in the McKenney book. McKenney was successful, however, in convincing James Hall, a prominent jurist and writer from Cincinnati, to become the editor of the project. Hall polished McKenney's prose and wrote biographies for the Indian leaders to be depicted, "of whom we knew nothing but the names," he wrote. After two years spent away from the project, McKenney was re-energized to push it toward completion. By

1836, he was able to convince Albert Newsam to complete all the lithographs from the Inman paintings. The edited text, the prints, and the captions were now ready to be seen by the public.

The first installment of the lithographs was mailed out to subscribers in 1837. It was an instant success, praised by all who saw it as one of the best examples of the printer's art yet created. Even the War Department purchased a copy, and then, impressed with the result, commissioned Charles Bird King to make portraits of the Sac, Fox, and Iowa Indians then visiting Washington. The new paintings, including portraits of Black Hawk

and Keokuk, were turned over to McKenney so that lithographs could be made from them and the images included in subsequent installments of the book. Each month, a new section of the lithographs and accompanying text was issued to the subscribers. Altogether, five printers eventually worked on the book. J.T. Bowen of Philadelphia took over the printing in 1837, committing forty people to working on the prints, including twenty-five women who hand-colored them. The first of the three volumes of Thomas L. McKenney and James Hall's *The Indian Tribes of North America with Biographical Sketches and Anecdotes of the Principal Chiefs,* was

74 LEFT *"Lap-Pa-Win-Soe, A Delaware Chief."*
This print was a copy of a painting by the Swedish
artist Gustavus Hesselius, made almost a century
before McKenney's time. McKenney wanted The
Indian Tribes of North America *to be a*
comprehensive study of all the Indian people, and
so he included this 1735 portrait of a Delaware
chief who had sold the lands of his people to
Thomas Penn, son of William Penn, and a group
of fourteen whites in the famous 1737 "Walking
Purchase." The Walking Purchase was a unique
method of acquiring land; the treaty stated that
the whites were entitled to the amount of land
between the Neshameny Creek and the Delaware
River that a man could walk in a day and a half.
The men picked to do the walking were very swift.

74 RIGHT *"Waa-Top-E-Not."* *A Ojibwa Indian*
from the Great Lakes region, Waatopenot appears
wrapped in a white trade blanket, holding his
"gunstock"-type war club, its wood painted blue
and decorated with patterns of brass tacks, its
lethal triangular metal blade gleaming below his
chin. The original portrait from which this print
was made was painted by James Otto Lewis at the
Fond du Lac council of 1826 and was later
copied by King.

75 *"Kee-She-Waa, A Fox Warrior,"* *Keeshewaa,*
"The Sun," was a noted Fox warrior and medicine
man and a friend of the Sac chief Keokuk.
McKenney wrote that Keeshewaa was "a firm,
onward, fearless chief, and of good character."
The painting from which this print was made was
probably painted by King in Washington about
1824.

published in 1837 and included 48 plates. After so many trials and setbacks over the course of seven years, McKenney must have been relieved to see it in print. But two more volumes remained to be completed.

The panic of 1837 and the resulting worldwide financial depression affected the publication of the remainder of the book. Frustrated, McKenney dropped out of the project for good, and publication did not resume until 1843. James Hall completed the text, and Rice and Clark of New York, the last printer to work on the project, issued the remaining volumes. By 1844, the final segment of the book had been published, fourteen years after Thomas McKenney initiated the project. The completed three volumes contained prints of 120 Indians, McKenney's history, and Hall's biographies. The book's high price of $120 made it available primarily to wealthy patrons, libraries, and museums.

Surprisingly, McKenney and Hall themselves received little credit and virtually no financial recompense for their hard work. It was the prints that astounded and fascinated people and made the book such a success. Just as McKenney, sitting in his War Department office, had been drawn to the King portraits, people who saw the completed McKenney and Hall *Indian Tribes* never tired of looking at the bold features and bright colors of the prints. The book influenced culture and cultural attitudes toward Indian people both in America and around the world. Some of the lithographs reappeared as transfer prints on china plates, in advertising art, and as models for artists who had never painted or

even seen a real Indian. For instance, John Gadsby Chapman probably used King's portraits in executing his huge oil painting *The Baptism of Pocahontas* for the rotunda of the U.S. Capitol in 1837-40. Samuel F. B. Morse used King's image of the Pawnee brave Petalesharro as a figure in his painting *The Old House of Representatives* in 1822. The far-reaching effects of King's portraits cannot be underestimated. They helped create an international consciousness of Indian people as tragic but noble red men of the forests and plains. That image would not be altered until after the Civil War.

Thomas McKenney's later years were filled with disappointment and penury. His wife had died in 1835, and his son, a wastrel, abandoned his father. Most of his brothers and sisters disowned him. He began a strange pattern of life, moving from hotel to hotel, from city to city, staying one step ahead of the bill collectors. He was unsuccessful at writing, politics, lecturing, and business. He long aspired to be restored to his position as commissioner of Indian affairs, but this, too, was denied him. He published a two-volume set of memoirs in 1846, a rambling, disjointed narrative that devoted most of its space to his 1826 and 1827 tours of the West and sought vindication of his conduct as commissioner of Indian affairs. The book did not sell well, and few people came to hear his lectures. Although he was virtually penniless during his final years, he insisted that a share of the receipts from his lectures go to the relief of American Indian people. The reason he gave the lectures, he wrote to a friend, was to "awaken the public's attention to the condition of the Indian tribes and to call forth an effort for the preservation of these unhappy people." Thomas McKenney had become a single-minded defender of Indians and Indian rights, but the public was indifferent to his message. He died suddenly in a Brooklyn, New York, boarding house on February 20, 1859, a forgotten man at age 74, whose four-line obituary listed him as having no survivors.

The bad luck that haunted Thomas McKenney throughout most of his life never touched Charles Bird King. In his later years, King gave many of his personal copies of portraits of both Indians and non-Indians to the Redwood Library in Newport, Rhode Island. He died on March 18, 1862, leaving one quarter of his estate, which totaled $38,000, to two Newport institutions, the Public School for Girls, and the Redwood Library. The 75 paintings he left to the Redwood upon his death brought the total number he had given that institution to about 215. Upon King's death, six portfolios of his sketches in pencil and in oils were sold at auction for $14.30 and forever lost to posterity. The Redwood Library eventually gave away 175 of King's paintings, the beginning of a pattern of dissipation and destruction of King's work that continues to the present day. In 1858, the majority of the Indian portraits collected by Thomas McKenney as commissioner of Indian affairs were given by the War Department to the new Smithsonian Institution. They were stored in a building designed by James Renwick, popularly known as "the castle," and displayed alongside a wonderful collection of 200 Indian scenes painted by John Mix Stanley in the 1840s and 1850s. Tragedy struck on January 24, 1865, when a fire raged through the gallery, destroying

76 TOP *"Nah-Et-Luc-Hopie."* Thomas McKenney said that this man was a Muskogee, a member of one of the "Five Civilized Tribes." Nahetluchopie told McKenney that the red spots on his hunting shirt marked the places where bullets had been fired into him during a murder attempt. Nahetluchopie's portrait was painted by King in 1825.

76 BOTTOM *"Timpoochee Barnard, An Ochee Warrior."* A brave warrior, Timpoochee Barnard fought against his own people beside Gen. Andrew Jackson during the Creek War. His portrait was painted by King in 1825.

77 TOP *"Tulcee-Mathla, A Seminole Chief."* This Seminole chief fought the whites in the Everglades. After the death of Osceola, he followed Billy Bowlegs until the surrender of 1842. Tulcee-Mathla was painted by King in Washington in 1825, before the hostilities between his people and the U.S. government erupted.

nearly all of the original works of King and Stanley. Just 66 of at least 184 Indian portraits once known to exist have survived, and many of them are copies King made from originals now lost and several are duplicates of the same figure. One hundred large engravings King gave to the Smithsonian Institution were also lost.

King's paintings have fared no better in more recent times. In 1970 the Redwood Library auctioned off 21 of King's Indian portraits, most of which were purchased by the Gulf States Paper Corporation of Tuscaloosa, Alabama. Even this collection was broken up when Gulf States Paper auctioned most of its portraits in 1993 at Sotheby's, nearly all of them entering private ownership. According to the catalogue complied by Andrew Cosentino in 1977 for the Smithsonian Institution, 211 of King's non-Indian portraits are known to survive, while only 17 of some 145 subject pictures (still lifes and landscapes) are known to exist.

Luckily, a series of sixteen studies King made in charcoal of Indian faces was discovered among family papers by a family descendant in 1974, adding immeasurably to King's surviving body of work. As a result of the dispersion and destruction of King's works over the years, however, very little remains for the scholar or

77 BOTTOM *"Thayendanegea, the Captain of the Six Nations."* *This print was taken from a portrait by an unknown artist of the Mohawk leader Thayendanegea, known to Euro-Americans as Joseph Brant. Brant was born about 1742 in the Ohio River Valley and grew up at Canajoharie Castle in New York's Mohawk Valley. He fought in the French and Indian War when he was just thirteen years old. Schooled in Connecticut, he visited England and sided with the British in the American Revolution. He and was an important factor in swaying four of the most powerful Iroquois tribes to fight alongside British troops and Loyalists. Brant participated in the Battle of Oriskany in 1777 and later waged guerrilla war on the American colonists in New York and Pennsylvania. His campaign was so successful that George Washington dispatched a small army under generals Clinton and Sullivan in 1779 to lay waste to the Iroquois country. Brant and his Mohawks were exiled to Canada at the conclusion of the war, where he translated the Book of Common Prayer into the Mohawk language. He died at Burlington, Ontario on November 24, 1807. This painting was a copy made by King to round out the story of the American Indian*

aficionado to see and appreciate. For the most part, we are left with a spare few portraits, their lithographic copies in McKenney and Hall's book, and the copies made by Henry Inman in the collection of the Peabody Museum at Harvard University.

Thomas McKenney and Charles Bird King were men of diverse interests who led very different lives. They were brought together at a seminal moment in American history, when vision and artistic talent were combined to create an artistic legacy of inestimable value. Their pioneering work would be augmented, even before the final volume of *Indian Tribes of North America* was published, by exciting new paintings by George Catlin and Karl Bodmer.

78 *"Wakechai, A Saukie Chief."* Wakechai came to Washington with a Sac and Fox delegation, signing a treaty with the United States on August 4, 1824, his name being third after that of Keokuk. This print is taken from a King portrait made during that 1824 visit. Also known as Crouching Eagle, Wakechai was the subject of a tale told to Thomas McKenney in the 1830s. Late in his life, apparently Wakechai was wasting away slowly from disease and felt a call from the Great Spirit to jump into the Mississippi, where a messenger would guide him to the spirit world. No messenger appeared, however, and Wakechai, wet and cold, dragged himself from the river and made his way back to his lodge, where he died the next day. He was buried on a bluff overlooking the river, still waiting for a messenger to guide him to the Great Spirit.

79 LEFT *"Mo-Hon-Go, An Osage Woman."*
Mohongo was probably one of the best-traveled women of her time, although it was never her ambition to be so worldly. In 1827, a strange French con artist named David Delauney was able to convince a group of seven Osage Indians, including Mohongo and her husband Kihegashugah, that he was a representative of the U.S. government and meant to take them on an official visit to Washington. The Osage accompanied Delauney down the Mississippi to New Orleans, where they boarded a ship for Washington. It was only when the ship landed in LeHavre, France, that the Indians were told that they would be, for a short time, the star attractions of a "Wild West Show." The Osage were exploited as they danced their way across Europe, making stops in France, the Netherlands, and Germany. When the popularity of the troupe waned, Delauney

abandoned them in Paris. Wandering about the city streets, the Osage could not speak French and refused to beg for food. To add to their plight, Mohongo was pregnant. Finally, they were brought to the Marquis de Lafayette, who kindly paid for their return to America. Smallpox struck on the Atlantic voyage, killing Mohongo's husband and two others. The survivors landed at Norfolk, Virginia, where they lived a hand-to-mouth existence until they were brought to the attention of Thomas McKenney. Mohongo and her son met President Andrew Jackson in 1830, who gave them the peace medal shown in this King portrait. Finally, after a three-year odyssey, Mohongo and her child were returned to her people in Kansas.

79 RIGHT *"Tish-Co-Han, A Delaware Chief."* This print, also a copy of a painting by the Swedish artist Gustavus Hesselius, was made in 1735 and shows another Delaware chief who signed the 1737 Walking Purchase treaty. The Delaware, who called themselves Lenni Lanape (True Men), lived in the modern-day states of Pennsylvania, New Jersey, New York, and Delaware.

The name Delaware comes from Lord De La Warr, the second governor of Virginia, and is not of Indian origin. The unusual squirrel-skin pouch around the chief's neck holds a clay pipe and tobacco. These paintings by Hesselius were rare forerunners of the Indian Gallery created by Thomas McKenney and King during the 1820s.

80 RIGHT *"Ahyouwaighs, Chief of the Six Nations."* Ahyouwaighs, also called John Brant, was the son of Thayendanegea (Joseph Brant) and Catherine, eldest daughter of the head of the turtle clan of the Mohawks. In the matriarchal society of the Iroquois, Catherine was allowed to make suggestions on the choice of chief, and she recommended her youngest son, John. Born September 24, 1794, Ahyouwaighs remained loyal to the British, as his father had before him. He led Mohawks against American forces during the War of 1812. Elected to the provincial parliament in 1821, Euro-Canadians protested that Brant was not a landholder and thus could not serve. Brant died before the controversy was resolved. The portrait from which this print was made was by an unknown artist.

80 LEFT *"Red Jacket, Seneca War Chief."* Although this print of King's 1828 portrait lists Red Jacket as a war chief, the old Seneca with the large George Washington peace medal around his neck was no warrior. Thomas McKenney compared Red Jacket to Cicero, the famous Roman orator, leading his people to war without participating in battle. Born about 1758 near of present-day Geneva, New York, Red Jacket was the nephew of the Iroquois religious leader Handsome Lake and the grandfather of Ely Parker, the first Native American to serve as commissioner of Indian affairs in 1868. At the beginning of the American Revolution, Red Jacket spoke out for neutrality, but when the Seneca, Mohawk, Onondaga, and Cayuga decided in council to support England, he went along. He fought little during the war, serving as a dispatch carrier, and was accused of cowardice by both Cornplanter and Joseph Brant. He became known as Red Jacket because of the British army coat he wore. After the war, Red Jacket became the principal spokesman for the Seneca and at times for the entire Iroquois League of Six Nations. As such, he was present at Canandaigua in 1794 and at Big Tree in 1797, during treaty negotiations at which large portions of Seneca lands were ceded. These cessions were due largely to the influence of Cornplanter and left the Seneca only a number of small reservations. Along with other Iroquois chiefs, Red Jacket visited President George Washington in Philadelphia in 1792 and received the large silver peace medal. Red Jacket was also painted by George Catlin. Advocating the retention of traditional Iroquois customs, Red Jacket was adamant in his opposition to Christianity, calling for a ban on all missionaries from Seneca territory. He also opposed the "longhouse religion" founded by his uncle Handsome Lake. In 1801, Handsome Lake accused him of witchcraft, damaging his reputation. Red Jacket's influence, under attack by the Christian Party, waned in the following years and was exacerbated by his drinking problem. In 1827, he was deposed as chief. When Red Jacket died in 1830, his wife let the local missionary give him a Christian burial, which went against Red Jacket's explicit wishes. He was later reburied at Forest Lawn Cemetery in Buffalo, when the city encroached upon his original burial site.

81 *"Ki-On-Twog-Ky or Corn Plant, A Seneca Chief."* This portrait of Cornplanter, a feared Seneca war chief, was originally painted by F. Bartoli in New York City in 1796. Cornplanter was born about 1735 to a Seneca mother and a white father named John O'Bail. During the American Revolution he sided with the British, fighting alongside Joseph Brant. After the war he became a frequent guest in the nation's capital, meeting with George Washington in the 1790s and Thomas Jefferson after 1800. Cornplanter was the half-brother of Handsome Lake, a Seneca warrior-turned-prophet, who in about 1800 founded a religion that mixed elements of Christianity and traditional Iroquois beliefs. Cornplanter represented the balance of power between the anti-European Red Jacket and Handsome Lake. Initially siding with his brother, Cornplanter shifted his allegiance later in his life to the Red Jacket faction. Cornplanter supported the United States in the War of 1812. He died in 1836, when he was nearly 100 years old.

82 *"Yoholo-Micco, A Creek Chief."* *A noted orator, Yoholo Micco was described by Thomas McKenney as "mild, his disposition sincere and generous." Not long after the completion of this portrait by King in 1826, Yoholo Micco voluntarily moved his large village from Tallapoosa County, Alabama, to the West. About fifty years old at the time, Yoholo Micco died of "the fatigues attending the emigration," according to McKenney.*

83 TOP *"Paddy-Carr, Creek Interpreter."* *The son of an Irishman and a Creek woman, Paddy Carr served as an interpreter for a delegation of Creek chiefs who came to Washington in 1826 to contest the treaty of Indian Springs. He was just 19 years old at the time of the meeting, when King painted his portrait. In later life, Paddy Carr* *became an ambitious man who loved racehorses, had three wives, and was the owner of nearly 80 slaves. He fought in the U.S. Army forces under Gen. Thomas Jesup against the Seminole. Despite his services to the whites, he was forced to relocate to the Indian Territory in 1847.*

83 BOTTOM *"Mistippee."* This Creek boy, the son of Yoholo-Micco, was an expert with a blowgun. Called a cohamoteker by the Creeks, the blowgun was a hollow reed eight to ten feet in length, according to McKenney, who tried it and found that the arrow had the speed and accuracy of a rifle ball. Mistippee's portrait was painted by King in 1826.

84 TOP *"Ledagie, A Creek Chief."* Ledagie was a member of one of the Creek delegations to Washington who protested the removal of their tribe to the West. King painted Ledagie's portrait in 1825.

84 BOTTOM *"Itcho-Tustinnuggee."* Thomas McKenney wrote that "Itcho means deer and Tustennuggee, warrior, so he is therefore known by the English name of Deer Warrior. . . . He is a partisan chief. One who hunts of choice, but fights when he is called upon to do so." Itcho-Tustinnuggee's portrait was painted by King in Washington in 1825. This Creek warrior wears a traditional turban headdress and woven sash.

85 *"Se-Loc-Ta, A Creek Chief."* Selocta, along with his father, Chinnaby, favored the whites during the Creek War and led the pro-white faction of their tribe. Their opponent was William Weatherford, a half-Creek, half-white chief who fought a bitter war against Gen. Andrew Jackson's forces until his capture. Selocta served as a guide and interpreter for Jackson, but as soon as armed resistance ended, the whites urged the Creeks to relocate in the West. Not even Selocta's faithful service could sway Jackson, and in 1825-26 he was forced to sign his Georgia lands over to the whites. The original portrait of Selocta was painted by King in 1825.

86 TOP *"Tah-Chee, A Cherokee Chief."*
Born about 1790, Tahchee was an early
emigrant, with his parents, to the lands west of
the Mississippi in Arkansas. He became an expert
hunter and studied the ways of the hunt with
other tribes, even the Osage, the enemies of the
Cherokee. He explored vast territories in the West
and was a true Indian "mountain man."
Tahchee, who was also known as Dutch, began a
one-man war with the Comanche over a
boundary dispute, and when he would not desist
from fighting, he was branded an outlaw by the
U.S. government. He later served as a guide for
the U.S. Army against the Comanche. George
Catlin met and painted Tahchee in 1834, but the
portrait from which this print was made was
probably painted during the 1820s in
Washington by King. The rough-
hewn Tahchee wears a lavender
hunting shirt with a knife
tucked in his sash, along with
a rakish turban and plume.

86 BOTTOM *"Spring Frog, A Cherokee Chief."*
Also known by the Cherokee names of Tooan Tuh
and Yoosto, Spring Frog supported the move west
and was one of the first of his people to do so.
Thomas McKenney remembered Tooan Tuh as "a
man of excellent disposition, and very correct and
honorable in all his dealings." His King portrait
was painted at an unknown date.

87 TOP *"David Vann, A Cherokee Chief."* Vann, a supporter of John Ridge, favored the resettlement of the Cherokee in the West. Thomas McKenney said of him that he had "more of white than of red blood in him, as his portrait manifests." The King portrait was completed in 1825.

87 BOTTOM *"John Ridge, A Cherokee."* Ridge, the son and namesake of the famous Cherokee leader who reluctantly supported removal by signing the Treaty of New Echota, supported his father's policies by writing editorials that appeared in the Cherokee-language newspaper, the Phoenix. He believed that whiskey peddlers were gaining a hold on the Cherokee nation, turning his people into alcoholics and preventing them from working their fields. They were so dissipated as a nation, Ridge claimed, that they could no longer defend themselves. Moving to the new lands in the West was the only solution, he argued, for in that way they could escape the evil influences of the whites. He eventually moved west with his Euro-American wife, where retribution awaited him. His foes dragged him from his bed in the middle of the night and slashed him to death. His father was shot down by assassins. Bitter feelings caused violence between the two Cherokee factions for many years to come. John Ridge's portrait was painted by King in 1825.

87

88 LEFT *"Yaha-Hajo, A Seminole Chief."* His name translates to "Mad Wolf," but Thomas McKenney thought this chief "mild and benevolent." He was reputed to be the best hunter in Florida and was the second principal war chief of the Seminole. Yaha-Hajo wavered between the factions that split his people when the government insisted on their relocation. At first siding with the progovernment faction led by Foke-Luste-Hajo, he eventually went over to the Micanopy faction. Yaha-Hajo was killed by U.S. soldiers during the Seminole War. His portrait was painted by King in 1825.

88 RIGHT *"Tuko-See-Mathla, A Seminole Chief."* When hostilities broke out in Florida over Indian removal in 1835, Tukosee-Mathla supported the U.S. government. He was killed by Osceola and his followers, who were determined to prevent removal to the West. Tukosee-Mathla was painted by Charles Bird King in 1826, when he was part of a Seminole delegation to Washington. The Seminole chief wears a hunting shirt of calico cloth, decorated with silver wrist- and armbands, a sash, and a combination gorget and peace medal. This rare full-length portrait shows Tukosee-Mathla with his flintlock rifle at the ready.

89 LEFT *"Micanopy, A Seminole Chief."* Micanopy, a feared Seminole war chief, violently opposed removal and helped lead the fight against U.S. forces in Florida. In 1832 a number of Seminole chiefs agreed to sign the Treaty of Payne's Landing, which allowed the cession of tribal lands to the whites and removal to Indian Territory. Micanopy refused to sign, and he supported younger warriors preparing to resist removal. He participated in the attacks of December 28, 1835, when Seminole warriors ambushed a force of 100 U.S. soldiers led by Maj. Francis L. Dade, who were traveling from Fort Brooke to Fort King. Only three of the white soldiers survived to tell the tale of what was soon called "the Dade Massacre." Micanopy agreed to relocation in July 1837 but was kidnapped by Osceola to keep him from surrendering. He finally surrendered to Gen. Jesup late in 1837. He told Jesup, "My warriors are all dead. . . . we have only women and children. . . . I can fight you no longer." Micanopy signed a treaty and was imprisoned for a time, before finally being allowed to move westward to Indian Territory. His portrait was painted by King in 1826. He died in 1849 at about 60 years of age.

89 RIGHT *"Nea-Math-La, A Seminole Chief."* Neamathla opposed the removal of his people to the West, and when Florida's territorial governor, William P. Duval, heard of his opposition, he used his influence among members of the tribe to have him deposed him as chief. Thomas McKenney wrote that the removal of Neamathla was "a curious instance of the anomalous character of the relation existing between our Government and the Indians; for while the latter are for many purposes considered as independent nations and are treated with as such, they are in all essential respects regarded and governed as subjects. "Neamathla not only opposed removal, but had also objected to the whites educating the Seminoles. He told Florida's governor Duval that they wanted "no schools such as you offer us. We wish our children to remain as the Great Spirit made them, and as their fathers are, Indians." Neamathla was painted by King in 1826. He continued to resist removal until he was captured by Alabama militiamen in 1836 and shipped West in shackles.

90 *"Payta-Kootha, A Shawanoe Warrior."* *Paytakootha, also known by the names Flying Clouds and Captain Reed, was a wandering ambassador for peace. He signed many treaties in the interests of peace with the whites, including the Treaty of Greenville in 1795. The date of the original portrait by King is not known.*

91 TOP LEFT *"Kish-Kal-Wa, A Shawanoe Chief."* *Kishkalwa fought the whites at the Battle of the Great Kanawha in 1774. When the Shawnee were moved west of the Mississippi in the early 1800s, friction resulted with tribes like the Osage, who claimed the lands where the resettled tribes were placed. In 1818, when he was about 80 years of age, Kishkalwa took part in a battle between the Shawnee, Delaware and Cherokee against the Osage in Missouri. He signed a treaty at a council between the Shawnee and Indian agents at St. Louis in November 1825, and later he led a delegation to Washington to meet the President. This King portrait was most likely completed during his Washington visit of 1826 or 1827.*

91 TOP RIGHT *"Ca-Ta-He-Cas-Sa-Black Hoof, Principal Chief of the Shawanoes."* Born about 1740, Catahecassa hated the whites and fought continuously from the time of Braddock's defeat in 1755 until his Shawnee were defeated by Gen. Anthony Wayne in the Battle of Fallen Timbers in 1794. Catahecassa signed the Treaty of Greenville in 1795, promising never again to fight the United States. The British in Canada were unsuccessful in getting him to change his mind, as were Tecumseh and his brother, the Prophet. Catahecassa visited Washington in 1802, asking for farming implements and livestock, believing that if his people became like the whites, they would be allowed to keep their lands. This print was taken from a portrait by an unknown artist. Catahecassa died in 1831 at Wapakoneta, Ohio, at about 90 years of age. He was one of the few lucky Shawnee who were not moved west.

91 BOTTOM *"Qua-Ta-Wa-Pea, A Shawanoe Chief."* Quatawapea led his Shawnee warriors in battle on the side of the United States during the American Revolution. In gratitude, he and his people were guaranteed a 40,000-acre tract of land in Ohio, but in 1831 the government forced him to move to the west side of the Mississippi. Thomas McKenney called Quatawapea a "sensible and brave Indian." During a visit to Washington in the early 1800s, President Jefferson personally placed the peace medal seen in the portrait around Quatawapea's neck. On a later visit to the capital in 1825, King painted Quatawapea's portrait.

92 **"Okee-Makee-Quid, A Chippeway Chief."**
This elaborately dressed chief made a birchbark canoe for McKenney at the Fond du Lac council. He wears a mantle or apron decorated with paint and feathers, over a brightly striped linen hunting shirt. His leggings are decorated with glass beads, as are his wide garters. In his right hand he holds a wooden war club and a small tobacco pouch, while in his left he holds a long-stemmed ceremonial pipe with a carved bowl of "Catlinite." Over his entire costume he wears a deerskin cloak dyed black, given to him by a Sioux chief when peace was made between the two tribes in 1825. His headdress, decorated with beads, feathers, and buffalo horns, gives him a unique appearance. The original portrait from which this print was made was painted by James Otto Lewis at the Fond du Lac council of 1826 and later copied by King.

93 TOP *"Shin-Ga-Ba-W'Ossin, A Chippeway Chief."* This chief, whose name translates to "Image Stone," was an important and influential figure among the Ojibwa. He urged peace with the whites, although he did not trust them. He signed the treaties of Prairie du Chien, Fond du Lac, and Butte des Morts. The $1,000 annuity paid to the Chippewa by the U.S. government was used, at Shingabaw'ossin's suggestion, to build a school for Ojibwa children at Sault Sainte Marie, on Michigan's upper peninsula. The original portrait from which this print was made was painted by James Otto Lewis at the Fond du Lac council of 1826 and was later copied by King.

93 BOTTOM *"J-Aw-Beance, A Chippeway Chief."* This portrait of a Chippewa chief is one of many copied by King from field portraits by James Otto Lewis. The Chippewa, or Ojibwa, lived in the upper Midwest, on the border of the United States and British Canada. McKenney described them as "wandering savages" who were "miserable and degraded," with "little ambition and few ideas." By writing about them in this fashion, he merely showed how little he knew about the Ojibwa. This tribe were fierce warriors who had driven the Sioux to the west and occupied vast areas of Canada. They were allied with the Ottawa and the Potawatomie, and lived in birchbark wigwams. They farmed, hunted, and gathered their food from the rich woodlands of the western Great Lakes. The fighting spirit of the tribe continues today. In 1968, three Ojibwas, Dennis Banks, George Mitchell, and Clyde Bellecourt founded the American Indian Movement (AIM) in Minneapolis. AIM is a militant group that continues to fight for Indian rights and improved social conditions, despite great controversy over their occupations of Alcatraz Island in 1969, the Bureau of Indian Affairs building in Washington in 1972, and the Wounded Knee site in South Dakota in 1973.

94 *"A Chippeway Widow."* James Otto Lewis painted this woman to show one of the unique customs of the Ojibwa. According to McKenney, upon the death of a husband, his widow would select some of his belongings and arrange them in a bundle, which she carried with her for one year. She was forbidden to remarry and could only be freed of the bundle by the relatives of her deceased husband, who could take it away when they felt she had mourned long enough.

95 *"Chippeway Squaw & Child."* *James Otto*
Lewis, at the Fond du Lac council, painted several
Ojibwa women, paintings that were later copied
by King and made into lithographs for Indian
Tribes of North America. *In this print, a Ojibwa*
woman is shown carrying her baby swaddled in a
cradleboard.

96 TOP *"Pee-Che-Kir, A Ojibwa Chief."* This chief, whose name means "Buffalo," was "a solid, straight formed Indian," according to McKenney. Here Peechekir holds a ceremonial pipe, its stem carved of wood and its bowl probably of the red stone later dubbed "Catlinite," after the artist George Catlin. His silver armband has an engraved symbol on it and may have been a gift from the British or U.S. government. Lesser chiefs often received silver armbands rather than peace medals. The original portrait from which this print was made was painted by James Otto Lewis at the Fond du Lac council of 1826 and was later copied by King.

96 BOTTOM *"Wesh-Cubb, A Chippeway Chief."* Weshcubb was known as a great and powerful warrior but was plagued by the fact that his son had become an A-go-kwa, that is, a homosexual. A-go-kwas were tolerated in nearly every Indian tribe, and the practice was an outlet for those who could not endure the physical hardships and fears associated with being a warrior. A-go-kwas dressed like women but were forced to live apart from the main band. Although shunned by tribal members, some men had sexual relations with them, and the A-go-kwas were thought to have great spiritual power. Unfortunately, more is usually made of Weshcubb's son than of Weshcubb, who was described by McKenney as "a good, fat, comfortable looking Indian."

97 TOP *"No-Tin, A Chippewa Chief."* No-Tin was described by Thomas McKenney as "a good smart Chippewa chief, a good hunter and a brave warrior." The original portrait from which this print was made was painted by James Otto Lewis at the Fond du Lac council of 1826 and was later copied by King.

97 BOTTOM *"Wa-Em-Boesh-Kaa, A Chippeway Chief."* McKenney carefully noted the attire of Waemboeshkaa, which he thought fitting for an Indian "king." His hat, which looked to McKenney like a crown, was made from feathers of a drake mixed with feathers from the head of a woodpecker. His wristbands were made of the same materials. He is also depicted with an elaborate ceremonial pipe, likewise decorated with feathers. Upon inquiry, McKenney found that Waemboeshkaa had no importance in tribal councils, despite his grand appearance. The original portrait from which this print was made was painted by James Otto Lewis at the Fond du Lac council of 1826 and was later copied by King.

98 LEFT *"Amiskquew, A Menominee Warrior."*
*This portrait was painted by James Otto Lewis at
the Butte des Morts council in 1827 and was later
copied by King. About Amiskquew, McKenney
stated that there was "nothing remarkable in his
history." The Menominee lived in Wisconsin and
ate wild rice for their subsistence. First
encountered by French explorers in 1634, they
made beautiful clothing, copper jewelry, and
woven pouches.*

98 RIGHT *"Mar-Ko-Me-Te, A Menominee
Brave."* *Markomete was part of a delegation that
signed a treaty in Washington in 1831, when
King painted his portrait.*

99 TOP *"Wa-Baun-See, A Pottawatomie Chief."* This influential war chief was first an ally of the British, participating in the attack on Fort Dearborn (today's Chicago) in the War of 1812. He signed a peace treaty with the United States in 1814 and in 1826 signed the Treaty of the Wabash in Indiana, which forfeited tribal lands to the United States. Wabaunsee was stabbed by a Potawatomi warrior that day, but he survived. Living to sign other treaties with the United States and to side against Black Hawk in 1832, Wabaunsee agreed to move his people west of the Mississippi in 1835, when this portrait was painted by King. In the painting, Wabaunsee wears a U.S. Army officer's coat, often given to loyal Indians along with peace medals, like the Andrew Jackson medal the chief wears around his neck. Wabaunsee settled on the Missouri River in Iowa, near Council Bluffs, where he died in 1848.

99 BOTTOM *"Me-Te-A, A Pottawatomie Chief."* Metea attended an Indian council at St. Joseph, Michigan, in 1827, and reached for a bottle of whiskey. Unfortunately, the bottle contained poison, and in a few short minutes he was dead. Metea had passed through many evolutions in his short life. Initially, he resisted U.S. power in the Midwest, fighting alongside the British in the War of 1812 and leading the ambush and massacre of American troops evacuating Fort Dearborn on August 15, 1812. He later made peace with the United States, attending a treaty council in Washington in 1821, and even urging the attendance of Potawatomi children at Euro-American schools. The original of this painting, which is now lost, may have been by Samuel Seymour.

101 "Wa-Pel-La, Chief of the Musquakees."

Born in 1787, Wapella was one of the three important chiefs of the Sac and Fox, the others being Keokuk and Powasheek. In 1837, Wapella was part of the delegation of Sac and Fox led by Keokuk to the East Coast. His portrait was painted in Washington by King. The Sac and Fox came to Washington to attend a peace conference with their enemies, the Santee Sioux. The conference resulted in five signed treaties but ultimately did not achieve its intended objective. In writing the treaties, the government managed to coerce the Indians into selling or exchanging vast amounts of their land, so that each of the opposing tribes left much poorer than when they arrived. Wapella's people were uncomfortably housed during their stay in Washington—34 men, women, and children were jammed into very tiny garret rooms at the Virginia Coffee House. Despite all these drawbacks, the Sac and Fox had a wonderful time in the capital. The Indians attended the theater, where from their box seats overlooking the stage they showered the lead actress with buffalo robes, headdresses, beaded belts, and moccasins. This disruption of her performance was taken in stride by the actress, who returned the favor by giving the Indians ostrich feathers. The Sac and Fox continued on to Boston, where they danced and spoke to a crowd. Wapella is shown wearing a mantle of white buffalo fur, decorated with feathers. Around his neck he wears a bear claw necklace and a peace medal, probably depicting Andrew Jackson. His head is wrapped in a silk turban. Wapella died while on a hunting trip near Ottumwa, Iowa, in 1842.

100 "Tai-O-Mah, A Musquakee Brave."

Although he was dying of tuberculosis, Taiomah made the long journey by steamboat and stagecoach to Washington in 1824. McKenney said that Taiomah belonged to a secret society among the Fox called the Great Medicine Society, which McKenney compared with the Masons. In the painting, Taiomah wears a bear claw necklace and silver armband. He died not long after his portrait was finished by King.

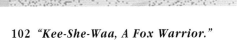

102 "Kee-She-Waa, A Fox Warrior."
Keeshewaa, the Sun, was a noted Fox warrior and medicine man and a friend of the Sac chief Keokuk. McKenney wrote that Keeshewaa was "a firm, onward, fearless chief, and of good character." The painting from which this print was made was probably painted by King in Washington about 1824.

103 "Ne Sou A Quoit, A Fox Chief."
Nesouaquoit came to Washington in 1837, unsuccessfully trying to claim money owed to his people by the U.S. government. The lithograph of Nesouaquoit is taken from an 1837 portrait made in Washington by King. A second portrait of Nesouaquoit, shown full-length in a seated position, was made by King in the same year; both paintings have survived. The name Nesouaquoit means "Bear in the Fork of a Tree."

104

105 *"Ap-Pa-Noo-Se, Saukie Chief."* Appanoose accompanied the delegation of Sac and Fox chiefs to Washington in 1837, where his portrait was painted by George Cooke. In the portrait Appanoose wears a decorative silver arm band and peace medal, possibly depicting Andrew Jackson. He carries a decorative "gunstock"-type war club with a lethal-looking iron point.

104 *"Kish-Ke-Kosh, A Fox Brave."* Kishkekosh, also a member of the 1837 delegation to Washington, is depicted in this George Cooke painting with a coup stick decorated with feathers and a "gunstock"-type war club. He wears a scalp tied around his neck. But his headgear nearly started a war between the delegation of Sac and Fox and the delegation of Santee Sioux in the capital city. When the two tribes were called together at the War Department, the Sac and Fox filed to the left of the meeting room, while the Sioux went to the right. The Sioux could not take their eyes off Kishkekosh's hat, and for good reason; he had made a raid on a Sioux village some time before, killing and scalping three warriors. He had taken the buffalo hat from one of the corpses. The tall, imposing Kishkekosh was finally persuaded with gifts and promises to leave his hat at the Virginia Coffee House before it caused further trouble.

105

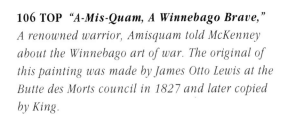

106 TOP *"A-Mis-Quam, A Winnebago Brave,"* A renowned warrior, Amisquam told McKenney about the Winnebago art of war. The original of this painting was made by James Otto Lewis at the Butte des Morts council in 1827 and later copied by King.

106 BOTTOM *"Hoo-Wan-Ne-Ka, A Winnebago Chief."* When Hoowanneka was painted by James Otto Lewis at the Fond du Lac council of 1826, he dressed exactly as he had presented himself to President Monroe in 1824 in a White House ceremony. He wears what appears to be a Jefferson peace medal, as well as silver arm and wrist bands. He carries a pipe-tomahawk, a popular trade item. Hoowanneka fought alongside the British in the War of 1812 but later made his peace with the United States. He signed treaties at Prairie du Chien in 1825 and Fort Armstrong in 1832.

107 TOP *"Tshi-Zun-Hau-Kau, A Winnebago."* This tall Winnebago warrior answered McKenney's questions about his unusual staff, saying that it was "the staff of life," and explaining what each of the marks and figures represented. McKenney said that they were "divisions of time, and certain changes of the seasons, to which were added signs indicating the results of certain calculations he had made respecting the weather." Tshizunhaukau, a medicine man and a magician, was part of the Winnebago delegation to Washington in 1828. McKenney insisted that Tshizunhaukau be painted by King holding his special staff. He also wears a peace medal and silver armbands and carries a fine pipe-tomahawk.

107 BOTTOM *"A Winnebago."* The Winnebago, whose home was among the beautiful lakes of Wisconsin, were fierce warriors. They called themselves Hotcangara ("People of the Big Speech"); Winnebago was a name they were called by their enemies, the Sac and Fox. The Winnebago lived in rectangular bark lodges and farmed the fields along the eastern arm of Green Bay. Over the course of several years and many broken treaties, they were forced to move west of the Mississippi to Nebraska. One of the Winnebagoes who lived through these years of great turmoil was painted in 1828 by King and is shown in this print. Part French, McKenney recalled that he was "a sensible, fluent speaker." He wears three silver peace medals around his neck, official signs of peace and friendship struck by the U.S. government and given only to high-ranking chiefs and warriors in each tribe.

108 *"Chono Ca Pe, An Ottoe Chief."* Another member of the 1821 O'Fallon delegation was Choncape, or "Big Kansas," the principal chief of the Oto. Noted for his fierce temper, Choncape nevertheless ruled his tribe fairly. His son was said to match him in explosive temperament. Choncape, in this print made from the 1821 King portrait, wears a bear claw necklace and a silver peace medal. He carries a "gunstock"-type war club with a decorative but lethal metal point.

109 *"No-Way-Ke-Sug-Ga, Otoe."* A member of an 1837 delegation to Washington, Nowaykesugga was one of the last Indians King painted for the government. Painted for war, he wears a decorative turban, a bear claw necklace, and a John Quincy Adams peace medal. His buffalo hide shirt is decorated with porcupine quills on the sleeve, and he holds a ceremonial pipe.

110 "Not-Chi-Mi-Ne, An Ioway Chief."

Notchimine was a fearless warrior who became a living legend within his tribe, and songs were sung about him by the women. In 1836, he grew weary of war and began to seek peace between his tribe and the Osage. Mediation by William Clark in St. Louis failed, but an 1837 conference in Washington was the source of a treaty between the two peoples. Notchimine was painted by King at the time of the Washington conference. He wears a calico shirt covered by a red blanket, an elaborately woven turban, and a James Monroe peace medal.

111 "Ne-O-Mon-Ne, An Ioway Chief."

Called a "warrior of repute" by McKenney, Neomonni, or "Cloud Out of Which the Rain Comes," was well respected by his people. Neomonni attended an 1837 treaty conference in Washington and had his portrait painted by King. McKenney, who by then was no longer commissioner of Indian affairs, showed Neomonni the first edition of his Indian Tribes of North America, with which the Iowa was pleased, recognizing many of the portraits.

112 *"Moa-Na-Hon-Ga, an Ioway Chief."*
This lithograph, which appeared in The Indian Tribes of North America by McKenney and Hall, can be compared with the portrait of the same chief done by Charles Bird King, shown in the second chapter of this book. This comparison is particularly useful, as it makes it possible to evaluate the great skill of Albert Newsam, the deaf-mute lithographer who had the task of using a lithographic pencil to copy King's paintings. His extraordinary faithfulness to the original bespeaks great artistic sensitivity, although it is unknown whether Newsam, like some of his contemporaries, used a rudimentary optical chamber to trace the outlines of his subjects.

113 *"Ma-Has-Kah."* Mahaska, or *"White Cloud,"* was the principal chief of the Iowa tribe when his portrait was painted by King in 1824. This lithograph was made from the original portrait and preserves the general feel of the painting, although it is very flat and two-dimensional. Mahaska is shown wearing a bear claw necklace, a peace medal, decorative feathers in his hair, and personal paint on his face. He carries a *"gunstock"*-style war club.

114 *"Shar-I-Tar-Ish, A Pawnee Chief."*
Sharitarish (Angry Chief) was an important
Pawnee leader who stood six feet tall. When
the principal chief of the Pawnee refused to
go to Washington with Benjamin O'Fallon in
1821, saying that it was beneath his dignity,
the ambitious Sharitarish gladly took his place.
He was well-liked in Washington and for a brief
time became chief of his nation upon his return
to his homeland. Within a few short months,
however, Sharitarish died of a fever. He wears a
buffalo robe turned hair side in, and a peace
medal of unknown origin.

115 *"Pes-Ke-Le-Cha-Co, A Pawnee Chief."*
Called "a firm, determined man, an expert hunter and a fearless warrior" by McKenney, Peskelechaco visited Washington with the 1821 O'Fallon delegation, when King painted his portrait. Peskelechaco wears a buffalo robe turned hair side in, with a horse painted on the tanned side. His peace medal appears to have the image of James Madison on it. Peskelechaco died in 1826 while defending his village against an Osage war party.

116 TOP *"To-Ka-Cou, A Sioux Chief."*
Tokacou, or "He That Inflicts the First Wound," was part of the society within his tribe that, like a police force, enforced the tribal rules. He signed treaties for the Yankton Sioux (Nakota) at Fort Lookout in 1825, Prairie du Chien in 1830, and Washington in 1837, when this painting was made by George Cooke. Tokacou wears a beautifully decorated shirt of buffalo or elk hide, decorated with beadwork and dyed human hair. He holds a sword that symbolizes his authority within the police society.

116 BOTTOM *"Esh-Ta-Hum-Leah, A Sioux Chief."* *Called "Sleepy Eyes," a loose translation of his Dakota name, Eshtahhumleah was a principal chief of his tribe, the Sisseton Sioux (Dakota). He signed major treaties at Prairie du Chien in 1825 and 1830, St. Peters in 1836, and Traverse des Sioux in 1851. His portrait was painted by King in 1824. Born about 1780 near present-day Mankato, Minnesota, he died in South Dakota on a hunting trip in about 1860. His remains were returned to Minnesota and are marked with a monument.*

117 *"Wa-Na-Ta, Grand Chief of the Sioux."*

Wanata was a chief of the Yanktonais band of the Sioux. The Yanktonais Sioux were one of three groups of people who spoke a related language. They were called "Sioux" by the French in an adaptation of the Ojibwa word Nadouessioux, *which means "adder" or "snake." Since the Ojibwa were the enemies of the Sioux, it is understandable that the people they were describing did not also call themselves snakes. Nakota, meaning "allies," is the term the Yanktonais Sioux used to describe their own people. The Nakota, composed of the Yankton and Yanktonais tribes, were the middle of the three Sioux nations, the eastern being the Dakota and the western the Lakota. Chief Waneta was born about 1795 in what is now South Dakota, and fought with the British against the Americans in the War of 1812. After the war he was invited to England and presented at court. In 1820 he plotted an attack on U.S. Fort Snelling in Minnesota, which was aborted when he was seized by the authorities. Wanata later became a friend of the United States, signing the treaties of Fort Pierre and Prairie du Chien in 1825. He died in 1848, when he was about 53 years old.*

GEORGE CATLIN: RESCUING THE INDIANS FROM OBLIVION

In 1868, Francis Catlin traveled across the Atlantic Ocean to Brussels, Belgium, to see his brother George for the first time in twenty-nine years. George Catlin, once a renowned painter of American Indian tribes, the man once hailed and feted on a tour of Europe, was living in a garret apartment, his only company a set of white mice he kept as pets. His daily routine involved sitting in a streetside café, writing memoirs of his travels among the wild Indian tribes of America and drawing sketches that he called "cartoons" of the incidents he recalled. Each day the 72-year-old Catlin ate the same meal of steak and potatoes in the café below his flat. Because he had grown deaf in his later years, he ate in silence, undistracted by the tumult of boisterous song and conversation around him. George Catlin told his brother that the cartoons he was busy sketching, coupled with the words he was writing about his experiences,

CATLIN'S INDIAN GALLERY:
In the Old Theatre,
On Louisiana Avenue, and near the City Post Office.

MR. CATLIN,

Who has been for seven years traversing the Prairies of the "Far West," and procuring the Portraits of the most distinguished Indians of those uncivilized regions, together with Paintings of their

VILLAGES, BUFFALO HUNTS, DANCES, LANDSCAPES OF THE COUNTRY &c. &c.

Will endeavor to entertain the Citizens of Washington, for a short time with an Exhibition of

THREE HUNDRED & THIRTY PORTRAITS & NUMEROUS OTHER PAINTINGS

Which he has collected from 38 different Tribes, speaking different languages, all of whom he has been among, and Painted his pictures from life.

Portraits of Black Hawk and nine of his Principal Warriors,

Are among the number, painted at Jefferson Barracks, while prisoners of war, in their war dress and war paint.

ALSO, FOUR PAINTINGS REPRESENTING THE

ANNUAL RELIGIOUS CEREMONY OF THE MANDANS,

Doing penance, by inflicting the most cruel tortures upon their own bodies—passing knives and splints through their flesh, and suspending their bodies by their wounds, &c.

A SERIES OF ONE HUNDRED LANDSCAPE VIEWS,

Descriptive of the picturesque *Prairie Scenes* of the Upper Missouri and other parts of the Western regions.

AND A SERIES OF TWELVE BUFFALO HUNTING SCENES,

Together with *SPLENDID SPECIMENS OF COSTUME*, will also be exhibited.

☞The great interest of this collection consists in its being a representation of the *wildest tribes of Indians in America*, and entirely in their *Native Habits* and *Costumes*: consisting of Sioux, Puncahs, Konzas, Shiennes, Crows, Ojibbeways, Assineboins, Mandans, Crees, Blackfeet, Snakes, Mahas, Ottoes, Ioways, Flatheads, Weahs, Peorias, Sacs, Foxes, Winnebagoes, Menomonies, Minatarrees, Rickarees, Osages, Camanches, Wicos, Pawnee-Picts, Kiowas, Seminoles, Euchees, and others.

☞In order to render the Exhibition more instructive than it could otherwise be, the Paintings will be exhibited one at a time, and such explanations of their Dress, Customs, Traditions, &c. given by Mr. Catlin, as will enable the public to form a just idea of the CUSTOMS, NUMBERS, and CONDITION of the Savages yet in a state of nature in North America.

The EXHIBITION, with EXPLANATIONS, will commence on Monday Evening, the 9th inst. in the old Theatre, and be repeated for several successive evenings, commencing at HALF PAST SEVEN O'CLOCK. Each COURSE will be limited to two evenings, Monday and Tuesday, Wednesday and Thursday, Friday and Saturday; and it his hoped that visiters will be in and seated as near the hour as possible, that they may see the whole collection. The portrait of OSEOLA will be shewn on each evening.

ADMITTANCE 50 CENTS.—CHILDREN HALF PRICE.

☞ These Lectures will be continued for *one week only*.

118 LEFT *Broadside Advertising "Catlin's Indian Gallery," Washington, D.C., April 1838.* The Indian Gallery of Catlin's paintings and artifacts from his western travels was a huge hit in New York. Its short run in Washington was prompted by political expediency, for Catlin wanted Congress to buy the entire gallery for the American people.

118 TOP RIGHT *"Male Caribou, A Brave," 1836.* This Ojibwa warrior was painted at Sault Sainte Marie in 1836. He wears a turban around his head and a medicine bag around his neck. As Catlin came to know American Indian people during his travels, he found that he was more interested in the relatively "unspoiled" Indians of the Far West than in those from tribes like the Ojibwa, who had sustained contact with Euro-Americans.

118 BOTTOM RIGHT *"Mouse-Colored Feather, A Noted Brave," 1832. This Mandan warrior posed for Catlin "with a beautiful pipe in his hand." Catlin noted that the man's hair was "quite yellow." The Mandan were a tribe of village Indians who had settled along the Missouri River in today's North Dakota. In 1832, Catlin became extremely fascinated with them, visiting them, painting them, and keeping notes about them.*

119 *Portrait of George Catlin, 1849, by William Fisk. In this portrait, the 53-year-old Catlin, stands with his palette and brush, dressed in buckskins inside an Indian lodge. An Indian warrior and his wife stand behind him, with Indian women and children outside in front of another tepee. By this point, Catlin had devoted his life to chronicling American Indian people, yet he had been away from America for a decade.*

In some ways, this portrait represents Catlin's glory days as an entrepreneur and showman. His wistful expression may reveal wishful thinking about a projected return to America. Catlin's biggest dream was to have the U.S. Congress buy his collection of paintings and artifacts as a permanent national resource dedicated to a "vanishing race." He was to be disappointed in his wish.

120-121 *"Ojibwa Troupe in London,"* **1844.**
*This composite drawing and series of portrait
studies was made by Catlin in London in 1844. It
details the members of the Ojibwa dancing
troupe, who made Catlin's gallery so popular for
over a year. The Ojibwa are dressed in all their
native splendor, with the men carrying war clubs
and ceremonial pipes.*

would once more bring him fame and fortune. But the artist was deluding himself. His era had passed, and with it had departed the Indian way of life he had observed during his youth in the American West.

George Catlin's artistic work comprised the first important pictorial record of western Indian tribes. No artist, in the period before photography, traveled more widely among as many different tribes or made as many portraits and scenes of Indians from life. Catlin's notes on Indian customs and cultures also constituted a valuable body of ethnological information. After completing the paintings, Catlin devoted himself to interpreting Indians for non-Indians in America and in Europe. Yet despite his incredible optimism, Catlin must have wondered at his failure in the latter half of his life as he sat day after day in the Brussels café.

Born in Wilkes-Barre, Pennsylvania, on July 26, 1796, George was the fifth of fourteen children of Putnam and Polly Sutton Catlin. Catlin's father, a veteran of the American Revolution, moved from New England to Pennsylvania to practice as a country lawyer shortly after the war. Putnam Catlin's fortunes declined, however, and the family moved from place to place when George was a boy. His happiest years were spent on a farm along the banks of the Susquehanna River in Broome County, New York. George later wrote that he had led an ideal boy's life, fishing in the rivers, hunting in the woods, searching for Indian artifacts, and listening to the stories of backwoodsmen. He grew up in an area where memories of Indians were strong, although Indian people themselves had been forced to move westward long before. In 1778, during the American Revolution, a force of Iroquois Indians and Americans loyal to the crown of England had swept down on the Wilkes-Barre area, killing many of the inhabitants in what became known as the Wyoming Valley Massacre. George's mother and grandmother had been held hostage for a short time, but both were subsequently released. As a result, the boy heard many stories about Indians during his youth, not all of them good.

George received his early education in Wilkes-Barre, where he learned mathematics, history, and classical languages at the local "academy." After five years there he was sent by his father to study law with Tapping Reeve in Litchfield, Connecticut. Reeve was one of the foremost instructors of young lawyers in the United States at that time. In his book *Letters and Notes on the Manners, Customs, and Condition of the North American Indians* (1841), Catlin recalled that he had managed to last at Reeve's school through a "siege with Blackstone and Coke," the major law texts of the time, although his mind was often on other things. He successfully completed the fourteen-month course in the autumn of 1818 and passed the Connecticut bar exam. But in his book *Life Amongst the Indians* (1857) Catlin said that during the next three years, as he returned to Pennsylvania to study law, "another and stronger passion was getting the advantage of me–that for painting, to which all of my love of pleading soon gave way; and after having covered nearly every inch of the lawyer's table (and even encroached upon the judge's bench) with penknife, pen and ink, and pencil sketches of judges, juries and culprits, I very deliberately resolved to convert my law library into paintpots and brushes, and to pursue painting as my future, and, apparently more agreeable profession."

By 1821, Catlin was in Philadelphia, exhibiting his work at the prestigious Pennsylvania Academy of Fine Arts and absorbing art instruction at the Philadelphia Academy. The mature Catlin stood about five foot eight, a thin, wiry man of about 135 pounds. He had blue eyes and dark hair, with a long scar on the left side of his face, received when a childhood friend threw a

122 *"Mandan Game of Tchung-Kee," 1832-33.* *The Mandans loved to play games, and Tchung-kee was a favorite. Nearly all Indian cultures loved to gamble on the outcome of games, including the Mandan. "The game of Tchung-kee [is] a beautiful athletic exercise," Catlin explained, "which they seem to be almost unceasingly practicing whilst the weather is fair, and they have nothing else of moment to demand their attention."*

122-123 *"Sioux Indian Council."* *This painting was probably painted in Catlin's studio from field sketches made in 1832. This sample nature scene puts Indian chiefs "in profound deliberation" in the foreground, emphasizing Catlin's vision of Indians as inseparable from the natural world they inhabited.*

tomahawk that bounced off a tree and cut him badly. The young man was quickly swept up in the artistic and scientific world of early nineteenth-century Philadelphia, which was still the largest and most cosmopolitan city in the United States.

A major component of the intellectual world of Philadelphia was the museum administered by the artist, inventor and naturalist Charles Willson Peale. Open for thirty-five years by the time Catlin saw it, Peale's museum was located in the "long room" on the second floor of Independence Hall, the historic building where both the Declaration of Independence and the Constitution had been adopted and signed. A truly unique institution, it displayed Peale's portraits of Revolutionary heroes, a mastodon skeleton, mounted birds and fish, and Indian artifacts, providing a comprehensive view of United States history and culture. Catlin may have been inspired by Peale's portraits of the explorer-heroes Lewis and Clark and the many items they brought back from the Far West, including Indian clothing, tobacco pouches, and ornamental belts. Artifacts from Stephen H. Long's 1820-21 expedition were also on display. There was certainly much of interest in the museum for a young man like George Catlin.

In addition to the museum, Philadelphia was home to the most important scientific minds in America, whose goal, like that of Charles Willson Peale's museum, was to catalogue the fascinating "new world" of America. These scientists wished to record every species of bird, to list every type of plant, to measure every quadruped, to discover the geographical distances across the continent, the length of rivers, the breadth of lakes–in short, to list and enumerate life and nature in America, which

they believed cried out for exploration, before it was changed forever by the surge of their own "civilization."

It may have been this spirit of inquiry that caused George Catlin to pursue his ambition to record and preserve the culture of American Indian people. His sojourns to Peale's museum and the intellectual climate of Philadelphia, perhaps coupled with the sight of a visiting Indian delegation or two, inspired Catlin's fertile mind to incorporate science into his art. Although Catlin had a natural artistic talent that he worked long hours to perfect, he was never able to compete with the classically trained artists of Philadelphia. He supported himself primarily by painting miniature portraits, which, in the era before photography, people commissioned and carried as keepsakes.

An important commission came to Catlin in 1824, when he was asked to paint the portrait of New York governor DeWitt Clinton. Catlin also made lithographs of the newly finished Erie Canal for an official souvenir booklet. His portraits were not enthusiastically received either by critics or by the public. By 1826 he had moved to New York City, where he continued to receive commissions and became a member of the National Academy of Design. During these years, New York was beginning its rise, soon to outstrip Philadelphia as the largest and most important city in America. Catlin's Erie Canal commissions took him to many areas of upstate New York. Through upstate friends he gained an introduction to Red Jacket, an important Seneca chief known for his resistance to Euro-American customs and religion. In 1826, Catlin was allowed to make a portrait of the aging Red Jacket and was excited at the thought of painting an Indian—the first in what he hoped would be a series of history paintings. But to Catlin, Red Jacket seemed too settled, too "civilized" in his log house with its stone fireplace. Catlin was

beginning to formulate a scheme of chronicling the "wild, uncivilized" Indians of North America. His half-formed plan contained elements of both science and art, for using his artistic talents he would document the lifeways of what he believed to be a "vanishing race."

Catlin felt trapped in his work of portrait and miniature painting. He told Secretary of War Peter B. Porter in an 1829 letter that he was "wasting my life and substance for a bare living." Catlin said he was interested in painting the history of the nation, and he asked for a position as an art instructor at West Point, or perhaps an appointment to an Indian agency in the field, where, he told Porter, in two years time he "could return with such a collection of portraits of the principal chiefs of different nations and paintings representing all their different manners and customs, as would enable me to open such a gallery, first in this country and then in London, as would in all probability handsomely repay me for all my labours, and afford me the advantage of a successful introduction beyond the Atlantic."

Catlin's voice here was that of an ambitious 32-year-old man wanting to make a name for himself in the art world by painting something unique, thereby gaining enough fame to establish a foothold in European and American artistic circles. Whether he envisioned devoting the rest of his life to chronicling American Indian people at this point is not known. We do know that he was not highly regarded in the art circles of his day. Thus, he needed to branch out and create his own niche, or else be forever forgotten as just another failed portraitist. Perhaps this is what he had in mind when he asked Secretary Porter to assist him.

Catlin was also undoubtedly looking toward his own personal future, for on May 10, 1828, he married Clara Gregory, the 20-year-old daughter of a prosperous Albany

124 "Strong Wind, Chippewa," 1834.
Strong Wind was one of the Ojibwa dancers Catlin met in London in 1843. Catlin described Strong Wind as "a half-caste, a young man of fine personal appearance and address."

125 "Strikes Two At Once, Oto," 1832.
Nowaykesugga, or "He Who Strikes Two at Once," was a distinguished Oto warrior.
While much of this canvas is unfinished, the figure of Nowaykesugga can easily be discerned, dressed beautifully in a hide shirt and leggings decorated with scalp-locks, eagle feathers, and porcupine quills, with a bear claw necklace.

126 *"One Horn, Lakota," 1832.* *The first portrait made by Catlin at Fort Pierre was of One Horn, or Hawonjetah, the principal chief of the Miniconjou Lakota. The Lakota were the westernmost tribe of the Sioux, and the Miniconjou were one of seven bands of the Lakota. One Horn took his name from the small shell hanging around his neck, which had once belonged to his father. When the portrait was completed, the Lakota were frightened by its power, for they had never seen a realistic image of a man on canvas before. Catlin might have had no more sitters, but the traders convinced One Horn that the portrait was an honor to his high status as chief. "His costume was a very handsome one," noted Catlin, "and will have a place in my Indian Gallery by the side of his picture. It is made of elk skins beautifully dressed, and fringed with a profusion of porcupine quills and scalp-locks; and his hair, lifted up and crossed, over the top of his head, with a simple tie, giving it somewhat the appearance of a Turkish turban."*

127 *"The Wolf, Kansas," 1832.* *The Kansa numbered only 1,500 in 1832, living in earthen lodges along the Kansas River. The Wolf was a "chief of some distinction," according to Catlin, "with a bold and manly outline of head, exhibiting an European outline of features, signally worth the notice of the inquiring world. The head of this chief was curiously ornamented, and his neck bore a profusion of wampum strings." The chief's importance is underscored by the peace medal he wears. Catlin painted several Kansa Indians at Cantonment Leavenworth in 1832.*

family. The Gregorys had far greater wealth and social status than the Catlins, so for George this was a very good match. The young couple settled in New York City, but there were few history paintings to make during these years, and Catlin remained frustrated. He managed to paint a delegation of Winnebago who visited Washington in 1828, and he also made trips to paint the Indians of the Iroquois Confederacy in upstate New York. At this time, Catlin surely saw the growing gallery of Indian portraits in the Washington office of Commissioner of Indian Affairs Thomas McKenney. McKenney encouraged Catlin in his work and gave him passes to visit Indian reservations. At the request of Red Jacket, Catlin painted a second full-length portrait of the elderly leader, with Niagara Falls in the background.

During this period, Catlin did not have enough money of his own to pursue his desire to paint American Indian people, yet he had little luck in establishing himself as a mainstream artist. He sought work in cities outside New York but was no more successful at gaining portrait commissions in Washington or Richmond than in New York. He did get an important assignment to paint

a group portrait of 101 delegates to the Virginia Constitutional Convention in 1830, but it seems that during the project Catlin finally became exasperated. Upon finishing the canvas with its masses of out-of-proportion figures and crude background, he dropped everything and, against the wishes of his wife and his family, headed for St. Louis and the beckoning West.

As he made his way west, Catlin probably had a very romantic idea about Indians in their own "primitive environment." Like Catlin, many easterners romanticized Indians and lamented the impending changes in their lives and customs—without recognizing the extent to which the changes that had already occurred. In St. Louis, however, Catlin would meet another stamp of men, those who knew and associated with real Indians. Some of these men, including Indian agents and fur trade barons, felt their mission was to Christianize and civilize the Indians as quickly and bloodlessly as possible. Others aimed to profit from Indians. Fur traders exploited their hunting and trapping skills, plying them with whiskey, often giving them worthless trade goods in exchange. As Euro-Americans moved farther west, they eyed

Indian lands and wondered if precious metals lay beneath them. and were always ready to move Indians off their traditional lands and farther west, negotiating treaties to make room for white settlers. As Catlin moved west by riverboat in 1830, he probably noticed the change in attitude of the populace as he moved closer to Indian country.

When his boat landed in St. Louis in 1830, Catlin had arrived at the edge of the western frontier. St. Louis was a small town of about 5,800 people; a large brick cathedral and a small brick courthouse were the only public buildings of note. The city was destined to grow and change rapidly during the next decade, but the town Catlin encountered still contained many old wooden French buildings from the colonial period, some dating back nearly to the founding of the town. St. Louis had been established in 1764 as a fur trading post by two French entrepreneurs, Pierre Laclede and Auguste Chouteau. Located on the Mississippi River, the site was ideal for north-south as well as east-west transport of commercial goods. Its levee, a flat bank along the river, serviced the many keelboats, pirogues, and canoes that brought furs down the Missouri River

128 TOP *Portrait of William Clark by Catlin, 1830.* Catlin was introduced to Clark on his first trip to St. Louis in 1830. The old explorer, still vigorous at age 70, took Catlin to conferences with American Indians. As the superintendent of Indian affairs at St. Louis, Clark was one of the most powerful federal officials of his time, negotiating treaties with Indian nations that convinced many to move west of the Mississippi. Without Clark's assistance and patronage, Catlin's western adventures could not have happened.

128-129 *William Clark's Map of the West, 1805-1838.* Originally compiled during and immediately following the Lewis and Clark expedition of 1804-1806, this map hung in Clark's Indian council chamber and museum in St. Louis. As fur traders, army scouts, explorers, and Indians came to St. Louis with new information, the map was amended. Eventually, it became the single most informed picture of the American West, and remained so until after Clark's death in 1838. Catlin consulted the map in 1830 and 1832 and learned directly from Clark about the topography of the Far West.

128 BOTTOM *"Cock Turkey, Repeating His Prayer, Kickapoo," 1830.* A follower of the Shawnee Prophet, Cock Turkey is depicted by Catlin in this early portrait "in the attitude of prayer . . . which he is reading off from the characters cut upon a stick that he holds in his hands." Many experts feel that this portrait was started in 1830 at Cantonment Leavenworth but was finished at a later date, as it shows greater artistic ability and polish resulting from Catlin's extensive field work in 1832.

129 *"Wolf on the Hill, Chief, Cheyenne," 1832.* In addition to the Lakota Sioux, Catlin also met a group of Cheyenne people at Fort Pierre. He painted Wolf on the Hill, who, he recalled, "was clothed in a handsome dress of deerskins, very neatly garnished with broad bands of porcupine quill-work down the sleeves of his shirt and his leggings, and all the way fringed with scalp-locks. His hair was very profuse, and flowing over his shoulders; and in his hand he held a beautiful Sioux pipe, which had just been presented to him by Mr. M'Kenzie, the Trader. This was one of the finest looking and most dignified men that I have

met in the Indian country." Cheyenne was the name the Sioux gave to the tribe; it means "People of a Different Speech." The Cheyenne called themselves Tsistsistas, meaning "the Beautiful People." Sometime in the late 1600s the Cheyenne were pushed out of the territory in Minnesota. In the late 1700s they gained the use of the horse and moved out onto the Plains to become semi-nomadic hunters of the buffalo. They stopped farming and making pottery during this transition. In about the year that this painting was made, the Cheyenne split into two groups.

and took trade goods back up to the Indians, who did most of the actual trapping. Just behind the levee were the remains of a steep limestone bluff, upon which the town had been built as insurance against periodic flooding. Settlers had spread west along the Missouri River, but St. Louis remained the largest community of any size in the region, the logical starting point for any journey farther west.

Of all the residents of St. Louis, Catlin needed to meet just one man in order for his project to be successful. William Clark, a legend in his own time, was superintendent of Indian affairs at St. Louis, and Catlin could not legally proceed into Indian country without a pass from him. Clark had traveled across the West to his Pacific in his famous exploration of 1804-1806 with Meriwether Lewis, and he was familiar with most western tribes, having negotiated with them at one time or another during his twenty-five-year tenure in the West. Of any non-Indian then alive, William Clark probably had the best overall understanding of the various tribes of the West, their politics, wars, and customs. Clark also possessed the most important map of the American West

then in existence. Originally drawn from sketch maps made on the 1804-1806 Pacific journey, the map had been constantly updated as mountain men and explorers visited Clark in St. Louis. The sum total of Euro-American knowledge of the geography of the West was compiled on this one piece of cartography.

In his book *Letters and Notes,* Catlin mentioned that the secretary of war had given him a letter of introduction to Clark and to "the commander of every military post and every Indian agent on the western frontier." Catlin probably had his first meeting with the famous explorer in Clark's Indian council chamber and museum, only a few blocks from the levee. Located next door to his home on a small bluff overlooking the St. Louis riverfront, Clark's museum was filled with a far more extensive group of Indian artifacts than Peale had on display in Philadelphia. From Taos to the Columbia River, from the Great Lakes to Louisiana, Clark had either visited or received visits from representatives of nearly every major Indian nation.

Luckily, Catlin impressed Clark immediately, and the aging explorer did all

130 "Rabbit's Skin Leggings, A Brave."
Named in his own language H Coa-H' Coa-Coates-Min, a Nez Percé warrior journeyed from the Pacific Northwest to St. Louis in 1831 with three other Indians, accompanied by white fur traders. Intrigued by the possibility that the power and wealth of the whites came from their Christian religion, the four Indians came to St. Louis seeking instruction by priests. Unfortunately, they were never able to find an adequate interpreter and could not communicate well enough to accomplish their goal. Tragically, two of the Indians, Black Eagle, chief of the Nez Percé, and Man of the Morning, a Flathead, died of disease during the winter. When the steamboat Yellow Stone *left the St. Louis levee in March*

1832, its passenger list included Rabbit's Skin Leggings. Unfortunately Rabbit's Skin Leggings, shortly after rejoining his tribe, was killed in battle with the Blackfeet. George Catlin made portraits of Rabbit's Skin Leggings, but it is not known whether they were painted in St. Louis or during the Yellow Stone's *visit to Fort Pierre. Rabbit's Skin Leggings wears an elkhide shirt decorated with porcupine quills sewn into colorful geometric patterns, as well as scalp locks. In his hair he wears feathers and silver medallions. His face is painted entirely in red. He forms the image of the quintessential western Indian, unspoiled by European contact, despite the fact that he had spent the winter in a growing city.*

1830
1832
1834
1835
1836

130-131 *Map of the Travels of George Catlin, 1830-1837.* *Catlin traveled over vast areas of the American West as he chronicled the appearance and customs of American Indian people. His sojourns can be broken down into five phases: an 1830 journey to Prairie du Chien and Cantonment Leavenworth, an 1832 journey up the Missouri River to Fort Union, including a sojourn with the Mandan, an 1834 trip through Arkansas to the Comanche country, an 1835 trip along the Mississippi, from New Orleans to Fort Snelling, and an 1836 journey to the Pipestone Quarry in Minnesota.*

131 *"St. Louis From the River Below,"*
1832-33. *The steamboat* Yellow Stone *set out for the West in March 1832. Four American Indians can be seen on the elevated deck in front of the smokestacks. The growing city of St. Louis is seen behind the boat. At least ten other steamboats are tied up near the shore, loading and unloading cargo. Within ten years, St. Louis would become one of the busiest ports in America. Already it was "destined to be the great emporium of the West," according to Catlin. "It is the great depot of all the fur trading companies to the Upper Missouri and Rocky Mountains, and their starting-place; and also for the Santa Fe, and other Trading Companies, who reach the Mexican borders overland, to trade for silver bullion, from the extensive mines of that rich country." The curious thing about Catlin's painting is that the* Yellow Stone *is headed downstream; it would have to turn around and steam 18 miles to the north to reach the mouth of the Missouri. One possible explanation is that since this was the first steamboat trip that planned to go all the way to Fort Union on the Yellowstone, the boat passed in review before the city before heading upstream. The jet of white steam from the whistle on board and the large decorative American flags lend credence to this hypothesis.*

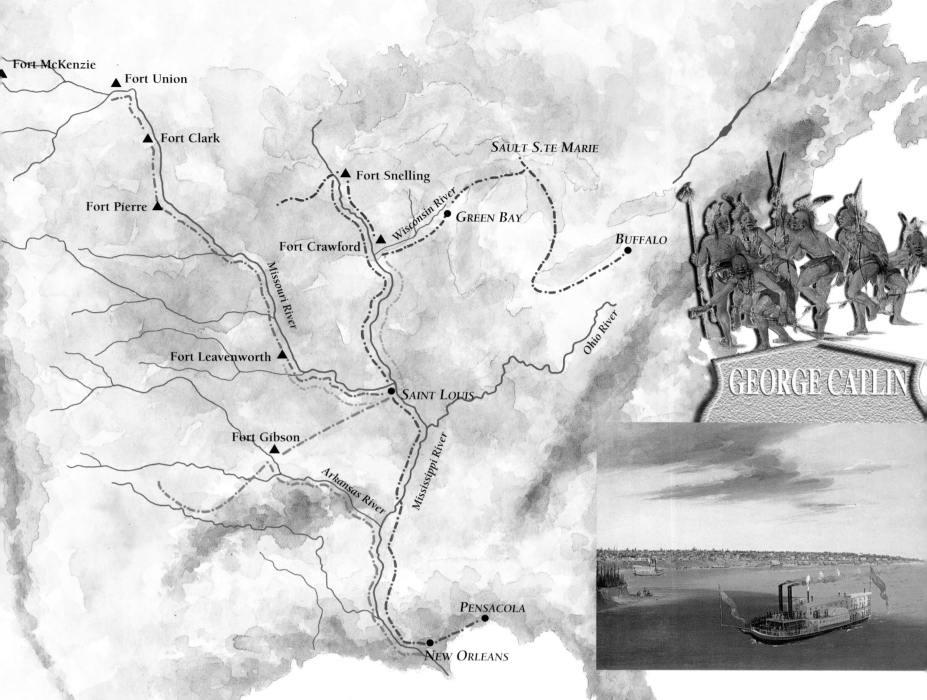

GEORGE CATLIN

he could to help and encourage the young artist. He gave Catlin an introduction to St. Louis society, which was an often bewildering composite of longstanding French residents and newer citizens from the United States who had arrived with the Louisiana Purchase of 1803. Factions had developed not only as a result of the influx of Americans but also over disputes involving real estate and the fur trade. Clark was able to assist Catlin in navigating these rough waters, gaining portrait commissions for him among the city's elite.

In July 1830, Clark allowed Catlin to accompany him on an official journey to negotiate a treaty at Prairie du Chien, in the present-day state of Wisconsin. The complicated treaty settled longstanding disputes with the Sioux, Sac and Fox, Omaha, Iowa, Oto and Missouri tribes. If Catlin made any sketches or paintings at the ceremony, they have not survived. On his return, however, Catlin painted his first scenes of western Indians near Cantonment Leavenworth, Kansas, including members of the Delaware, Kaskaskia, Kickapoo, Peoria,

Piankashaw, Potawatomi, Shawnee, and Wea tribes. At that time, Cantonment (later Fort) Leavenworth was the westernmost outpost of the U.S. Army. Catlin's first trip to the West had been a success, primarily due to his friendship with William Clark. In early 1831, Catlin returned to the eastern United States for a visit where he added to his fledgling collection of Indian portraits by painting Menominee and Seneca delegations to Washington.

By December 1831, Catlin felt ready to risk everything and begin his great adventure: a trip to the Far West to paint the Indians of the plains in their natural surroundings. Upon his arrival in St. Louis, Catlin was able to practice by painting portraits of an Assiniboin and a Creek chief bound for Washington. During early 1832, he made preparations for a trip to the Upper Missouri River region. His destination was Fort Union on the Yellowstone River, 2,000 miles up the Missouri from St. Louis, located near what is today the border of North Dakota and Montana. Catlin turned once again to his friend and benefactor, William

Clark, for advice and another consultation with his master map of the West. In addition, many fur trappers and traders in St. Louis offered the young man guidance. The journey would be difficult, amenities would be few, and there were many unknown factors. Few non-Indians had ever visited the area where Catlin was headed.

A voyage to the Upper Missouri in 1832 could be compared with a Space Shuttle mission in the 1990s—a select few, specially trained people had made the trip, primarily for commercial or official reasons. Most French, Spanish, and later American fur trappers and traders had endured the backbreaking journey on keelboats. Equipped with sails, keelboats had to be propelled by other means when the wind was not blowing. They could be propelled by men who walked along the edges of the deck in unison, pushing against the shallow bottom of the river with long poles. In places where the river ran deep, keelboats had to be "cordeled," or hauled by ropes attached to the bow. The crew walked on

132-133 *"Arikara Village of Earth-Covered Lodges," 1832.* This Arikara village, located downstream from the Mandan, consisted of 150 earthen lodges, on the west side of the Missouri River. Once friendly and helpful to the whites, most notably in the aid they gave the Lewis and Clark expedition, the Arikara had changed overnight when one of their principal chiefs died during a visit to Washington. Swearing everlasting enmity, the Arikara attacked white traders and trappers and any Indian allies of the whites. Catlin avoided their village, both on his passage up river and on his return by pirogue, but he sketched it for posterity as the Yellow Stone steamed past in 1832.

133 *"Band of Sioux Moving Camp," 1837-1839.* This painting shows a band of Lakota moving their camp. The process fascinated Catlin, who wrote in Letters and Notes: *"For this strange cavalcade, preparation is made in the following manner: the poles of a lodge are divided into two bunches, and the little ends of each bunch fastened upon the shoulder or wither of a horse, leaving the butt ends to drag behind on the ground on either side. Just behind the horse, a brace or pole is tied across, which keeps the poles in their respective places, and then upon that and the poles behind the horse, is placed the lodge or tent, which is rolled up, and also numerous other articles of household and domestic furniture, and on the top of it all, two, three, and even (sometimes) four women and children! Each one of these horses has a conductresss, who sometimes walks before and leads it, with a tremendous pack upon her own back; and at others she sits astride of its back, with a child, perhaps, at her breast, and another astride of the horse's back behind her, clinging to her waist with one arm, while it embraces a sneaking dogpup in the other. In this way five or six hundred wigwams may be seen drawn out for miles, creeping over the grass-covered plains."*

shore, pulling the boat foot by foot up the Missouri, against a swift current and around floating tree limbs and other debris called "snags." The physical difficulty of this journey had kept all but the most resolute and hardy from making it.

In addition to the transportation problems was the uncertainty of Indian-white relations. For nearly seventy years, the fur trade had been conducted from St. Louis with the village Indians of the Missouri, the Mandan and Hidatsa people, primarily for beaver pelts to be made into fashionable hats. After 1822, when the factory system of trading was ended by congressional fiat, the work of trapping was no longer primarily performed by Indian people. Instead, Euro-Americans called mountain men, hired by fur trade companies in St. Louis, spread out over the West in an ever-more-difficult search for the dwindling beaver. Many Indian people were not happy or comfortable with these white invaders in their homelands. The

even before the arrival of Europeans. With settlers pushing into the Ohio River Valley and the Great Lakes region by the early 1830s, Indian people were being pushed ever westward, inevitably bumping into one another and causing tensions to rise between tribes. It was into this volatile situation that George Catlin would be traveling as he journeyed to Fort Union in 1832.

Unlike earlier travelers, however, Catlin's trip up the Missouri would be made not on a keelboat but in one of the new steamboats that were beginning to ply the western waters. In the spring of 1832, when the ice was breaking up on the Mississippi River in the spring of 1832, the American Fur Company's 130-foot steamboat *Yellow Stone* made ready to sail. She would be the first steamboat ever to attempt the passage up the Missouri all the way to Fort Union. Her iron boilers belched white smoke from the wood they burned, the heat of the fire turning water to steam. The pressure of the steam

Arikara, once friendly to Euro-Americans, were now so hostile that just passing through their territory on the river could be very dangerous. The powerful Lakota people, called the Teton Sioux by the French, were a major impediment to travel up the Missouri. Warlike and sometimes aggressive, they often demanded presents and tribute from trappers passing through their country. Farther up the river lived the Blackfeet, who killed several Euro-American trappers each year who defied their wishes and traveled into their region. In a realm of political alliances, trading partners, and traditional enemies that rivaled those of Europe in complexity, the relations of Indian tribes in the West had been complicated

drove a piston that turned a waterwheel, driving the boat effortlessly upstream. Catlin's voyage on the *Yellow Stone* was part of a somewhat dangerous experiment, for although the steam vessel would save untold labor and add a great deal of speed to the trip, snags lurking below the surface on the muddy water could easily rip the hull open if the skipper was not cautious.

On March 26, 1832, Catlin boarded the *Yellow Stone* for his journey up the Missouri. His trip was arranged courtesy of Pierre Chouteau, the influential manager of the American Fur Company and virtual ruler of the company's western trading posts and forts. Accompanied by Chouteau himself, some rough trappers, a small group of

134 LEFT *"Buffalo Hunt Under the Wolf-Skin Mask,"* *1832-33.* An ancient method of hunting buffalo that dates to the era before horses is illustrated in this painting. A hunter would put on the hide and persona of a wolf, creeping slowly with his spear into the herd of buffalo. Buffalo were accustomed to having wolves in their midst and were not bothered by them, since wolves attacked only the very sick or old in a herd. The ruse of the wolfskin apparently worked, especially if the hunter was careful to wipe out any trace of a human scent. Crawling slowly up to the side of his prey, he had to thrust his spear deeply into the animal's body and penetrate the heart, or risk the wrath of a two-ton beast who might trample or gore him.

134-135 *"Buffalo Chase with Bows and Lances,"* *1832-33.* In Letters and Notes, *Catlin* described this painting: "I have represented a party of Indians in chase of a herd, some of whom are pursuing with lance and others with bows and arrows. The group in the foreground shews the attitude at the instant after the arrow has been thrown and driven to the heart; the Indian at full speed, and the laso dragging behind his horse's heels. The laso is a long thong, of rawhide, of ten or fifteen yards in length, made of several braids or twists, and used chiefly to catch the wild horse. . . . In running the buffaloes, or in time of war, the laso drags on the ground at the horse's feet, and sometimes several rods behind, so that if a man is dismounted, which is often the case, by the tripping or stumbling of the horse, he has the power of grasping to the laso, and by stubbornly holding on to it, of stopping and securing his horse, on whose back he is instantly replaced, and continuing on the chase."

134 BOTTOM RIGHT *"Buffalo Chase, Bulls Making Battle with Men and Horses,"* *1832-33.* "The buffalo is a very timid animal," wrote Catlin, "and shuns the vicinity of man with keenest sagacity; yet, when overtaken, and harrassed or wounded, turns upon its assailants with the utmost fury. In their desperate resistance the finest horses are often destroyed; but the Indian, with his superior sagacity and dexterity, generally finds some effective mode of escape."

Missouri, so the boat was tied up to the shore each evening. In addition, stops were made to give supplies to forts and trading posts and to take furs on board. The first stop was at the village of the Ponca, near the mouth of the Niobrara River in present-day Nebraska. As Catlin spoke to the chief of the Ponca, through an interpreter, the Indian lamented the fact that white men were beginning to settle in the territory of his people, who were making ready to move farther west. The chief confirmed what Catlin most feared—that the lifeways of Indian people were changing so rapidly, in a very few years they would be gone forever.

With a renewed sense of purpose, Catlin reboarded the steamboat, which continued to chug slowly upstream, occasionally grounding on hidden sandbars and often struggling around snags. Huge herds of animals, including buffalo, elk, and antelope, could be seen on the shores. "From day to day we advanced," wrote Catlin, "until at last our boat was aground; and a day's work of sounding told us at last there was no possibility of advancing further until there should be a rise in the river." As a result, Pierre Chouteau, eager to reach Fort Pierre and impatient with the delay, decided to take a party of twenty men two hundred miles overland to the fort, located at the mouth of the Teton River. Eager for adventure, Catlin volunteered to go along, enlisting several of the men to

Indians returning home, the U.S. Indian agent John F.A. Sanford, and a huge cargo of supplies for the forts upriver, Catlin set out on the adventure of his life. He recalled: "I sat out alone, unaided and unadvised, resolved (if my life should be spared), by the aid of my brush and my pen, to rescue from oblivion so much of their primitive looks and customs as the industry and ardent enthusiasm of one lifetime could accomplish."

As the *Yellow Stone* chugged up the river, Catlin sat on deck and painted small canvases chronicling the landscape. Although distorted in their depiction of verdant green grasslands and somewhat repetitious, Catlin's paintings were the first authentic records of the appearance of the Far West along the Missouri River. Placed end to end, the canvases provided a good overview of the topography of the Missouri River Valley.

It took three months for the *Yellow Stone* to wend its way upriver. Travel after sunset was far too dangerous on the tricky

135 *"Buffalo Chase, A Single Death," 1832-33.*
In several paintings made over the course of his career, George Catlin chronicled the dangerous work of Indian buffalo hunters. The Plains tribes, as well as many midwestern tribes, subsisted on the gifts provided by the buffalo, for shelter, clothing, food, and tools. This painting shows a hunter ready to let an arrow fly into the animal's side. If the arrow misses the heart of the prey, the dangerous

buffalo might turn on its attacker. Catlin described a buffalo hunt of this type in Letters and Notes, *saying that the hunter "generally strips himself and his horse of his shield and quiver and every part of his dress which might be an encumbrance . . . grasping his bow in his left hand, with five or six arrows ready for instant use. In his right hand or attached to his wrist is a heavy whip, which he uses without mercy."*

135

assist him by carrying his artist's materials on their backs.

Subsisting by hunting buffalo along the way, after a week the party arrived at Fort Pierre. Catlin was struck by the appearance of the fort, a wooden stockade surrounded by nearly six hundred buffalo-hide tepees of the Teton Sioux people. Fort Pierre was an important trading center, where beaver and buffalo hides were brought for shipment through St. Louis to the East Coast and Europe. The stay at Fort Pierre lasted longer than expected, because the *Yellow Stone* continued to be hung up downriver. This gave Catlin an even greater opportunity to

paint portraits and learn about the Sioux people.

When Catlin painted these Indians, he threw off the conventions that had dominated his previous portraits. He felt pressed for time, as though he could not work fast enough to record what he was seeing. He began each canvas by quickly outlining the features of his subject with broad brushstrokes, then spent a great deal of time on the face, emphasizing each Indian as an individual. He made careful notations as to the dress, hairstyle, and objects carried by each Indian, so that he could add such fine details to the canvas when he returned to his eastern studio. He used only about a dozen colors and kept his canvases rolled in a large cylinder for easier transport. His palette became increasingly brighter and more vivid as he continued to paint western Indians. In formulating this palette, Catlin was affected by the vibrant clothing and gorgeously decorated accessories carried by Indian people. When painting subjects in the field, he applied his colors in thin strokes, with plenty of linseed oil mixed in, so that the canvases would dry quickly and not crack when they were rolled up and stored for travel. Although the Sioux people were at first suspicious of Catlin's great power in being able to paint realistic and recognizable versions of human beings, one of their chiefs convinced

136 "The Smoked Shield, Kiowa," 1834-35.
After the excitement of his journey up the Missouri in 1832, Catlin took a year off to finish his numerous partially started canvases. In 1834 he received permission to accompany Col. Henry Dodge and his dragoons into the country of the Comanche. Catlin traveled up the Arkansas River by steamboat to meet the dragoons at Fort Gibson. Near the fort, Catlin observed a virtual "melting pot" of Indian cultures, where Plains tribes, former woodland tribes like the Osage, and newly displaced members of the "Five Civilized Tribes"

from the Southeast all came into uneasy contact. Smoked Shield, a Kiowa warrior, was "near seven feet in stature, and distinguished, not only as one of the greatest warriors, but the swiftest on foot, in the nation. This man, it is said, runs down a buffalo on foot, and slays it with his knife or his lance, as he runs by its side." The Kiowa had been allied with the Comanche since about 1790. They had originated in what is now Montana, migrated southward and picked up the use of the horse along their journey, and eventually settled on the Arkansas River.

136-137 *"Sioux Dog Feast."* *Catlin's invitation to partake of this feast was a special honor accorded him by the Lakota. The Lakota kept dogs for many purposes, some for hunting and as watchdogs and pets, others to pull travois loaded with household goods from one camp to another. Still others were kept as meat animals, and several Lakota ceremonies involved eating dog* meat, *which was considered to be a special treat. In this painting we see Catlin and his companions Kenneth McKenzie, John F.A. Sanford, and Pierre Chouteau within a special marquee set up for the feast, two large tepees pitched together without closing the circle of either, thus giving shelter from the west winds at sunset. Catlin said that 150 men sat down to* enjoy the feast. *On the flag staff the Sioux placed a white flag and ceremonial pipes, "both expressive of their friendly feelings towards us." The iron kettles, full of dog meat were placed in a row in the center of the circle, while several Indians appear to be lighting their ceremonial pipes, a signal that the feast is near its end and that the participants have finished eating.*

them that artist's "medicine" was good and not evil.

Catlin described the Sioux as "one of the most vigorous and warlike tribes to be found, numbering some forty or fifty thousand, and able undoubtedly to muster, if the tribe could be moved simultaneously, at least eight or ten thousand warriors, well mounted and well armed." In Catlin's time, the mighty Sioux still fought and hunted primarily with bows and arrows or long lances; very few firearms of any quality or accuracy had fallen into their hands. The Teton Sioux, who called themselves Lakota, were the westernmost of three related groups of people with similar languages. Within the Lakota were seven tribes. Over the course of a century, the Lakota had mastered the horse and become completely mobile hunters and gatherers. By 1832,

they were pushing smaller tribes of Indians aside to increase the size of their hunting grounds.

While Catlin was at Fort Pierre, the Sioux who were encamped nearby indulged in games, sports, and dances, which he was able to record pictorially and in writing. These ceremonies included the Sun Dance, a ritual in which men endured great pain, hunger, and thirst while seeking spiritual visions. Their blood was spilled from chest wounds where skewers were placed, which, connected with leather thongs to a central pole, were stretched taut by the dancing and the pulling of the men themselves. Eventually, after many hours of self-torture, the men were able to free themselves when the weight of their bodies pulled the skewers out through their flesh and muscle. The Sun Dance, held each

summer, was thought to renew the life of the tribe and to ensure bountiful harvests and successful hunts. George Catlin was one of few Euro-Americans to witness this ceremony.

With the arrival of the *Yellow Stone* at Fort Pierre, the men wasted no time in proceeding farther up the river. If the boat were held up too long, water levels in the river would drop, and it would be stranded until the following year. Chugging 800 more miles against the current, the *Yellow Stone* reached Fort Union in June. Located near today's North Dakota-Montana border, Fort Union was two thousand miles northwest of St. Louis, an American Fur Company outpost in the middle of Assiniboin country. The fort was established three years before Catlin saw it. Two hundred feet square, built of stone, the fort housed "eight or ten log

**138-139 *"Comanche Feats of Horsemanship,"*
*1834-35.*** *As the dragoons in Catlin's party
watched, the Comanche on the white horse put on
a show of horsemanship like nothing they had
ever before seen. "The distance between the two
parties was perhaps half a mile, and that a
beautiful and gently sloping prairie; over which
he was for the space of a quarter of an hour,
reining and spurring his maddened horse, and
gradually approaching us by tacking to the right
and the left, like a vessel beating against the wind.
He at length came prancing and leaping along till
he met the flag of the regiment, when he leaned
his spear for a moment against it, looking the
bearer full in the face, when he wheeled his horse,
and dashed up to Col. Dodge, with his extended
hand, which was instantly grasped and shaken.
We all had him by the hand in a moment,
and the rest of the party seeing him received
in this friendly manner, instead of being
sacrificed, as they undoubtedly expected,
started under 'full whip' in a direct line
towards us, and in a moment gathered, like
a black cloud, around us!"*

**139 *"Little Spaniard, A Warrior, Comanche,"*
*1834.*** *Also known by the Comanche name
Hisoosanches, Little Spaniard was one of the
leading warriors of his tribe. He was called Little
Spaniard because he was half-Spanish and half-
Comanche. Catlin explained that this was the
warrior who "dashed out so boldly from the war-
party, and came to us with the white flag raised
on the point of his lance. . . . I have here
represented him as he stood for me, with his
shield on his arm, with his quiver slung, and his
lance of fourteen feet in length in his right hand.
This extraordinary little man, whose figure was
light, seemed to be all bone and muscle, and
exhibited immense power, by the curve of the
bones in his legs and arms." He was dressed only
in a breechclout, with leggings decorated
with long fringes and moccasins.
His long hair is braided and the
ends are tied with red cloth.*

140 LEFT *"The Open Door, Shawnee," 1830.* The younger brother of Tecumseh, known as Tenskwatawa or the Prophet, was in his sixties by the time Catlin painted his portrait. Several decades before, the Prophet had tried to form an alliance of all Indian tribes to drive the whites back across the Ohio; his dream was shattered by the defeat at Tippecanoe Creek in 1811 and by the defeat of the British in the War of 1812. When Catlin painted him, the Prophet was traveling from tribe to tribe along the Missouri, with his "medicine or mystery fire" and a "sacred string of beads." Young warriors accepted the fire, promising never to let it die, and they touched the string of beads as a sign of their dedication to the Prophet's cause. Catlin painted this portrait at Cantonment Leavenworth, Kansas. Another portrait of Tenskwatawa was painted by James Otto Lewis in Detroit in 1823 and copied in 1829 by Charles Bird King.

140 RIGHT *"Chee-A-Ka-Tchee, Wife of Nottoway, Iroquois," 1835-36.* Nottoway's wife and child wear clothing that is Ojibwa in character rather than Iroquois. The baby's cradleboard has bells, trinkets, and a cross hanging from its bar.

houses and stores," wrote Catlin, noting also that 40 to 50 men and 150 horses resided within its walls. By 1832 the post was a major rendezvous site for many tribes, who often crossed great distances to reach it. Even among tribes who were bitter enemies, the fort was recognized as a neutral ground for purposes of trade. The commander of the fort was an American Fur Company employee named Kenneth McKenzie, who welcomed Catlin heartily and treated him to large feasts of delicious frontier food.

Staying for over a month, Catlin painted portraits of the chiefs of surrounding tribes, averaging five or six partially finished paintings each day. He watched as the *Yellow Stone*, now loaded with a year's catch of furs, turned back for St. Louis. When his work was finished, Catlin planned to travel on his own by canoe or pirogue, spending time among the Upper Missouri tribes and returning to St. Louis when winter approached.

During his western sojourn, he was able to take part in several buffalo hunts with the Indians, which he later sketched and painted. His realistic portrait work soon made Catlin a legend among the Indians, and crowds of dignitaries from many tribes descended upon the fort. Setting up a studio in one of the fort's bastions, Catlin sat on "the cool breach of a twelve-pounder" cannon as he worked at his easel. Tribal chiefs placed their warriors, armed with spears, at the door as guards to keep the curious from interrupting the portrait work.

When a contingent of Blackfoot Indians had journeyed to Fort Union to trade, Catlin spent a great deal of time painting them. The Blackfeet were a large and powerful tribe of about 50,000 people, whose territory extended well into Canada and out to the Rocky Mountains. Suspicious of outsiders, they had successfully resisted the

141 *"Nottoway."* Catlin painted this portrait of Nottoway sometime in 1835 or 1836, probably either at Fort Snelling or Sault Sainte Marie. Nottoway, an Iroquois, was found living with the Ojibwa, far from his tribe's original hunting grounds in New York State and into the Ohio Valley. Catlin stated "This was an excellent man, and was handsomely dressed for his picture. . . . He seemed to be quite ignorant of the early history of his tribe, as well as of the position and condition of its few scattered remnants, who are yet in existence. . . . [T]hough he was an Iroquois, which he was proud to acknowledge to me . . . he wished it to be generally thought, that he was a Chippeway."

142 " Mah-Ta-Toh-Pa, Mandan," 1832.
Mahtatohpa, which means "Four Bears," was the second chief of the Mandan. He spent an entire morning preparing for this portrait, not arriving at Catlin's makeshift studio until noon. "I looked out of the door of the wigwam," Catlin recalled in Letters and Notes, *"and saw him approaching with a firm and elastic step, accompanied by a great crowd of women and children, who were gazing on him with admiration, and escorting him to my room. No tragedian ever trod the stage, nor gladiator ever entered the Roman Forum, with more grace and manly dignity than did Mah-to-toh-pa enter the wigwam, where I was in readiness to receive him. He took his attitude before me, and with the sternness of a Brutus and the stillness of a statue, he stood until the*

darkness of night broke upon the solitary stillness." Mahtatohpa wore a shirt made of two mountain sheep skins, with bands of decorative porcupine quills sewn the length of each arm over the seams, and the bottom finished off with ermine skins. His leggings were made of deer skin, with bands of porcupine quills along the seams, mixed with the scalp-locks of enemies. The headdress consisted of eagle feathers set in ermine, extending to the ground in the back, with two highly polished buffalo horns set in the crown. Catlin enjoyed long talks with Mahtatohpa during his stay with the Mandan, and he was treated to feasts of buffalo ribs, marrow fat, and a pudding of prairie turnips and buffalo berries by the second chief.

efforts of white mountain men to penetrate their country, preferring to do the trapping and trading themselves and bring their goods to Fort Union. Initially astounded by Catlin's ability to accurately render friends and loved ones, the Blackfeet, like the Sioux, eventually accepted Catlin's powerful medicine as good. A Blackfoot medicine man who finally consented to sit was so pleased with his portrait that he gave Catlin his entire costume, starting Catlin's personal collection of Indian artifacts.

After a few weeks, Catlin feared that he might miss seeing and recording some of the other fascinating cultures William Clark had described, and so in mid-July he packed his belongings, including many Indian artifacts, into a pirogue. A narrow wooden boat navigated with paddles and a tiller, a pirogue could not be managed by one man in the swift current of the Missouri River. Catlin brought along two French-Canadian voyageurs named Ba'tiste and Bogard on his long journey back to St. Louis. He often stopped to paint views of the countryside and speculate about the geology of the areas through which they passed. In addition to the large number of Indian artifacts and artist's implements packed on board, the porigue also boasted a fully grown, domesticated war eagle (given to Catlin by Kenneth McKenzie) perched on a six-foot post at the prow of the craft. The pirogue must have been a remarkable sight as it flowed with the current into the land of the Mandan.

Catlin and his companions stopped for a long period with the Mandan, a people who planted crops, hunted buffalo, and lived in large, conical earthen lodges. A small, peaceful tribe of but 2,000 people, they lived in two villages near the present city of Bismarck, North Dakota. The American Fur Company located Fort Clark near the

143 TOP *"Mah-To-Toh-Pa, Mandan," 1832.*
Catlin devoted more pages of Letters and Notes *to the Mandan than to any other tribe. During July and August 1832, he enjoyed learning as much as he could about these fascinating people. The Mandan, a tribe of about 2,000 , lived in earthen lodges along the Missouri River. They called themselves See-pohs-ka-nu-mah-ka-kee, or "People of the Pheasants," and lived in two villages, about two miles apart, near present-day Bismarck. Their location at the center of a complex network of trade brought them into contact with Indians of many tribes as well as European fur traders, who had been bargaining with them for nearly a hundred years. Catlin thought that the permanency of village life enabled the Mandans to enjoy "the comforts, and even luxuries of life." Woefully uninformed regarding the extensive contact between the Mandan and Europeans,*

Catlin thought that the variety of skin, hair, and eye color he observed was evidence of the then-popular myth that the Mandan were descendants of Welsh colonists who had come to North America before Columbus. If Catlin thought highly of the Mandan, his regard for Mahtatohpa was astronomical. He called the Mandan chief "the most extraordinary man, perhaps, who lives at this day, in the atmosphere of Nature's noblemen." Catlin felt that Mahtatohpa was "the favorite and [most] popular man of the nation," although he was the tribe's second chief. The first chief, called Wolf Chief, was in Catlin's view "a haughty, austere, and overbearing man, respected and feared by his people rather than loved." In this portrait, Mahtatohpa is shown in mourning, with a few locks of his hair cut off, and scars from the Okeepa ceremony are visible on his chest and arms.

Mandan villages in 1831, and the company's agent, James Kipp, greeted Catlin warmly. The Mandan people were very hospitable, giving Catlin all the information he could wish about their culture, while believing him to be a person possessing great medicine because of his artistic ability. They literally lined up to have their portraits painted and to watch Catlin's magic brushstrokes become recognizable images of their loved ones and neighbors. Catlin spent hours talking with Four Bears, the second chief of the tribe, learning about

143 BOTTOM *Self-Portrait of George Catlin Painting Mahtatohpa. This sketch, painted in oil on canvas, shows the artist creating the portrait of Mahtatohpah on the opposite page. This image was used as the frontispiece to Catlin's book* Letters and Notes *when it appeared in 1841. Catlin reported that Mahtathopa suvived the smallpox epidemic of 1837, although he "watched every one of his family die about him, his wives and his little children . . . and wept over the final destruction of his tribe" before he starved himself to death. Other sources say that Mahtotohpa died of smallpox. In addition to Catlin's portraits, Mahtatohpa as also painted by Karl Bodmer in 1834.*

144 *"The Dog, Lakota," 1832*. On his final day at Fort Pierre, Catlin was painting the portrait of a man named Mahtocheega, or Little Bear, a distinguished chief of the Hunkpapa band of Lakota. Catlin chose to show him in profile. Looking at the artist's work, a rival from another band named Shonka, The Dog, taunted Little Bear, saying that he was but half a man. Little Bear immediately called The Dog a coward, provoking a fight outside Catlin's tepee. Little Bear was killed, the side of his face that was not shown in the painting having been shot away. The Lakota camp was in an uproar as Catlin hastily packed his supplies and fled to the safety of the fort. He boarded the Yellow Stone the next day to continue his journey upriver. He later learned that The Dog was killed by some of Little Bear's followers in the Black Hills.

145 *"Two Crows, Hidatsa," 1832*. Two Crows was painted in a "handsome shirt, ornamented with ermine, and necklace of grisly bear's claws," according to Catlin's 1848 catalog of his paintings. Two Crows' shirt bears paintings depicting his exploits, while beautiful porcupine quill work in a decorative strip enhances the seam of the shirt's arm. Quills of porcupines were flattened and dyed various shades by Indian people throughout most of North America, then woven and sewn into intricate patterns that could be affixed to clothing made of hide. Glass beads, some made by Indians but most imported from Europe, gradually replaced quill work as the nineteenth century wore on. In the fall of 1832 Catlin made a special trip back up the Missouri to see the Hidatsa village.

ceremonies and rituals such as the Okeepa, which Catlin was allowed to witness. The four-day Okeepa ceremony was similar to the Sun Dance but infinitely more brutal to its participants. Catlin described it as a "torture" ceremony, and although he could not understand the full religious significance of it, he left a detailed written record of his observations, the only ones ever made of this ritual.

After a month with the Mandan, Catlin traveled back up the river eight miles to visit another village tribe, the Minnetarees, or as they called themselves, the Hidatsa. The Hidatsa then lived in three villages of about 1,500 people. Their largest village of 40 to 50 earthen lodges arose amid cornfields. As with the Mandan, Catlin found much of interest among the Hidatsa, but with the coldness of autumn in the air, Catlin, Ba'tiste, and Bogard once again turned their pirogue downriver. At the Mandan village they recovered their baggage amid a warm good-bye. Catlin genuinely liked the Mandan and was

impressed by the fact that contrary to the reports of whites, Indians did not lie, steal, or cheat. Catlin would be devastated to hear, five years after his visit, that a smallpox epidemic introduced by fur traders killed nearly every person among the Mandan.

Slowly continuing his return to St. Louis, Catlin often went ashore to climb the surrounding hills and contemplate the wild, endless beauty of the unspoiled West. The Missouri River Valley, he said, was a "place where the mind could think volumes." He returned to the Cantonment Leavenworth area, where he painted Iowa, Kansa, Missouri, Omaha, Oto, and Pawnee Indians who had camped around the fort to trade.

Catlin arrived back in St. Louis in October 1832, having painted or sketched out more than 130 canvases in 86 days. He did not consider his field work to be finished for the season, however. An important "war" with Indians in Iowa and Illinois had occurred in his absence, and

the Sac leader, Black Hawk, was imprisoned just eight miles to the south of St. Louis, at Jefferson Barracks. Black Hawk had defied the U.S. government, which wished to take the land of his people. His defiance had been short-lived, however, and his small force was defeated by a U.S. Army force at the Battle of Bad Axe. After the battle, Black Hawk and the other leaders of the resistance were brought to St. Louis in chains. Catlin limned all the prisoners, including Black Hawk's two sons, before finally returning to his wife in New York in late December.

After his epic journey, Catlin began the work of completing his unfinished paintings. During 1833 he used his sketches to paint in the details of the dramatic landscapes, buffalo hunts, prairie fires, and nighttime dances of the Indian peoples he had encountered. Once they were completed, he traveled with Clara to show his paintings in Pittsburgh, Cincinnati, and Louisville. Catlin's 140 finished and framed pictures were praised

This woman's name was Juahkisgaw, and she was painted with her baby at Fort Snelling in Minnesota in 1835. Catlin mentions that the baby's umbilical cord was "hanging before the child's face for its supernatural protector." Many tribes carried their umbilical cord with them throughout their lives. It was placed in a special sealed pouch, which was worn around the neck on a thong under the clothing, or perhaps carried in a warrior's medicine bag. "The woman's dress was mostly made of civilized manufactures," Catlin continued, "but curiously decorated and ornamented according to Indian taste."

by Cincinnati editor James Hall, later to write the text for Thomas McKenney's *Indian Tribes of North America.* His paintings were unique to the people who viewed them, since so few had any idea of the appearance or customs of Indians in the Far West. For the vast majority of Euro-Americans, Catlin's paintings were their first pictorial glimpse of this region's inhabitants

Catlin's knowledge and respect for Indian people showed in his paintings. He wrote in 1841: "I have seen a vast many of these wild people in my travels, it will be admitted by all. And I have had toils and difficulties, and dangers to encounter in paying them my visits; yet I have had my pleasures as I went along, in shaking their friendly hands, that never had felt the contaminating touch of money, or the withering embrace of pockets; I have shared the comforts of their hospitable wigwams, and always have been preserved unharmed in their country. And if I have spoken . . . with a seeming bias, the reader will know what allowance to make for me, who am standing as the champion of a people, who have treated me kindly, of whom I feel bound to speak well, and who have no means of speaking for themselves."

Catlin had gone west with an idealized notion of Indians. After taking a serious look at real Indian people and recording every detail he could, he returned with a different perspective. He treated his sitters with dignity—none are portrayed as "generic" Indians. Their personality traits come through in nearly every portrait. His portraits of women, some posing with their children, showed them as people, not curiosities. Unlike the paintings of Charles Bird King and other early artists, Catlin's portraits definitely highlight the specifically Indian features of his subjects; they do not look like Caucasians wearing Indian clothing. Moreover, Catlin had matured as an artist. Through practice and through the excitement he felt about his subject matter, he had developed a personal style and a vastly improved technique.

After a winter in New Orleans, Catlin left Clara behind and went off on another adventure. In 1834, he was given permission by Secretary of War Lewis Cass to accompany Col. Henry Leavenworth's First U.S. Dragoons in making initial diplomatic contact with the Comanche of

the Southwest. The Comanche were tough warriors who attacked and harassed trappers and traders who passed through their territory. The Santa Fe Trail, an important trade route between St. Louis and the then-Mexican town of Santa Fe, had been constantly disrupted by Comanche raids, making diplomatic contact almost impossible. In April, Catlin arrived at Fort Gibson on the Arkansas River, near present-day Tulsa, Oklahoma, by steamboat. At that time Fort Gibson, established in 1824, was the southwesternmost outpost of U.S. authority. Unlike the fur trade forts on the

147 *"Tchow-ee-put-o-kaw," Creek 1834.*
This Creek woman wears beautiful jewelry made of beadwork and turquoise disks.

Upper Missouri, Fort Gibson was an outpost of the U.S. Army, garrisoned by troops.

Many Indians who settled near Fort Gibson had been "removed" from their ancestral homelands in the East to these new "reservations" of land set aside for them. Seeing these Indians was another sign to Catlin that Indian life was changing forever. For two months he painted Cherokee, Choctaw, Creek, and Osage Indians; he also witnessed and painted scenes of the Choctaw people playing a unique ball game.

In June Catlin left with the dragoons (light cavalry) commanded by Col.

Leavenworth on their cross-country journey to make contact with the Comanche. He marveled at the Red River country through which they passed as he rode a superbly trained horse named Charley. After they had traveled many hard days over hundreds of miles, a Comanche party suddenly appeared. They were so numerous that they might easily overwhelm the dragoons. The Comanche made no hostile moves, however; instead, they put on an unforgettable display of horsemanship. Riding their unsaddled ponies, the Comanches demonstrated their skill in leaning completely over to the flank of the horse, where they could not

be seen by the dragoons, firing arrows from under the horse's head. As the unaimed arrows fell harmlessly in the distance, the dragoons wondered if they were going to be attacked or welcomed as friends. Finally, the leader of the group rode across the prairie and directly up to an officer, shaking his hand. After a general round of handshaking, laughter and relief, the Comanches led the group into their village in the foothills of the Wichita Mountains.

Catlin made paintings of the Comanche chiefs, their village, their horsemanship, and a buffalo hunt. But he had already been feeling the effects of a high fever when the dragoons set up their camp, and

148-149 *"Comanche Meeting the Dragoons,"*
1834-35. In this painting, Catlin recorded the
meeting of the U.S. Dragoons and the Comanches.
He recalled that "On the fourth day of our march
. . . we discovered a large party at several miles
distance, sitting on their horses and looking at
us. . . . Col. Dodge ordered the command to halt,
while he rode forward with a few of his staff, and
an ensign carrying a white flag. I joined this
advance, and the Indians stood their ground until
we had come within half a mile of them. We then
came to a halt, and the white flag was sent a little
in advance, and waved as a signal for them to
approach; at which one of their party galloped out
in advance of the war-party, on a milk white
horse, carrying a piece of white buffalo skin on
the point of his long lance in reply to our flag."

149 *"Red Thunder, Son of Black Moccasin,*
Hidatsa," 1832. Catlin recalled in Letters and
Notes *that Red Thunder was reputed to be "one of
the most desperate warriors of his tribe." He
painted Red Thunder "at full length, in his war-
dress, with his bow in his hand, his quiver slung,
and his shield upon his arm. In this plight, sans*
headaddress, sans robe, and sans everything that
might be an useless encumbrance—with the body
chiefly naked, and profusely bedaubed with red
and black paint, so as to form an almost perfect
disguise, the Indian warriors invariably sally
forth to war."

150 *"He Who Kills the Osages, Missouri,"*
1832. *Catlin identified this subject, who was the chief of the Missouri tribe, as "an old man" with a "necklace of grisly bears' claws, and a handsome carved pipe in his hand." The pipe is made from the red stone later dubbed Catlinite, and includes a beautiful carved animal effigy near the bowl, created by He Who Kills the Osages himself. Probably painted on Catlin's second visit to Cantonment Leavenworth in 1832, He Who Kills the Osages was also later painted by Charles Bird King in Washington.*

151 *"Black Hawk, Sac and Fox," 1832.*
Black Hawk, or Muk-a-tah-mish-o-kah-kaik, according to Catlin's phonetic pronunciation, led the Black Hawk War of 1832. Catlin met him in October 1832, immediately following his Missouri River sojourn, at Jefferson Barracks, a military post south of St. Louis. Black Hawk was imprisoned at the time the portrait was painted. Catlin noted that Black Hawk sat for the picture in his war dress, with strings of wampum in his ears and around his neck, "and in his hand, his medicine-bag, which was the skin of a black hawk, from which he had taken his name, and the tail of which made him a fan, which he was almost constantly using." Black Hawk was about 65 years old when this portrait was painted. Catlin saw Black Hawk once more, at an 1836 treaty council held at Rock Island, during which the Sac and Fox relinquished 256,000 acres of land on the Iowa River. Catlin noted that the once-proud Black Hawk was "looked on as an object of pity. With an old frock coat and brown hat on, and a cane in his hand, he stood the whole time outside of the group, and in dumb and dismal silence." Black Hawk was also painted by Charles Bird King in 1837.

he fell severely ill soon after. On the return journey along the Canadian River, many of the dragoons, along with Catlin, were too sick to ride and had to be transported on stretchers. Col. Leavenworth left many of his men behind at a camp as he traveled on to meet the Pawnee Picts, another tribe with whom he wished to negotiate. Catlin was too sick to argue or care about being left behind. Roughly a third of the 455 men on the 1834 dragoon expedition died and were buried along the trail before the troop returned to Fort Gibson. Catlin was lucky to survive.

After a short recuperation, Catlin was eager to be reunited with his wife, who was staying near St. Louis. He decided to ride the 540 miles to St. Louis alone on his

horse, Charley. Fighting off the effects of fever, he recuperated on the trail. Meeting Clara in Alton, Illinois, the young couple took a steamer downriver to New Orleans and from there journeyed to Pensacola, Florida, to stay with George's younger brother James.

In early 1835 George and Clara returned to New Orleans, where Catlin showed his paintings and lectured on Indians to enthusiastic crowds. The Catlins then took a leisurely steamboat trip up the Mississippi, from New Orleans to Fort Snelling, Minnesota. There he painted the Chippewa, or as they called themselves, the Ojibwa people. Catlin was disturbed by the Indians he observed at Prairie du Chien, Wisconsin, who were addicted to whiskey and were

having difficulty adapting to Euro-American lifeways. Paradoxically, Catlin preferred to imagine what the area would look like when finally settled by whites, when it would include "cities, towers and villas." He was resigned to the fact that change was inevitable, even though he lamented that the Indian cultures he was growing to love would be destroyed. Catlin's last stop of the summer was the Sac and Fox village, where he made two portraits of Chief Keokuk.

In early 1836, Catlin decided to make one last trip west, to visit the legendary Pipestone Quarry, where the Indians of many nations acquired a special red stone for use in making the bowls for their ceremonial pipes. Arriving in Green Bay, Wisconsin, Catlin painted Ojibwa and

152 *"Keokuk on Horseback, Sac and Fox,"* *1835.* Catlin described Keokuk, the principal chief of the Sac and Fox, as *"a man of a great deal of pride, [who] makes truly a splendid appearance on his black horse. He owns the finest horse in the country, and is excessively vain of his appearance* *when mounted in all their gear and trappings. He expressed a wish to see himself represented on horseback, and I painted him in that plight. He rode and netted his prancing steed in front of my door, until its sides were a gore of blood."*

153 *"Keokuk, Sac and Fox," 1835.* In Letters and Notes *Catlin called Keokuk "a dignified and proud man with a good share of talent, and vanity enough to force into action all the wit and judgment he possesses, in order to command the attention and respect of the world. . . . In this portrait I have represented him in the costume, precisely, in which he was dressed* *when he stood for it, with his shield on his arm, and his staff (insignia of office) in his left hand. There is no Indian chief on the frontier better known at this time, or more highly appreciated for his eloquence, as a public speaker, than Kee-o-kuk."* Keokuk was also painted by Charles Bird King in 1837.

Menominee people and met an Englishman named Robert Sherrill Wood, who traveled with him by canoe and horseback to the quarry. It was a sacred place to Indian people, and although Catlin was ordered to turn back several times by Santee Sioux people, he defied their wishes and pressed on. Upon his arrival, he speculated about the geological conditions that could have produced the unique red rock. Eventually, Catlin's samples were declared to be a new, undiscovered mineral, dubbed Catlinite by Charles Thomas Jackson, a leading mineralogist.

154 LEFT *"Pipestone Quarry on the Coteau Des Prairies, Minnesota," 1836-37.*
Catlin's last major foray into the West was to seek out the famous Pipestone Quarry.
As long as he had been studying Indian people, Catlin had seen their sacred pipes, most of which consisted of two sections: a long wooden stem and a bowl made of carved stone. More often than not, the western tribes had pipes whose bowls were made of a unique red stone, all of which came from the same quarry.
The quarry was located in a secluded spot and not open to whites, although the site formed a neutral ground, even for members of warring tribes. In the painting, Catlin includes figures of Indian people for scale, even placing one man on the far right to show the size of the boulders called the Three Maidens, and people atop the cliff to show its height.
Catlin rearranged some the elements, exaggerating the height of the quartzite ledge above the red stone, and moving the Three Maidens to the right to bring them into the composition. Today the Pipestone Quarry is protected by the National Park Service, but its stone is still used by Native American people.

154 RIGHT *"The Cheyenne, A Republican Pawnee," 1832.* *Although the Pawnee lived in permanent villages of earthen lodges, they switched to tepees in the summer, like the ones shown behind The Cheyenne in this picture. By the early 1700s, the tribe had divided into four bands, the Skidi, the Grand, the Tapage, and the Republican. At the time Catlin painted this unfinished canvas, at Cantonment Leavenworth in 1832, the Pawnee were suffering at the hands of Euro-Americans. Their traditional hunting grounds had been invaded by the Delaware, who had been moved west from the eastern seaboard, during the government's systematic relocations. Their numbers had been reduced by half through diseases introduced by Euro-Americans, particularly smallpox. This warrior, called The Cheyenne, or Teahkeraleerecoo, wears his hair in a scalp-lock, and has decorated his ears with earrings, beads, and mussel shell ornaments. The most striking thing about him is his face paint, in the shape of a hand, which meant that he had killed an enemy in hand-to-hand combat. Around his neck he wears a large silver peace medal. He holds a ceremonial pipe in his left hand, a horse-whip in his right.*

At the end of 1836 Catlin was in Utica, New York, with his paintings, preparing them for a New York exhibition. He had been short of money during his years of sojourning among the Indians, depending upon the good graces of many benefactors to make his trips, while spending winters with relatives. Luckily, Clara's father and brother were relatively wealthy and could support her while her husband traveled.

Catlin's Indian Gallery opened in Clinton Hall, New York City, on September 25, 1837, and was an instant hit, providing a pictorial view of the West unknown and unguessed at by most Americans. Few pictures of the West had been made up to this time, and verbal descriptions in the journals of Lewis and Clark and Maj. Stephen H. Long and in the writings of Washington Irving could not do justice to the vastness and openness of the landscape. Nor could they convey the actual appearance of western Indians, in their brilliant and proud regalia. *The United States Gazette* declared that "perhaps no one since Hogarth has had, in so high a degree, the facility of seizing at the moment the true impression of a scene before his eyes, and transferring it to the canvas."

Catlin basked in the first public praise he had received as an artist. His Indian Gallery was crowded with viewers. Indeed, many could not believe what they were seeing and put the pictures down as a hoax. In addition to his paintings, Catlin's collection of artifacts was also displayed: spears, clubs, lances, bows and arrows, and clothing, and even a full-size buffalo hide tepee were on view, representing the material culture of several tribes.

Each night Catlin lectured at Clinton Hall, trying to persuade his audiences that Indians were neither noble warriors nor bloodthirsty savages, just people whose culture was different from the white culture of eastern America. Eventually, the crowds grew so dense that Catlin had to move the collection to a larger hall, the Stuyvesant Institute on Broadway. With his new-found fame, Catlin took able to take up the cause of the Indian people, criticizing those among his fellow white Americans— including the fur company people—who discounted Indian culture and encroached upon their lifeways. False and dishonorable

155 *"Double Walker, Omaha," 1832. Catlin painted this warrior in an attitude of smoking his ceremonial pipe, with the smoke escaping from his mouth. He wears a peace medal and leggings fringed with scalps.*

156 *"Osceola, The Black Drink, A Warrior of Great Distinction," 1838.* *One of Catlin's finest portraits was made at a great price, for it was created during the final days of the great Seminole leader. The artist traveled to South Carolina's Fort Moultrie specifically to paint the captive Osceola. He painted him "precisely in the costume, in which he stood for his picture, even to a string and a trinket. He wore three ostrich feathers in his head, and a turban made of vari-coloured cotton shawl—and his dress was chiefly of calicos, with a handsome bead sash or belt around his waist." It is not known how Osceola died; he may have been poisoned by his captors, or fallen prey to disease. Or, weary of imprisonment and bitter with hatred for the whites who had defeated him through treachery, he may have willed his own death on January 30, 1838. A lithograph of Osceola from an unknown source was included in McKenney and Hall's* Indian Tribes of North America.

treaties were stripping Indians of their lands, Catlin reported, which could eventually lead only to conflict between Indians and whites.

Catlin closed the exhibition in December when he learned that the Seminole leader Osceola had been incarcerated at Fort Moultrie in Charleston, South Carolina. A leader of the Seminole resistance against white encroachment, Osceola could not be defeated by the military in battle, so deception had been used to capture him: Asked to parley with the Americans under a flag of truce, Osceola had instead been taken prisoner when he came in unarmed. Catlin rushed to the scene of his imprisonment to paint his portrait, with a commission from the Bureau of Indian Affairs. The portrait is one of Catlin's most finished and carefully considered pieces. Not only does it reveal his regard for Osceola, but the painting's subtitle, *A Warrior of Great Distinction,* reinforces his respect. Osceola was in declining health, chained and in a cell as Catlin painted and talked with him. He died the day after Catlin left him. Many said he died of a heart broken from the loss of his country and the inevitable removal of his people to the West.

Catlin had risen from obscure artist to national celebrity and was now presenting himself as a spokesman for American Indian people. His next move was a logical one: to try to preserve his collection intact so that it would be cared for and seen by fellow Americans of his own day and in the future. To convince the U.S. Congress to purchase it, Catlin brought his exhibit to Washington in April 1838. Congress did not see the wisdom of buying the collection, however, so Catlin took his paintings on the road to Baltimore, Philadelphia, and Boston. In 1839 he again displayed his work in New York and

157 *"The Cloud, A Chief, Seminole." This portrait, painted at Fort Moultrie in 1838, depicts one of the Seminole chiefs incarcerated with Osceola. Catlin noted that The Cloud had "distinguished himself in the war." In contrast to Osceola, The Cloud was "a very good-natured, jolly man, growing fat in his imprisonment."*

158

158 *"Pigeon's Egg Head (The Light), Assiniboin," 1831.* Catlin painted this portrait of The Light in St. Louis in 1831, as the Assiniboin was traveling to Washington. The artist recorded that The Light "appeared as sullen as death in my painting-room—with eyes fixed like those of a statue, upon me. In his nature's uncowering pride he stood a perfect model; but superstition had hung a lingering curve upon his lip, and pride had stiffened it into contempt." The reticence with which The Light posed for Catlin would be duplicated throughout the artist's western travels, as each new tribe had to be convinced that his powers were good and not evil.

Philadelphia, threatening to take it to Europe if Congress did not purchase it. Even when he lowered his price to $60,000, however, he could not get Congress to buy. His goal had shifted from chronicling the Indian tribes of North American to achieving congressional purchase of the collection. But his dream of safeguarding the collection through government purchase would remain unfulfilled for the remainder of his life.

In December 1839 he sailed for Liverpool, England. When Catlin arrived there, the success of his exhibition seemed assured. By February 1, 1840, the eight tons of paintings and artifacts that comprised his exhibit were opened to the public in Egyptian Hall, in London. A total of 485 portraits and landscapes hung on the walls, surrounding a Crow tepee and other artifacts, and costumes. Catlin was seen as a rustic backwoodsman from America with much to tell British audiences, especially scientists, about Indian people and their cultures. He was a success in British society and wrote home to his family: "You will rejoice to hear that I am well, although almost half crazy with the bustle and excitement I have been continuously under in this great and splendid city—amongst nobody but strangers. . . . [I] have pursued steadily and unflinchingly my course, and have at last succeeded in making what they call a 'decided hit.'" During the first year the exhibit was shown in Egyptian Hall, 32,500 people paid a total of $9,433 to see it.

That summer Clara arrived from America with their two daughters (born in 1837 and 1838). Catlin went to work on a book about his western experiences called *Letters and Notes on the Manners, Customs, and Condition of the North American Indians.* Even after attendance at his exhibit flagged, Catlin continued to live in high style and to spend money as quickly as it came in. To

revive interest in his Indian Gallery, he began to present what he called Tableaux Vivants, staged recreations of Indian dances, songs and war rituals. Catlin's brother Burr and nineteen Europeans dressed up as Indians for these programs. Unfortunately, receipts did not increase.

When he could not find a publisher for *Letters and Notes,* Catlin financed it himself, raising over $8,000 by subscription for the two volumes and 312 carefully drawn illustrations. Catlin personally managed the book's layout, printing, and distribution. Upon its release in October 1841, it became an instant classic. Although it was wordy and sometimes inaccurate and presented an itinerary that was difficult to follow, it was well-received by critics in Europe and America. Many American reviewers commented that Catlin seemed biased toward the Indian perspective and viewed the book as a critique of American society. *Letters and Notes* is still consulted by ethnologists for its valuable eyewitness reports of Indian people relatively unaffected by whites. But in its day it was an expensive book, costing 3,000 American dollars. Catlin had to depend on publishing

houses in Europe and America to sell it, thus eliminating the healthy profit he had hoped to make.

Catlin, by now the father of three children, had to cut back on expenses. In 1842, since receipts were down in London, he accepted an offer from the Mechanics Institute in Liverpool to set up his exhibit there. During the winter of 1843, a tour through several English towns and Dublin with his Tableaux Vivants show received a mixed response. With the final display of his exhibit in Manchester, Catlin announced to the press that he was taking his artifacts and paintings back to America.

Before he could leave, however, a Canadian named Arthur Rankin convinced him that another chance remained for success. Rankin had brought from America a group of Ojibwa Indians, who performed authentic traditional dances. The combination of Catlin's Indian paintings and artifacts and the Ojibwa dancers could not help but be a success, Rankin argued. Once more Catlin brought his show to London, where the Ojibwa were indeed a draw. They performed for Queen Victoria, and such notables as Charles Dickens came to see

159 *"Pigeon's Egg Head (The Light),*
Assiniboin, Going to and Returning from
Washington," 1837-39. When Catlin traveled up
the Missouri River in 1832, he shared the deck with
this Assiniboin man, dressed in European style.
Catlin recorded the man's name as Wijunjon, or
"Pigeon's Egg Head," but the man's actual name
was Ahjonjon, "The Light." The son of a chief of the
Assiniboin, Ahjonjon was returning to his village.
from a visit to Washington to see the President.
Catlin observed how the visit had changed the
warrior. Catlin had first met Ahjonjon in 1830 in
St. Louis. "He was dressed in his native costume,"
which was classic and exceedingly beautiful; his
leggings and shirt were of mountain goat skin,
richly garnished with quills of the porcupine and
fringed with the locks of scalps taken from his
enemies heads." But Ahjonjon loved Washington,
with its parties and dances. Upon the young man's
return from the East, Catlin had reason to think
that his manner and dress had been significantly
altered. In addition to his uniform coat and
epaulettes, Ahjonjon wore "a high-crowned beaver
hat, with a broad silver lace band, surmounted by
a huge red feather, some two feet high; his coat
collar, stiff with lace, came up higher than his ears,
and over it flowed downward to his haunches, his
long Indian locks, stuck up in rolls and plaits, with
red paint." Ahjonjon strolled the deck whistling
"Yankee Doodle," with two whiskey bottles peeking
out of his back pockets. When he was reunited with
his people, they were like strangers to one another.
The stories he told of the white man's world were
too unbelievable to be true, they concluded, so
Ahjonjon was obviously a liar. He continued to
strut about in his Euro-American clothes, even
as they wore out, and insisted upon telling
unbelievable stories of the East. Finally, as he was
trying to explain to a young man the immensity of
a Washington building, the man could stand it no
longer and killed The Light. Catlin reflected upon
the incident many times in his writings and felt it
epitomized not only the vast changes in their
cultures, but also the inability of some cultures to
reach a common meeting ground.

159

them. Dickens, in an essay entitled "The Noble Savage," described the Indians as "squatting and spitting" on a table in the center of the hall, in between "dancing their miserable jigs, after their own dreary manner." On the other hand, Dickens noted that Catlin, "in all good faith, called upon his civilized audiences to take notice of their symmetry and grace, their perfect limps, and the exquisite expression of their pantomime; and his civilized audience, in all good faith, complied and admired." But Catlin, for the first time, was accused of exploiting his collection. A falling-out with Rankin ended the engagement three months early.

In late 1843 Catlin retired to the British countryside to write and prepare lithographs for a book called *The North American Indian Portfolio*. Catlin promised his family that he would return home after the book was published and he had recouped some

money. But once more he reneged on his promise, this time when a band of Iowa Indians arrived in London, many of whom Catlin had met years before. In the summer of 1844, he rented Egyptian Hall once again, with the Iowa dancing nightly in Catlin's Indian Gallery. In the autumn, Catlin took the Indians on a European tour. But tragically, the Iowa were struck by disease, and two of them died during the winter. Despite this setback, they agreed to accompany Catlin to Paris in the spring of 1845.

At first, Catlin's gallery was hailed in Paris, as it had been in London, as a must-see event. King Louis-Philippe received the Iowa dancers personally, while George Sand and Victor Hugo visited the gallery. But disaster struck after the Iowa left for America. In July, Catlin's wife Clara, exiled for so many years, suddenly died of

pneumonia, leaving behind four children. Receipts were dwindling, even after another group of Ojibwa began dancing. Catlin stored the collection and began a tour of Europe with the Ojibwa, but eight of the Indians caught smallpox in Brussels, and two died. Catlin helped to nurse the others back to health, and when they were well, he saw them off as they departed for England. This second tragedy of Indian deaths after exposure to European diseases convinced Catlin to end his attempts at staging "Wild West Shows."

Returning to Paris with four small children to support, he began to work on copying selected Indian paintings, commissioned by Louis-Philippe. Bad luck continued to pursue him, however, for his young son died of typhoid in 1846. After delivering the fifteen Indian subjects to Louis-Philippe, Catlin was asked to paint a series of twenty-nine scenes

commemorating the voyages of the French explorer LaSalle, for which he would receive $100 each. Just as the paintings were nearly completed, mobs of people began to take over the streets of Paris in the revolution year of 1848. The King and Queen fled the country, and Catlin was never paid for his work. He was barely able to get out of France with his three daughters and his collection.

Catlin returned to London and rented a studio-residence-showroom, publishing a book he called *Eight Years' Travels and Residence in Europe*. The book was a disappointing collection of anecdotes about and descriptions of the uncomfortableness of the Ojibwa and Iowa dancing troupes in Europe, and it did not sell well. Catlin received a small number of commissions, but his personal fortunes continued to decline. He borrowed money against the worth of his collection—and against the certainty, in his own mind, that Congress would one day buy it. He sent letters to Congress and to the British Museum, offering to sell his collection, but despite the backing of influential people, his offers were refused.

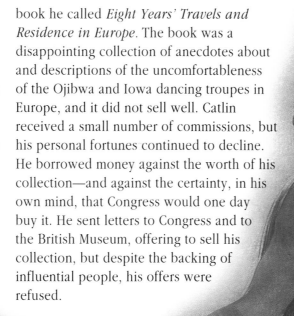

160-161 *"Ball Play of the Choctaw—Ball Down,"* 1834-35. *The Choctaw ball game was a form of lacrosse. Catlin, in* Letters and Notes, *states that it was "no uncommon occurrence for six or eight hundred or a thousand of these young men, to engage in a game of ball, with five or six times that number of spectators, of men, women and children, surrounding the ground, and looking on. And I pronounce such a scene, with its hundreds of Nature's most beautiful models, denuded, and painted of various colours, running and leaping into the air, in all the most extravagant and varied forms, in the desperate struggles for the ball, a school for the painter or sculptor, equal to any of those which ever inspired the hand of the artist in the Olympian games or the Roman forum." Players could move and pass the ball to one another only by means of the nets at the ends of the sticks—they could not use their hands. The object of the game was to throw the ball through the enemy's goal. There were no other rules, no penalties for roughness, and no referees! The first team to score 100 goals won the game.*

161 *"He Drinks the Juice of the Stone, in Ball-Player's Dress,"* Choctaw, 1834. *The Choctaw were forced to move from Mississippi to Arkansas beginning in 1830. Catlin encountered the tribe near Fort Gibson in 1834, while adjusting to life in their new homeland: "Whilst I was staying at the Choctaw agency in the midst of their nation, it seemed to be a sort of season of amusements, a kind of holiday; when the whole tribe almost, were assembled around the establishment, and from day to day we were entertained with some games or feats that were exceedingly amusing: horse-racing, dancing, wrestling, foot-racing, and ball-playing, were amongst the most exciting; and of all the* catalogue, the most beautiful was decidedly that of ball-playing. This wonderful game, which is the favourite one amongst all the tribes, can never be appreciated by those who are not happy enough to see it." He Drinks the Juice of the Stone—according to Catlin, "the most distinguished ball-player of the Choctaw nation—posed for the artist in his game clothing. His breechclout is covered with a "tail" of horsehair, which is secured with a beaded belt. A "mane" of horsehair is worn around the neck, topped off by a turban decorated with feathers. The two sticks he holds were used to catch and throw the ball. Ball players were not allowed to wear other clothing, or moccasins on their feet.*

162 "Little Wolf, Iowa," 1844. *This beautiful portrait shows the warrior Little Wolf in all his finery. Festooned with earrings and necklaces made of beads and wampum, his face is painted red for battle. His necklace of grizzly bear claws surmounts two peace medals, one silver and one bronze. His scalp-lock is augmented with a horsehair roach. Unlike the bulk of the paintings reproduced in this book, this portrait was not painted on the Plains of North America. Begun in London and completed in Paris, it was one of two paintings that Catlin entered in the Salon of 1846. William Truettner calls it "the masterpiece of [Catlin's] European career." Little Wolf was one of the dancers in Catlin's Indian Gallery; his wife and child fell victim to disease during their stay in Europe.*

163 "No English, Peoria," 1830. *An influential man with his tribe, No English was also a dandy. Catlin painted him in curious war paint, "with a looking-glass in his hand." His beautiful feathered hat and nose ring were typical of his tribe, but they were taken to a higher level of fashion by No English. The stories of diminishing, displaced tribes like the Peoria and Wea must have given Catlin a sense of urgency in his work.*

By 1852 Catlin was completely broke by 1852 and heavily in debt. An unwise investment in a Texas land company prompted his creditors to demand payment of their loans. Unable to pay, Catlin was thrown into debtor's prison. A friend sailed across the Atlantic to escort the three young Catlin girls back to America and helped get Catlin out of prison. Catlin went to Paris, where once again he begged the U.S. Senate to buy his collection and once again was rejected. With nowhere to turn, Catlin was on the verge of breaking up his collection and selling his precious paintings at auction. His life had been a continual downhill slide from the moment he sailed to Europe. The integrity of the collection was saved only by the arrival of American locomotive manufacturer Joseph Harrison, Jr., who happened to be traveling in Europe. Learning of Catlin's plight, Harrison paid off Catlin's debts (now $40,000) in exchange for the paintings, which he sent to America to be stored in his Philadelphia factory.

Finally freed from a mountain of debt and worry about his collection, Catlin's original ambition returned. In 1853 he traveled to South America to search for gold, paint landscapes, and most importantly, begin a series of paintings documenting South American Indians. By 1857, he had sketched many South American tribes and made a trip to the West Coast of the United States, where he sketched California Indians.

In the early 1860s, Catlin returned to Europe and settled in Brussels, where he began painting scenes of the American West from memory. He used his over 300 sketches of South American and West Coast Indians to create a second collection of paintings. Now deaf, he lived as a recluse for over ten years in Brussels, painting more than 600 subjects and writing another book called *Life Amongst the Indians* (1867), containing entertaining, carefully written stories for young readers. Catlin also finished detailed essays on the Okeepa ceremony, defending his original observations as they had appeared in *Letters and Notes* against critics who doubted he had really witnessed the ceremony in 1832.

Catlin continued to dream that he would one day make a triumphant return to the United States. Still trying to get Congress to purchase his paintings, he offered to sell the two collections for $120,000, sadly forgetting that the majority of the first collection was now owned by Joseph Harrison and was lying about a boiler factory in Philadelphia.

George Catlin finally returned to the United States in late 1870, after thirty-two years in Europe and South America. In October 1871 he set up his new collection of paintings in a New York City gallery, but the press and public took little notice. In early 1872 he moved to Washington, D.C., where an old friend, Joseph Henry, now secretary of the Smithsonian Institution, let him have the use of a room in the Smithsonian castle building. Both men had hopes that Congress would finally purchase Catlin's paintings, some of which were hung in a hallway on the second floor of the building. But congressmen, like the general public, had almost completely forgotten Catlin.

Far from being intrigued by Indians, most Americans in 1872 were interested in pushing them aside, as more and more land was opened to white settlement following the Civil War. Americans interested in the country's "manifest destiny," the notion that the United States would inevitably stretch unbroken from ocean to ocean, saw Indians as a nuisance who either had to assimilate to the ways of Euro-Americans or be forever marginalized. The stated Indian policy of the Grant administration was called the "Peace Policy," but the army's attempts to round up Indians and place them on mostly worthless tracts of land touched off the last of the Indian wars with the Plains, desert, and Modoc tribes.

In October 1872 George Catlin became seriously ill and was transported to Jersey City, New Jersey, where he was tended by his daughters. He died on December 23, 1872, at the age of 76, and was buried in Brooklyn's huge Greenwood Cemetery beside his wife and son. He was never able to fulfill his early goal of painting the lifeways of all American Indians; nor did he ever return to the productivity he experienced in the early 1830s. But Catlin's name will forever be synonymous with his dream of preserving Indian lifeways. It is estimated that Catlin painted forty-eight tribes, completing at least 310 unique portraits and 200 genre scenes. Although he never achieved lasting success with his traveling gallery and Wild West Shows and was denied his greatest goal—government acquisition of his entire collection—Catlin remained an optimist and a dreamer to the end.

Catlin's artistic creations languished for many years. The original Indian Gallery, purchased by Joseph Harrison in 1852, remained stored in his Philadelphia factory until 1878, suffering fire and water damage. In 1878, a federal official named Thomas Donaldson worked with Spencer F. Baird, secretary of the Smithsonian Institution, in persuading Harrison's widow to donate the remains of the Indian Gallery to the Smithsonian. It is there that the bulk of Catlin's work survives. Donaldson compiled a catalog of the remaining works in 1885, over 900 pages in length, which included 445 of the 585 original paintings. Catlin's second collection of drawings, which he called his "cartoon collection," was created during his European sojourn at the end of his life. Following his death, the cartoon collection was inherited by Catlin's daughters. The

American Museum of Natural History acquired this collection in 1912 but eventually sold it. By 1965, it was owned by Paul Mellon, who generously donated 351 cartoons to the National Gallery of Art.

In addition to the Smithsonian and National Gallery collections, a group of 35 oil portraits of Upper Missouri Indians commissioned by Maj. Benjamin O'Fallon of St. Louis survives in the Field Museum, Chicago; and a series of his watercolors is in the collection of the Thomas Gilcrease Institute of Tulsa, Oklahoma. Other small collections of Catlin's work exist in several other American repositories.

Although Catlin had originally been an inspiration for many young artists, including John Mix Stanley, Charles Deas, Paul Kane, Carl Wimar, George Caleb Bingham, and others, he trained no followers, and his work had been largely forgotten by the 1870s. The influence that his Indian Gallery had on Euro-American perceptions of the West lasted until just after the Civil War, when new attitudes about settlement and new images of the Plains Indian wars, including photographs, began to alter it. It was only when the paintings were rediscovered by anthropologists at the Smithsonian Institution that they began to be seen as important documents. In the late 1940s, historians such as Bernard DeVoto and ethnologists like John C. Ewers finally assured Catlin's position in American history.

His rehabilitation was far too long in coming. He was the first major painter to seek out American Indian people in their own country. His concern for them was evident in his painting, his writing, and his actions on their behalf. The indelible images he created influenced a generation of American perceptions of the look and character of the West and remain important historical documents today. Although he often felt like a failure during his lifetime, Catlin's original goal of chronicling the vanishing, unspoiled lifeways of American Indian people was a resounding success.

164-165 "Battle Between Sioux and Sac and Fox." *This battle between Indian tribes, not witnessed by Catlin but imagined many years later, was painted in Paris in 1846-48. It demonstrates how Catlin fondly remembered his days on the prairie, and the stories he recalled and wished to illustrate.*

167 RIGHT *"Bread, Chief of the Tribe, Iroquois," 1831*. With one trip to St. Louis under his belt, George Catlin returned east in 1830 and was able to paint several chiefs who were visiting Washington. Bread, an Oneida chief, impressed Catlin, who noted that he was a "shrewd and talented man, well educated—speaking good English—is handsome, and a polite and gentlemanly man in his deportment." Catlin thought that Bread was part European. The portrait was painted in Washington, where Bread signed a treaty in January 1831. The removal of part of the Oneida people from New York State to Green Bay, Wisconsin, must have been one more sign to Catlin that the lifeways of American Indian people were changing forever.

166 *"He Who Has Eyes Behind Him, Plains Cree, 1831, also known as Broken Arm."* This warrior accompanied The Light to Washington in 1831-32. The ornaments he has woven into his hair are called hair pipes; the smooth shells of sea creatures were harvested in the Bahamas and prepared in New Jersey for trade with the Indians on the frontier. The Cree were associated with the land that became British Canada, extending from the Ottawa River in Quebec to the Saskatchewan River in western Canada. A subgroup of the Cree migrated onto the Plains, adapting to a true Plains lifestyle, living in buffalo-hide tepees rather than birchbark wigwams.

167 LEFT *"Grizzly Bear, Chief of the Tribe, Menominee," 1831*. Grizzly Bear led a delegation of fifteen Menominee to Washington and "there commanded great respect for his eloquence, and dignity of deportment." This portrait was probably painted in the nation's capital in January 1831, when the fourteen delegates of the Menominee nation negotiated and signed a treaty to sell a portion of their tribal lands to the government.

168-169 *"Horse Chief, Grand Pawnee Head Chief," 1832.* This painting shows the principal chief of the Grand Pawnee, wearing a buffalo skin hair-side-in, and a peace medal. Catlin sketched many portraits of the Pawnee quickly, never finishing them, although this one is complete.

169 TOP *"Bird That Goes to War, A Tapage Pawnee."* In an unfinished Pawnee portrait, Catlin still manages to capture the sitter faithfully and present him as an individual. Catlin was far more excited by his portraits of Upper Missouri Indians than by those he made of Indians who had had more contact with whites. This may be the reason that so many of his Pawnee portraits were never completed.

169 BOTTOM *"Brave Chief, A Skidi (Wolf) Pawnee," 1832.* The Skidi Pawnee migrated the farthest north of the four Pawnee bands and settled along the Platte, Loup, and Kansas Rivers (Republican fork) in Nebraska. They are sometimes referred to as the Northern Pawnee. Brave Chief wears a peace medal and has eagle feathers and an arrow in his scalp-lock. His painted hands signify that he defeated and killed an enemy in hand-to-hand combat.

170 *"Buffalo Bull, A Grand Pawnee Warrior,"*
*1832. Buffalo Bull, or Ladookea in his own
language, a member of the Grand Pawnee tribe,
was painted by Catlin wearing his personal
symbol—of the head of a buffalo—painted on his
face and breast. The Grand, Tapage, and
Republican Pawnee were referred to as the
Southern Pawnees, and they lived along the
Arkansas River until about 1770, when they
migrated northward to join the Skidi. Their move
was forced by the loss of the fur trade with
France, which had been defeated by England in
the French and Indian War and been driven out
of North America in 1763.*

171 *"Big Elk." This man's name was pronounced
"Om-pah-ton-ga" in his own language. He was
the principal chief of the Omaha tribe, as
evidenced by the fact that he wears the largest-
sized peace medal issued by the U.S. government.
His black face paint symbolizes the death of an
enemy killed in combat. Big Elk was painted by
Catlin at Cantonment Leavenworth in 1832; he
was also painted by Charles Bird King in 1821.*

172 TOP *"Sioux Indian Council, Chiefs in Profound Deliberation," 1832-37.*
Catlin left no account of this incident, and it may be a conjectural scene painted from his imagination. He shows a group of chiefs gathered around a fire on the prairie, perhaps on a war party.

172-173 *"Self-Torture in Sioux Ceremony,"*
1835-37. Catlin witnessed this scene, a part of the
Sun Dance ceremony, near Fort Pierre in 1832:
"I went to a little plain at the base of the bluffs,
where were grouped some 15 to 20 lodges of the
Tiny-ta-to-ah band. We found him naked, except
for his breech-cloth, with splints or skewers run
through the flesh of both breasts, leaning back
and hanging with the weight of his body to the t
op of a pole which was fastened in the ground
and to the upper end of which he was fastened by
a thong which was tied to the splints. In this
position he was leaning back, with nearly the
whole weight of his body hanging to the pole, the
top of which was bent forward, allowing his body
to sink about half-way back to the ground. . . . He
held in his left hand his favorite bow, and in his

right, with a desperate grip, his medicine bag."
Catlin continued, *"In this condition, with the*
blood trickling down over his body, which was
covered with white and yellow clay, and amidst a
great crowd who were looking on, sympathizing
with and encouraging him, he was . . . to stand
and look at the sun, from its rising in the morning
'till its setting at night; at which time, if his heart
and his strength have not failed him, he is 'cut
down,' receives the liberal donation of presents . .
. and also the name and the style of a doctor, or
medicine-man, which lasts him, and ensures him
respect, through life." Catlin saw only a portion of
the Sun Dance ceremony, in which warriors shed
their blood for the renewal of the tribe and the
earth each year. Their blood sacrifice also brought
visions for their own well-being.

173 BOTTOM *"Black Rock, A Two Kettle*
Chief, Lakota," *1832.* Catlin stated that Black
Rock was *"a constant and faithful friend of Mr.*
McKenzie" and described him as a *"tall and fine*
looking man, of six feet or more in stature; in a
splendid dress, with his lance in his hand; with
his pictured robe thrown gracefully over his
shoulders, and his headdress made of war-eagles'
quills and ermine skins, falling in a beautiful
crest over his back, quite down to his feet, and
surmounted on the top with a pair of horns
denoting him . . . head leader or war chief of his
band." Each eagle feather in the headdress was
earned by the chief in battle—they were awarded
for *"counting coup."* *"Coup"* was the act of
striking an enemy with a stick, a lance, a war
club, or best of all, one's bare hands. One had to
boast of the coup afterward and have witnesses.
Feathers could be placed at four different
attitudes, symbolizing a first, second, third, or
fourth coup. A full war bonnet could hold up to
thirty feathers, and then tail pieces could be
attached. Each feather had to be obtained by the
warrior himself, from an immature bald eagle.
Remaining feathers might be traded to others for
use as decoration, but not for headdresses. The
Two Kettles were one of the seven tribes of the
Lakota nation.

174-175 *"Scalp Dance, Lakota,"* 1835-37.
After a successful raid on enemies, scalps were brought back to the village to be presented to sisters or mothers. Catlin described the scalp dance in Letters and Notes: *"The Scalp-dance is given as a celebration of a victory; and amongst this tribe, as I learned whilst residing with them, danced in the night, by the light of their torches,* *and just before retiring to bed. When a war party returns from a war excursion, bringing home with them the scalps of their enemies, they generally 'dance them' for fifteen nights in succession, vaunting forth the most extravagant boasts of their wonderful prowess in war, whilst they brandish their war weapons in their hands. A number of young women are selected to aid* *(though they do not actually join in the dance), by stepping into the centre of the ring, and holding up the scalps that have been recently taken, whilst the warriors dance (or rather jump), around in a circle, brandishing their weapons, and barking and yelping in the most frightful manner, all jumping on both feet at a time."*

175 *"War Dance, Sioux," 1845-48.* *"Each warrior, in turn, jumps through the fire, and then advances shouting and boasting, and taking his oath, as he 'strikes the reddened post.'" This painting, made much later, when Catlin was in Europe, was composed from sketches made at Fort Pierre in 1832.*

176-177 *"Sioux Indians on Snowshoes Lancing Buffalo."* *Snowshoes aided winter buffalo hunts, allowing the hunter, according to Catlin, "to glide over the snow with astonishing quickness, without sinking down or scarcely leaving his track where he has gone." A winter hunt was easier because deep snows impeded the flight of the animals, and buffalo bulls were separate from the cows. Although Catlin never spent a winter in the West with the Indians, he probably based this painting on verbal descriptions and his personal experiences of hunting buffalo in other seasons.*

177 *"Buffalo Chase in Winter," 1832-33.* *Autumn buffalo hunts usually yielded enough meat to stand a tribe through the winter. Winter hunts were conducted, however, to obtain buffalo robes to trade with the Euro-Americans often for enormous profits. The anthropologist John C. Ewers points out that Catlin never saw the winter hunt scene portrayed here, for the Indians are dressed in summer clothing. These winter paintings were an attempt by Catlin to present a well-rounded picture of Indian life to the Euro-American public, despite the fact that his time with each tribe was limited. Although not accurate in all their particulars, they are nevertheless important for the general feeling that Catlin evoked.*

178 "Eagle's Ribs, Piegan Blackfeet," 1832.
When Catlin reached Fort Union on board the
Yellow Stone, he had arrived at the westernmost
point of his journey. It was at Fort Union that he
met and painted the notorious Blackfeet. Eagle's
Ribs, a Blackfoot warrior, openly boasted that the
seams of his shirt and leggings were decorated
with hair from eight scalps of white trappers, as
well as some of his Indian enemies. "I have
painted him at full length," Catlin noted, "with a
head-dress made entirely of ermine skins and
horns of the buffalo. This custom of wearing
horns beautifully polished and surmounting the
head-dress, is a very curious one, being worn
only by the bravest of the brave; by the most
extraordinary men in the nation." Catlin also
depicted the warrior holding a lance and two
medicine bundles. The Blackfeet were a
confederacy of tribes that controlled a huge
expanse of the northeastern Plains, from the
North Saskatchewan River in Alberta to the Upper
Missouri in Montana. The three principal groups
were the Blackfeet (Siksika), who lived farthest to
the north; the Bloods (Kainah), named because
they painted their bodies with red clay; and the
Piegans (Pikuni), which means "Poorly Dressed,"
to the south. The Blackfeet were seminomadic
hunters who lived year-round in tepees and
subsisted on buffalo.

**179 "Medicine Man, Performing His
Mysteries Over a Dying Man, Blackfeet,"
1832.** Catlin painted The White Buffalo in his full
medicine man regalia, as he tried to revive a
Blackfoot chief who had been shot by a Cree
enemy at Fort Union. Spectators, including
Catlin, formed a ring of 30 to 40 feet in diameter
around the dying man; then a hush fell over the
crowd, "and nothing was to be heard, save the
light tinkling of the rattles upon his dress, as he
slowly moved through the avenue left for him. . . .
He approached the ring with his body in a
crouching position, with a slow and tilting step.

His body and head were entirely covered with the
skin of a yellow [grizzly] bear, the head of which
(his own head being inside of it) served as a
mask; the huge claws of which were dangling on
his wrists and ankles; and in one hand he shook
a frightful rattle and in the other brandished his
medicine spear." The ritual lasted for half an
hour, a dance in imitation of the grizzly bear,
"until the man died; and the medicine-man
danced off to his quarters and packed up, and
tied and secured from the sight of the world, his
mystery dress and equipments."

180 *"Buffalo Bull's Back Fat, Blackfeet,"*
1832. A principal chief of the Bloods (Kainah), in
the Blackfoot language his name was pronounced
"Stumickosucks," according to Catlin. "Backfat"
was the hump on a buffalo's back, "the most
delicious part of the buffalo's flesh." Catlin, in
Letters and Notes, described Stumickosucks as "a
good-looking and dignified Indian, about fifty
years of age, and superbly dressed; whilst sitting
for his picture, he has been surrounded by his
own braves and warriors, and also gazed at by
his enemies, the Crows and Knisteneaux,
Assiniboins and Ojibbeways; a number of
distinguished personages of each of which tribes,
have laid all day around the sides of my room;
reciting to each other the battles they have fought,
and pointing to the scalp-locks, worn as proofs of
their victories, and attached to the seams of their
shirts and leggings. This is a curious scene to
witness, when one sits in the midst of such
inflammable and combustible materials, brought
together, unarmed, for the first time in their
lives." William Truettner, the foremost chronicler
and student of Catlin's art, considers this
painting Catlin's masterpiece.

181 *"White Buffalo, Blackfeet," 1832.*
Wunnestow, The White Buffalo, was a powerful
medicine man in the Blackfoot nation. Catlin
recorded that he had captured the "looks and
very resemblance' of an aged chief, who combines
with his high office, the envied title of mystery or
medicine-man, i.e. doctor—magician—prophet—
soothsayer—jongleur—and high priest, all
combined in one person, who necessarily is
looked upon as 'Sir Oracle' of the nation...
[O]n his left arm he presents his mystery-drum or
tambour, in which are concealed the hidden and
sacred mysteries of his healing art."

182-183 *"'Brick Kilns' Clay Bluffs, 1900 Miles Above St. Louis", 1832.* *During his return journey to St. Louis by pirogue in 1832, Catlin went ashore to examine these volcanic formations. He was determined to record every aspect of the West, including its geology. He wrote in* Letters and Notes *that the "whole country behind us seemed to have been dug and thrown up into huge piles, as if some giant mason had* been there mixing his mortar and paints, and throwing together his rude models for some sublime structure of a colossal city . . . and in the midst of his progress, he had abandoned his works to the destroying hand of time, which had already done much to tumble them down, and deface their noble structure." *Catlin also speculated on the volcanic nature of the formations and the possible action of water and erosion upon them.*

183 TOP LEFT *"Thighs, Wichita," 1834.* The Wichita were sometimes called the "Tattooed Pawnee" or the "Pawnee Picts" in the nineteenth century. Catlin wrote in Letters and Notes *that "amongst the women of this tribe, there were many that were exceedingly pretty in feature and in form; and also in expression, though their skins are very dark . . . . [They] are always decently and comfortably clad, being covered* generally with a gown or slip, that reaches from the chin quite down to the ankles, made of deer or elk skins." Thighs was a Wichita girl who, along with another girl from her tribe named Wild Sage, had been held prisoner by the Osage. Part of the mission of Col. Dodge's dragoons in 1834 was to return Thighs to her people. The freedom of the two girls was purchased by a minister named Schemmerhorn.

183 RIGHT *"The Six, Plains Ojibwa," 1832.* "The chief of that part of the Ojibbeway tribe who inhabit these northern regions," Catlin explained, "is a man of huge size; with dignity of manner, and pride and vanity, just about in proportion to his bulk. He sat for his portrait in a most beautiful dress, fringed with scalp locks in profusion; which he had snatched, in his early life from his enemies', and now wears as proud trophies and proofs of what his arm has accomplished in battles with his enemies. His shirt of buckskin is beautifully embroidered and painted with curious hieroglyphics, the history of his battles and charts of his life."

184 *"Wolf Chief, Head of the Mandan Tribe,"*
1832. *Hanatanumauk, or Wolf Chief, was the principal chief of the Mandan people. Catlin thought him "a haughty, austere, and overbearing man, respected and feared by his people rather than loved." Wolf Chief's portrait was the first to be painted in the Mandan village, and the people were astounded that Catlin had created a likeness that they could recognize. Wolf Chief wears an unusual headdress composed of a raven's feathers, and he carries a highly, ornamented ceremonial pipe.*

185 *"Mint, A Pretty Girl, Mandan," 1832.*
Mint, whose name in her own language was Shakoha, was twelve when her portrait was painted. Like many Mandan people, she has a white streak in her hair. Catlin was fascinated with this anomaly of the Mandans, that people "of both sexes, and of every age, from infancy to manhood and old age, [have] hair of a bright silvery grey; and in some instances almost perfectly white." Catlin noted that the trait seemed to be hereditary, and that one in ten Mandans seemed affected by it. The women seemed very proud of their gray hair, he said, and grew it so that it fell over their shoulders and in some cases as low as their knees. Catlin described Mint as a "belle" who was famous for her "conquests, not with the bow or the javelin, but with [her] small black eyes, which shoot out from under [her] unfledged brows, and pierce the boldest, fiercest chieftain to the heart."

186-187 *Mandan Foot War Party in Council,* 1832. *This war party is resting just outside the Mandan village after returning from an unsuccessful raid on the Arikara. While "following the trails of their enemy . . . they were attacked by a numerous party, and lost several of their men and all their horses." Catlin painted them "seated on their buffalo robes, which were spread upon the grass, with their respective*

weapons laying about them, and lighting their pipes at a little fire which was kindled in the centre—the chief or leader of the party, with his arms stacked behind him, and his long head-dress of war-eagles' quills and ermine falling down over his back, whilst he sat in a contemplative and almost desponding mood, was surely one of the most striking and beautiful illustrations of a natural hero that I ever looked upon."

187 TOP *"Archery of the Mandan,"* 1835-37. *In this popular Mandan game, each man would try, one at a time, to shoot as many arrows as he could into the air before the first one hit the ground. Some Mandan warriors could put as many as eight arrows up at one time, "thrown from the same bow."*

187 BOTTOM *"Mandan Scalping an Enemy,"* *1835-37.* Although Catlin never mentioned witnessing a scalping, he probably based this painting on verbal accounts from warriors he interviewed. He noted in Letters and Notes *that the scalp "is a patch of skin taken from the head of an enemy killed in battle, and preserved and highly appreciated as the record of a death produced by the hand of the individual who possesses it; and may oftentimes during his life, be of great service to a man living in a community where there is no historian to enrol the names of the famous—to record the heroic deeds of the brave, who have gained their laurels in mortal* combat with their enemies." In order to be considered a genuine scalp, the piece cut away "must contain and show the crown or centre of the head; that part of the skin . . . where the hair divides and radiates from the centre." Over the years historians have debated whether Europeans introduced the practice of scalping to American Indians, or whether the practice existed in North America prior to 1492. Historian James Axtell has proven fairly conclusively that scalping was practiced by many Indian tribes before the advent of the Europeans. The Europeans exploited and spread it as a means of paying bounties for the number of enemies their Indian allies killed.

188-189 *"Rainmaking Among the Mandans,"* *1837-3.* Hair of the White Buffalo stands on the roof of a Mandan lodge calling to the skies for rain. Inside the lodge, medicine men perform mysteries, while young volunteers stand atop the lodge throughout the day: "Each one has to hazard the digrace which attaches (when he descends at sundown) to a fruitless attempt; and he who succeeds acquires a lasting reputation as a Mystery or Medicine man."

189 *"Interior View of the Medicine Lodge, Mandan O-Kee-Pa Ceremony," 1832.* On the second day of the Okeepa, The Old Bear left his lodge and began dancing through the streets; the young men emerged from their lodges who were to make the sacrifice and endure the four days of torture. The Old Bear led them to the medicine lodge, where they would stay until the end of the ceremony. Mahhatohpa personally led Catlin and James Kipp into the medicine lodge at this point. It was an extraordinarily high honor for an outsider to be invited to witness the most sacred

for the candidates to face their ordeal. They came forward, one at a time, already weak from four days of fasting and no sleep. Catlin recalled, "An inch or more of the flesh on each shoulder, or each breast, was taken up between the thumb and finger by the man who held the knife; and the knife, which had been hacked and notched to make it produce as much pain as possible, was forced through the flesh below the fingers, and was followed by a skewer which the other attendant forced through the wounds (underneath the muscles, to keep them from

ritual of the Mandan people. During the next few days, the young men fasted and were exhorted by the medicine man and the elders to face their coming ordeal bravely. The beginning of their test came on the fourth day, when at about noon a solitary figure approached the village, his naked body painted black with white rings and large white fangs painted on his face. Around his waist was an enormous red male sexual organ of carved wood. This was Okeeheede, the evil one. He ran quickly into the village, scaring the women and children, finally joining in the bull dance and losing his power, then submitting to gradual attacks by the women and children in which his red organ was wrested from his body and he was driven back out onto the prairie. The woman who had captured the organ harangued the crowd for a time, then ordered the bull dance stopped. Then the Pohk-hong began: It was time

being torn out), as they were hacked. There were then two cords lowered from the top of the lodge, which were fastened to these skewers, and they immediately began to haul him up. He was thus raised until his body was just suspended from the ground, when the knife and additional splints were passed through the flesh in a similar manner on each arm below the shoulder, also below the elbow, on the thighs, below the knees." Each candidate was thus prepared, hanging from the ceiling of the lodge by stout cords attached to skewers in their breasts; their personal shields, bows, and other items, including buffalo skulls, were attached to skewers on their thighs and elbows and hung as weights. The attendants then spun the candidates around using long poles, until the agony of the young men made them cry out to the Great Spirit, and they finally fainted from the pain.

190 *"Tal-Lee, Osage," 1834. Catlin noted:*
"Amongst the many brave and distinguished
warriors of the tribe, one of the most noted and
respected is Tal-lee, painted at full length, with
his lance in his hand—his shield on his arm, and
his bow and quiver slung upon his back. In this
portrait, there is a fair specimen of the Osage
figure and dress, as well as of the facial outline,
and shape and character of the head, and mode
of dressing and ornamenting it with helmet crest,
and the eagle's quill."

191 LEFT *"Wa-Ho-Beck-Ee, Osage," 1834.*
In Letters and Notes, *Catlin wrote that the Osage*
were among the tribes "who shave the head, cut
and slit their ears very much, and suspend from
them great quantities of wampum and tinsel
ornaments. Their necks are generally ornamented
also with a profusion of wampum and beads; and
as they live in a warm climate where there is not
so much necessity for warm clothing, as amongst

the more Northern tribes . . . their shoulders,
arms, and chests are generally naked, and
painted in a great variety of picturesque ways,
with silver bands on the wrists, and oftentimes a
profusion of rings on the fingers." Catlin noted
that Wahobeckee was the handsomest man of
his tribe.

191 RIGHT *"Clermont, First Chief of the*
Tribe, Osage," 1834. This portrait was made at
Fort Gibson and shows some of Catlin's growth as
an artist, the figure being nicely proportioned
and life-like. According to Letters and Notes,
Clermont was the "head-chief of the Osages at this
time . . . the son of a very distinguished chief of
that name, who recently died; leaving his son his
successor, with the consent of the tribe. I painted
the portrait of this chief at full length, in a
beautiful dress, his leggings fringed with scalp-
locks, and in his hand his favourite and valued

war-club." Catlin felt that the Osage were the
tallest men in North America, and other
contemporary observers agreed: "very few of the
men, at their full growth, . . . are less than six feet
in stature, and very many of them six and a half,
and others seven feet. They are at the same time
well-proportioned in their limbs and good-
looking; being rather narrow in the shoulders,
and, like most very tall people, a little inclined to
stoop. . . . Clermont's father had established trade
relationships with St. Louis fur outfits, yet
vigorously opposed liquor and other temptations
of the whites."

192 *"He Who Carries a Wolf, A Distinguished Brave," 1834.* This distinguished Comanche warrior "piloted the dragoons to the Camanchee village." His name came from the fact that he carried a medicine bag made from the skin of a wolf. He Who Carries a Wolf holds his shield in the painting, and a whip in his right hand. The Comanche ranged over a huge area in the American Southwest, including parts of the modern states of Kansas, Texas, New Mexico, Oklahoma, and Colorado, as well as northern Mexico. They became skilled horse breeders and trainers, with huge herds of horses, which they captured in raids and sometimes traded with other tribes. By about 1790, the Comanche had allied themselves with the Kiowa and were the most feared tribe in the Southwest. They were called "The Lords of the Southern Plains."

193 *"Comanche Mounted War Party," 1834-37.* Catlin criticized the appearance of the Comanches, saying that they were "in stature, rather low, and in person, often approaching to corpulency. In their movements, they are heavy and ungraceful; and on their feet, one of the most unattractive and slovenly-looking races of Indians that I have ever seen; but the moment they mount their horses, they seem at once metamorphosed, and surprise the spectator with the ease and elegance of their movements." Catlin declared the Comanche to be "the most extraordinary horsemen that I have seen yet in all my travels, and I doubt very much whether any people in the world can surpass them." Warriors sometimes had personal herds numbering 200 horses. Stealing horses from other tribes increased one's status within the Comanche culture.

194 TOP *"Comanche Lodge of Buffalo Skins,"*
1834-35. Once Catlin arrived in the Comanche
country, he quickly became too ill to paint or
record what he saw. But he was able to make
some very fine paintings before he collapsed. The
Comanche lodges, he wrote, were "made of
buffalo skins, in the manner precisely of the Sioux
and other Missouri tribes." The village, "with its
thousands of wild inmates, with horses and dogs,
and wild sports and domestic occupations,
presents a most curious scene; and the manners
and looks of the people, a rich subject for the
brush and pen."

194-195 *"Comanche Village, Women Dressing*
Robes and Drying Meat," *1834-35.*
"In the view I have made of it, but a small
portion of the village is shewn," wrote Catlin,
"which is as well as to shew the whole of it,
inasmuch as the wigwams, as well as the
customs, are the same in every part of it. In the
foreground is seen the wigwam of the chief; and
in various parts, crotches and poles, on which the
women are drying meat, and 'graining' buffalo
robes." Catlin has often been criticized for
painting tepees as though they were all of the
same size and shape.

195 *"Bow and Quiver, First Chief of the*
Tribe," *1834.* Catlin described the principal chief
of the Comanche as a "mild and pleasant looking
gentleman, without anything striking or peculiar
in his looks; dressed in a very humble manner,
with very few ornaments upon him, and his hair
carelessly falling about his face and over his
shoulders. . . . The only ornaments to be seen
about him were a couple of beautiful shells worn
in his ears, and a boar's tusk attached to his
neck, and worn on his breast." The Comanche
attacked members of other Indian tribes who
came into their country. In 1829 they even
attacked a U.S. Army wagon train that was
mapping the Santa Fe Trail between Missouri and
New Mexico. The mission of Col. Dodge in 1834
was therefore seen as crucial to continued
commerce along the Santa Fe Trail.

196-197 *"Tobacco, Lakota," 1832.* The second chief of the Oglala Lakota, Tchandee, "The Tobacco," was one of the bravest warriors of his tribe. He is depicted with his hair tied up in somewhat the same fashion as One Horn, with eagle feathers representing the important coups he has counted. The porcupine quill work on his war shirt is especially vivid in this portrait.

197 *"Blue Medicine, Santee Sioux," 1835.* A medicine man whom Catlin painted at Fort Snelling, Minnesota, in 1835, Blue Medicine appears "with his medicine or mystery drum and rattle in his hands, his looking-glass on his breast, his rattle of antelope's hoofs, and drum of deer-skins." Blue Medicine was part of the Tingtatoah band of the Santee Sioux (Dakota).

198-199 *"View on the St. Peters River, Sioux Indians Pursuing a Stag in their Canoes,"* *1836-37.* *This painting was sketched out during Catlin's journey to the Pipestone Quarry in 1836. It shows Dakota Sioux hunters pursuing a stag trying to swim away from them.*

199 TOP *"Big Eagle, Santee Sioux (Dakota),"* *1835.* *Big Eagle was painted in 1835 at Fort Snelling, Minnesota. Located on the Mississippi River in modern-day Minneapolis, Fort Snelling was an official U.S. Army outpost. Big Eagle was a chief of the O-hah-kas-ka-toh-y-an-te band of the Eastern Sioux, the Dakota. These Indian people had had far more direct contact with Euro-Americans than the Lakota Sioux, whom Catlin painted in 1832 on the Missouri River.*

199 BOTTOM *"Sioux Worshiping at the Red Boulders."* *This scene depicts Dakota Sioux supposedly "worshiping" red boulders. The Dakota had painted these three rocks red to represent a buffalo cow and two calves. Catlin did not understand that American Indian cultures did not distinguish between animate and inanimate objects. Oftentimes when Europeans thought that Indians were worshiping an inanimate object, they were really associating it with other objects or animals; the connection to them was vital, one being a part of the other. The Dakota at the Red Boulders might have been communing with buffalo that came to that spot, praying for a return of the herd and good hunting. There are many other possible explanations that often escaped literal-minded Euro-American observers.*

200-201 *"Indian Family Alarmed at Approaching Prairie Fire," 1846-48.*
This painting was made in Paris in 1846-48, one of Catlin's many conjectural scenes that show the hold the West continued to have on his imagination. Prairie fires, which moved swiftly and caused terrible destruction, were a real hazard for Indians of the region. The mobile Plains tribes were used to breaking camp in as little as fifteen minutes time, as they are seen doing in this painting. If the fire moved too quickly, the family might have to abandon their belongings to try to outrun it on their swift horses.

KARL BODMER: "OVER THERE I HAD FRIENDS"

202 TOP *Portrait of Karl Bodmer by Loys Delteil, 1894.* The Swiss-born Bodmer is shown here sixty years after his American visit. In later years he became reclusive and turned out pedestrian magazine illustrations. His early glories as an illustrator of the American landscape and American Indian people, however, assure his continued fame.

202-203 *"Banks of the Missouri."* *"This is a view of the* Yellow Stone *hung up on a sandbar on May 15, 1833. The frustrating delays in travel allowed Bodmer to make detailed sketches and watercolors from life, showing the boat in the distance. Unlike George Catlin, who often composed his scenes from memory many months or sometimes years after the fact, Bodmer's paintings have an incredible immediacy and almost photographic fidelity to their subject.*

203 LEFT *"Pasesick-Kaskutau, Assiniboin."* *Ready for a hunt, this man is dressed warmly for an autumn day on the Plains. Not posed in the usual finery of most warriors, he gives us a truer picture of the day-to-day appearance of men going about the work of providing for the tribe. On October 21, 1833 Prince Maximilian noted in his journal that "several Assiniboins, whom we have not seen before, arrived successively. Among them was a man wearing his winter dress, having on his head a badger's skin, by way of cap, and gloves, which are very rare among the Indians. His name was Pasesick-Kaskutau (nothing but gunpowder), and Mr. Bodmer took an admirable full length portrait of him."*

In the winter of 1834, harsh winds blew across the Dakota plains, and cold wisps of snow penetrated between the narrow cracks in the walls of a ramshackle log cabin. The light coughing of a weak, sick man covered with buffalo robes came from a corner bed, while a younger man, bundled against the chill that the fire on the hearth could not disperse, stood at an easel, painting a portrait of a Hidatsa warrior in all his finery. The rude cabin was within the walls of Fort Clark, located adjacent to the Mandan village of Mih-Tutta-Hang-Kush on the Missouri River. The sick man was a German prince named Maximilian, a scholarly man of science who had come to North America to study the flora, fauna, and indigenous peoples of this "new world." The young artist was Karl Bodmer, a Swiss national who

had been hired by the prince to illustrate his travels and discoveries. Now, in the unbelievably harsh winter weather of the great plains, the prince was ill and wondered if he would ever see his homeland again. No matter what happened, however, Prince Maximilian knew that this journey had been one of the highlights of his life, and that the artwork already completed by Karl Bodmer would immortalize them both.

Still, the importance of the journey and the artwork it spawned would not always seem to them so clear or positive, particularly after the journey was over. The prince was a sensitive and generous man, ultimately disappointed by the results of his North American voyage. Bodmer was a moody and demanding artist, rarely

202

203 RIGHT *"Sih-Chida, Mandan."* *Sih-Chida was an Indian artist who was fascinated by the work of Maximilian and Bodmer. They in turn were captivated by him and noted his progress in understanding form and perspective. With art supplies Bodmer gave him, he drew pictures of the Europeans and of his Mandan friends. Sih-Chida, whose name means "Yellow Feather," wears many decorations of otter skin, including a tippet around his neck and trailers at his feet. The prince noted that he was "very polished in his manners, and possessed more delicacy of feeling than most of his countrymen."*

deferential even to his royal patron. "Over there I had friends," Bodmer stated late in his life, referring to the Indian people he met and painted in North America. After he executed his elegant, finely crafted watercolors during the North American trip, Bodmer never again seemed to hit his stride as an artist. Perhaps he lamented the fact that he had never returned to the land where he had enjoyed such adventures in his youth, where, in fits of nostalgia, he decided he had been truly happy. Bodmer, unlike Thomas McKenney and George Catlin, never became obsessed with chronicling America's Western frontier or disseminating that information to a worldwide audience. Many frustrations plagued him, however, and with the exception of his North American work, he never fulfilled the promise of his enormous artistic talent.

Karl Bodmer's American paintings are important for more reasons than their fine draftsmanship. He created his own vision of America in the prephotography era, chronicling the West with an intensity and truthfulness unmatched until cameras were taken out on the frontier. Compounding Bodmer's natural curiosity and huge artistic talent was the fact that he was a European. Everything he saw was new and exotic to him. Americans and Indians alike seemed different and intriguing, and he painted both with the same curiosity and scrutiny.

What emerges from his work is a portrait of America as it was from 1832 to 1834, poised on the threshold of the industrial age. Factories that manufactured cloth, foundries that made iron and steam engines for railroads and ships, mills that produced lumber, firearms, and traps—all were slowly becoming more important than home manufactures. People were growing dependant upon goods they purchased rather than items they made at home. America was growing in other ways. The fur trade still dominated the far West, but thousands of homesteaders were moving into Indiana, Illinois, Missouri, and Michigan. Immigration to America was growing with each passing year. Within a decade, wagon trains of pioneer farmers would set out across the plains, and by 1850 the United States would stretch from the Atlantic to the Pacific.

How Karl Bodmer got to America, and

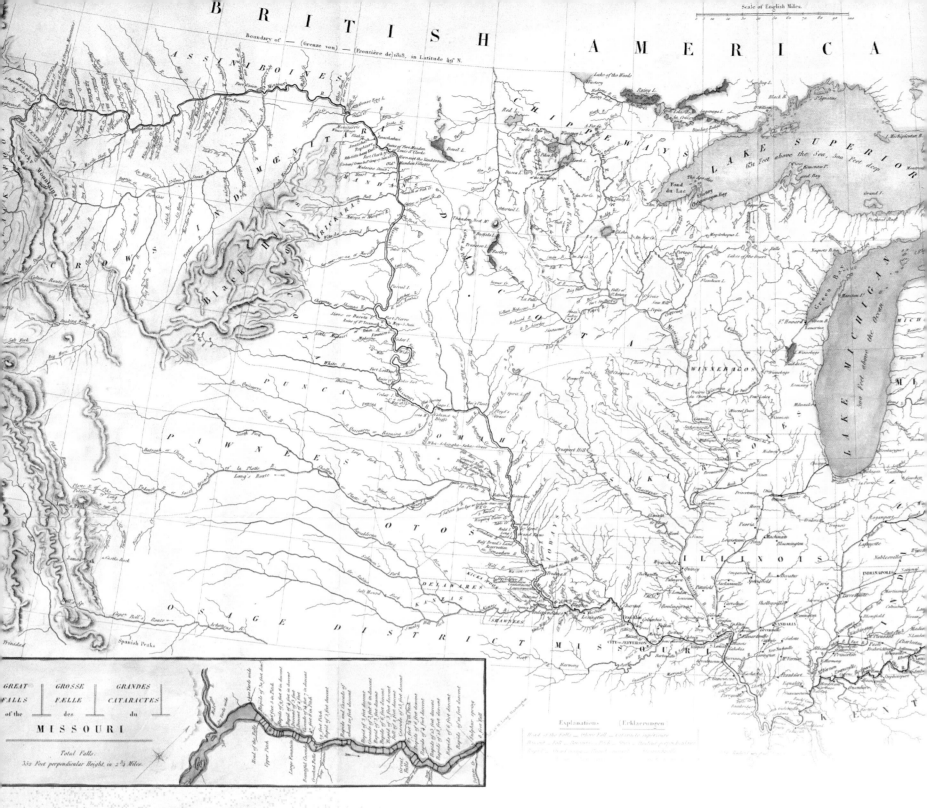

GREAT | GROSSE | GRANDES
FALLS | FÆLLE | CATARACTES
of the | des | du
MISSOURI

Total Falls:
352 Feet perpendicular Height, in 2¾ Miles.

the details of his incredible experiences there, read more like a novel than history. Unfortunately, Bodmer did not write of his experiences; since Prince Maximilian did, we must follow Maximilian and Bodmer as a team throughout their travels. The written narrative tells us about the America Maximilian saw; the visual record shows us Bodmer's America.

Karl Bodmer was born in Zurich, Switzerland, on February 11, 1809, the son of a cotton merchant named Heinrich Bodmer and his wife Elisabeth Meier. Showing promise in art, at the age of thirteen he was apprenticed to his uncle, an engraver named Johann Meier, and he worked in Meier's shop for ten years. Meier had been trained by two of the best artists in Switzerland, Johann Heinrich Füssli and Gabriel Lory. Along with his older brother, Rudolf, Bodmer traveled about Switzerland with his uncle, learning how to produce watercolor paintings, sketches, and aquatint engravings. Although many sources state that Bodmer was trained in Paris, there is no evidence of this. It is

now thought that Bodmer's only artistic training was from his uncle.

Bodmer began his career by producing romantic landscape scenes of Switzerland and the Rhineland, some of which were published. Neither an adequate market for art nor adequate support for an artistic community existed in Switzerland at this time, and Karl moved to the German Rhineland, where he could paint romantic compositions incorporating the castles, hillsides, vineyards, and river life surrounding him. In 1831 a book containing scenes of the Moselle Valley, painted by Karl Bodmer and engraved by Rudolf Bodmer, was published in Koblenz.

Bodmer's opportunity to go to America came through a German prince named Alexander Philip Maximilian of Wied-Neuwied, who in late 1831 was planning a two-year trip to the New World, to culminate in a hunting and exploring jaunt in the Rocky Mountains. Maximilian, a naturalist with an established reputation, planned to write a book detailing his experiences. His family

ruled a principality called Neuwied, located on the Rhine near Koblenz, Germany. He had been born on September 23, 1782, the eighth of ten children, in an eighteenth-century castle, and was a veteran of the Napoleonic wars. He had been captured at the Battle of Jena in 1806, and his brother had been killed serving in Wellington's army during the peninsula campaign. After repatriation in a prisoner exchange, Maximilian won the Order of the Iron Cross at Châlons and was part of the victorious allied army that swept into Paris in 1814.

Maximilian's primary interests were not military, however, but scientific. He had been educated by Johann Friedrich Blumenbach of Göttingen, a professor of anatomy and natural history who was compared favorably with Linnaeus and Buffon, and whose star pupil had been scientific explorer Alexander von Humboldt. Maximilian had been instilled with the theories of Blumenbach, which addressed the question of "race" and how human beings had developed and migrated throughout the world. Blumenbach believed

204-205 *Map of the Travels of Prince Maximilian and Karl Bodmer.* *From 1832 to 1834, Maximilian and Bodmer undertook an incredible odyssey across the North American continent, from Boston through Pennsylvania and Indiana to St. Louis, and from there up the Missouri River to Fort McKenzie, halfway across the modern state of Montana. They spent the winter of 1833-1834 with the Mandan at Fort Clark, returning to Europe through New York in the summer of 1834. The journey was successful by any criterion, not only for the distances traveled but for information gathered, and artwork produced. The prince's illness in 1834 was the only negative incident during the entire journey—quite a statement considering the primitive modes of transport the Europeans used to reach a wild and inaccessible area.*

205 RIGHT *Portrait of Prince Maximilian of Wied.* *Prince Maximilian was already known in scientific circles for his pioneering work in the jungles of Brazil. Traveling in North America under the name "Baron Braunsberg," the prince was a short, pudgy man nearing 50, who dressed almost continually in green hunting garb. His journal of the 1832-34 visit to America still makes fascinating reading. The quotes in the picture captions in this chapter come from the prince's journal.*

that non-European races were at different and lower stages of development, and he pondered whether they could someday work their way up to the same cultural and scientific level as whites. Perhaps, thought Blumenbach at some point in history, they had formerly been on the same level or even superior to European cultures, then degenerated in a long slide toward "barbarism." In the early nineteenth century, these questions were somewhat new and carried a great deal of weight with the scientific community. The thinkers of the era saw the world not as a static, unchanging place, but as a fluid environment, in which animals had lived and become extinct, and in which human cultures had evolved, risen into full flower, and disintegrated.

Maximilian's connection with Blumenbach brought him into contact with the great Alexander von Humboldt as well. Von Humboldt was an adventurer-scientist who possessed "a versatility of genius which I have never seen equaled," declared no less a source than Goethe. Humboldt's goal was to

assemble and publish all knowledge of the physical world, even as such knowledge was growing exponentially during the early nineteenth century.

By 1815, Maximilian, inspired by Blumenbach's theories and von Humboldt's explorations in South America, traveled to Brazil with the German naturalists Georg Wilhelm Freyreiss and Friedrich Sellow. For two years they explored the jungles of the Brazilian rainforest and lived among native peoples. Upon his return, Maximilian wrote a two-volume report on his voyage, similar to von Humboldt's *Voyage to the Equinoctial Regions,* entitled *Reise nach Brasilien in den Jahren 1815 bis 1817.* Maximilian illustrated the report himself, and although his sketches were redrawn by his talented brother and sister, they were still the weakest aspect of the work, attacked by European critics upon the book's release in 1821.

In preparation for his 1832 trip to North America, then, he logically sought out an accomplished artist who spoke German and could stand the rigors of sea and overland

206-207 *"The Steamboat* Yellow Stone.*"*
Prince Maximilian, accompanied by Bodmer and
hunter David Dreidoppel, arrived in the United
States in 1832 for an examination of the country
both scientific and ethnological, centering on
American Indians of the West. In 1833, one year
after George Catlin's ascent of the same river,
Maximilian, Bodmer, and Dreidoppel left St. Louis
for the adventure of their lives. The Yellow Stone,
making its third annual ascent of the river, this
time bound only as far as Fort Pierre, became
hung up frequently on sandbars along the way.

This watercolor by Bodmer, painted on April 19,
1833, shows the boat near Fort Osage, Missouri,
having part of its cargo removed to lighten its load
so that it can be floated off the sandbar. This is
probably the best pictorial representation of the
Yellow Stone *ever made. The 1833 trip was the*
Yellow Stone's *last up the Missouri. In 1835 she*
was sold to men who took her to Texas, where she
plied the Brazos River and had a role in the fight
for Texas independence. The Yellow Stone *was last
seen in Galveston Bay in 1837 and thereafter is lost
to history, her fate unknown.*

206 BOTTOM *"Mouth of the Big Sioux River."*
This watercolor shows the confluence of the Big
Sioux River with the Missouri, near modern Sioux
City, Iowa. The Yellow Stone *steamed past this
point on May 8, 1833. This typical view of the
Missouri River in the 1830s shows the absence of
any development along its shores, as well as river
snags peeking up out of the water near the far
side. This detail is a testament to Bodmer's
abilities as an artist.*

207 TOP *"View of the Missouri River Near Fort Leavenworth."* *This unfinished view, painted on April 20 or 21, 1833, shows the Missouri River below Cantonment Leavenworth. Maximilian described the "tall, slender forest trees, [which] grow among picturesque rocks; the beautiful flowers of the red bud tree, bright green moss, and a thick carpet of verdure, chiefly consisting of the leaves of the May-apple. We were now in the free Indian territory, and felt much more interested in looking at the forests, because we might expect to meet with some of their savage inhabitants."*

voyages. The 23-year-old Bodmer seemed to fit all of the prince's criteria. It is not known how the two met; perhaps they had mutual acquaintances, or perhaps the prince had seen Bodmer's scenes of the Moselle Valley. At any rate, Maximilian asked, and Bodmer was eager to go on the adventure. The prince offered a salary of 33 thalers per month, in addition to the all-expense-paid trip. He imposed some conditions, however: Bodmer would have to provide his own art materials, including paints and brushes, and he would also be expected to assist in collecting artifacts and specimens and to help hunt for food. But the most difficult and demanding condition of all was that the prince would retain ownership of all the artwork Bodmer produced during the journey. Bodmer could make copies of the work for himself, but he would have to obtain permission from the prince to exhibit them. In the contract, Maximilian also warned Bodmer that he himself lived simply and that no amenities should be expected on the journey.

Bodmer balked at these last conditions, brazenly telling the prince that 33 thalers was not enough money, and that he wanted more freedom to retain and display his artwork. The prince gave in to Bodmer's demands, granting him a salary of 45 thalers a month and freedom to publish landscapes after a set period. Maximilian was worried that Bodmer's artwork might be shown to the public before his own book on the trip was prepared and published. Bodmer agreed to this more reasonable set of conditions and signed a contract with the prince on April 25, 1832.

Maximilian's itinerary was hazy. In letters to friends, he stated that he wished to examine the flora and fauna of North America, and that he aimed particularly to study the Native American people, comparing them to the people with whom he had lived in Brazil. But he had no defined route in mind, although he mentioned the Upper Missouri region, Louisiana, and New Mexico. In his book on the voyage, *Travels in the Interior of North America*, Maximilian stated that he wanted "to pass some time in the chain of the Rocky Mountains."

With these rather undefined goals, Prince

Maximilian and Karl Bodmer, accompanied by an experienced hunter and taxidermist named David Dreidoppel, set out for America on May 17, 1832, from Helvoetsluys, the Netherlands. The American brig *Janus* took six weeks to cross the Atlantic, landing at Boston on July 4, 1832. Bodmer was miserable during the voyage, so seasick that he was able to paint very few scenes. When they gratefully left the ship in Boston, the prince and his companions were treated to the patriotic music, sumptuous food, militia parades, and boisterous games of an American Independence Day celebration. It was an interesting introduction to the United States.

Maximilian saw little that engaged him until he toured Charles Willson Peale's Museum in Philadelphia. No longer housed in Independence Hall, the museum was now administered by the late Peale's son, Titian. Maximilian praised the museum in his *Travels* as being different from those he had seen in Boston and New York, which he declared were mere "accumulation[s] of all sorts of curiosities . . . hung up without any order." Fewer "trifling nicknacks" had been admitted to the Peale Museum, where he admired the mastodon skeleton, Indian artifacts from the Lewis and Clark expedition of 1804-1806, and paintings executed during the 1819-1820 Stephen Long expedition by Titian Peale and Samuel Seymour.

The German prince was astounded to discover that after a thorough search of bookstores and print shops, he could not find good representations of American Indian people. The era's really fine images had yet to be published or else had not yet been created. Even as the prince searched Philadelphia for images, George Catlin was painting Indians far to the West along the Missouri River. It would be several years before the public would see these portraits, and several more years before they were published. Meanwhile, Thomas McKenney was in the midst of preparing the lithographs of the Charles Bird King paintings in Philadelphia. Before the end of his visit to Philadelphia, the prince would see these images, mentioning them in his *Travels*. In fact, Maximilian and Bodmer may have seen some of the original King paintings or the Henry Inman copies of

208 *"Study of an Elk."* This beautiful nature study, painted on September 19, 1833, was made in the Badlands along the Missouri River. Bodmer not only rendered the elk but also drew a cross-section of the animal in the interest of science.

208-209 *"White Castles on the Missouri."* On July 25, 1833, as the Flora was approaching the Badlands, it passed white sandstone rock formations along the Missouri that reminded the travelers of castles on the Rhine. Maximilian wrote that as they got a closer view, "the resemblance naturally vanishes; but from Mr. Bodmer's sketches one will easily see . . . a group of pronghorn antelope on the sand bar, with some swimming the river."

209 BOTTOM *"Nodaway Island."* A steamboat like the Yellow Stone could not carry enough wood for her boilers for a lengthy upriver journey like that to Fort Pierre, so at likely spots along the route, men were sent out to cut wood. On April 25, a wood-cutting detail landed at the mouth of the Nodaway River, and the prince used the time to search for specimens. Bodmer, who accompanied the him, painted this Arcadian scene, including deer and birds in flight. Maximilian noted that the "numerous horse-chestnuts were in full leaf; the white ash was in flower, as well as many species of pear and plum, which looked as if covered with snow, and formed a beautiful contrast with the red masses of the flower of the Cercis. In a dark glen in the forest, we observed a long Indian hut, which occupied almost its whole breadth, and must have served for a great number of persons."

them. Many historians have speculated that the King/Inman works influenced Bodmer in his approach to Indian portraits when he reached the West. Considering the way Bodmer handled the ethnological details, this is quite possible.

In Philadelphia the prince waited for the arrival of his equipment, which was not shipped from Boston because of a cholera epidemic then raging on the East Coast. Cholera was mankind's worst epidemic since the Black Death, and Maximilian had good reason to fear the disease and to keep clear of it. The spread of this disease to North America in 1832 was part of a pandemic that began in India in 1816, and reached the Ganges delta about 1826. In three more years it came to the Caspian Sea and by 1830 was spreading across Russia and the Near East. During 1831 and 1832 the disease reached Mecca and the Islamic world, the Black Sea, and Europe. Irishmen packed in the holds of emigrant ships brought it to Canada early in 1832, from which it spread down the Atlantic coast and the Great Lakes to the Mississippi.

The disease was frightening because its cause was unknown and there was no treatment or cure. Once a person was infected, cholera could kill in a matter of hours. Severe diarrhea and vomiting led to complete prostration and fluid loss as the victim's face grew thin, wrinkled, and hollow, while the skin turned blue. In a few hours, or at most a few days, the infected person either died in agonizing pain or rounded the corner and began to mend. Medical science has since discovered that the virus was transmitted through water, milk, or other foods that had been contaminated with excreta of patients or carriers, but this was not known at the time. Even today cholera remains a deadly disease, although it can now be treated through vigorous intravenous replacement of fluids.

Because of the cholera epidemic, the prince changed his travel plans He avoided the Erie Canal route to the West through upstate New York in favor of the "savage grandeur" of the Delaware Water Gap and

the "National Road" into central Pennsylvania. When he finally received his supplies, he moved westward into Pennsylvania's Lehigh Valley. All along their route, Maximilian and Dreidoppel searched for animal and plant specimens, fossil remains, and ancient Indian sites, while Bodmer made sketches and watercolor renderings. Before striking out for the Midwest, the party returned to eastern Pennsylvania to prepare animal specimens for shipment to Europe. Finally, in late September 1832, Maximilian left with Dreidoppel for a utopian community called New Harmony, located on the Wabash River in Indiana. Bodmer's hunting rifle had exploded a few days before, cutting open his left thumb and burning his hand badly, so he stayed behind to recuperate.

Maximilian found both a trove of information and learned companions with whom to share it at New Harmony, where the reunited party arrived on October 19, 1832. A village of 600 people, New Harmony manufactured cigars and whiskey, while

processing beef, pork, and corn for shipment
down the rivers to New Orleans for export.
The community had an extensive library of
books and manuscripts on America, and more
than its share of celebrated intellectuals.
Thomas Say and Charles-Alexandre Lesueur,
two of America's most important scientists,
were in residence at New Harmony that
winter. Say, an entomologist, had
accompanied Stephen Long's 1819-20
expedition to explore the great plains and the
Rocky Mountains, and Maximilian wanted to
learn as much as he could from his
experience. Lesueur, an artist-naturalist, was
an expert on American wildlife. The prince
enjoyed their company immensely, until he
became ill with symptoms "nearly resembling
cholera." While the prince recovered, Bodmer
made sketches. For five months Maximilian
read every important book yet published
on the West and American Indians and
participated in philosophical discussions with
Say and Lesueur.

Just as the prince was becoming close to
the two scientists, a bond also developed

between Maximilian and Bodmer, making them far more than patron and hired artist. In a letter reprinted in *Karl Bodmer's America,* the prince wrote his brother August as early as May 17, 1832 that his artistic colleague was "a lively, very good man and companion, seems well educated, and is very pleasant and very suitable for me; I am glad I picked him. He makes no demands, and in diligence he is never lacking." On November 20, Maximilian again wrote his brother, conveying his excitement at the incredible body of work Bodmer was creating for him. "If only I could show you, my dear August, our good landscape painter, Carl, Mr. Bodmer's portfolio. How many times you would exclaim: 'Oh, excellent! Beautiful! Beautiful!' He now has seventy pages of sketches . . . from which you will be able to travel very vividly here with me. God grant that we will all experience this joyous moment healthy and happy together again!!!"

As the prince recovered his health, he began to make short journeys into the Indiana and Illinois countryside. He was appalled by the fact that the Euro-American settlers indiscriminately cut down trees on public land to build their homes, flatboats, fences, and fires. They did not stop when

they had the wood they needed, but continued to destroy the native forests just to clear the land. By contrast, the German states had managed their forests for hundreds of years. In the prince's view, the settlers had driven out the Indians with their wanton destruction of a precious resource and then gone on to alter the landscape to the point where wildlife could no longer survive. Maximilian's acute perceptions on this topic correctly summarized the effects of the vanishing frontier, convincing him that he had arrived in America just in time to glimpse the last vestiges of its pristine wilderness— and perhaps even more important, to witness the culture of its disappearing Indian inhabitants.

Meanwhile, Bodmer, perhaps bored with the prince's philosophical activities, volunteered to take a journey down the Mississippi River to Louisiana. Maximilian had contemplated this trip from the outset, for he had business to conduct with the banks in New Orleans. In addition to taking care of these matters for the prince, Bodmer could be the eyes and ears of his employer en route. On January 3, 1833, Bodmer left for New Orleans by steamboat, painting, sketching, and keeping a journal of his

210 *"Head of a Buffalo."* One of Bodmer's best nature studies, this is also one of the first accurate depictions of the animal that was so important to survival on the Great Plains.

210-211 *"Landscape with Herd of Buffalo on the Upper Missouri."* Amidst the incredible rock formations in the early morning light of July 14, Bodmer's eyes were greeted with the sight of dozens of grazing buffalo.

observations along the way. Bodmer marveled at the various forms of river craft he observed on these western waterways, the true highways of America at that time. He was also impressed by the rapid change in the weather as the steamboat moved southward, reporting that "we came in two days from total winter into the most beautiful spring!" He observed that Natchez, Tennessee, was a "bad and dirty place, notorious on account of its gamblers and disorderly women." Surprisingly, it was not until New Orleans that Bodmer first saw an

American Indian, a Choctaw "living in a sadly inactive condition." Bodmer sketched many Choctaws, once the proud rulers of forests in Alabama and Mississippi, now removed by treaty from their homelands to Indian Territory, in what is now Oklahoma. Many Choctaws had not moved West but instead eked out a living on the streets of New Orleans, Natchez, and other river towns.

During Bodmer's solo journey, he honed his talents at landscape and portrait renderings, becoming acclimatized to the

new, surprising, and fascinating world of America, while leaving behind many of his preconceived European notions of romantic New World landscapes and pristine environments. Bodmer returned to New Harmony in February 1833.

By March, Maximilian was ready to set off for the West. The party steamed down the Ohio and up the Mississippi to St. Louis, where they arrived on March 24, 1833. George Catlin had first seen the same levee three years earlier and had departed from it for the Upper Missouri just three months

212 *Unusual Elevations on the Upper Missouri.* *These paintings were made by Bodmer on July 9, 1833. "Near Lewis and Clarke's Bighorn Island, we again saw most singular summits on the hills," wrote the prince. "Entire rows of extraordinary forms joined each other, and in the lateral valleys we had interesting glimpses of this remarkable scenery... It were to be wished that the geologist and the painter might devote a considerable time to examine this part of the country, step by step."*

Indians, Maximilian and Bodmer were observers, aware of the injustice they were seeing but noting it as just a sad fact of American life.

The prince and his party spent the following few weeks stocking up on the supplies and trade goods they would need for their journey and waiting for their ship to sail. Clark provided them with passports to the western territory, introduced them to the town's leading citizens, and showed them his museum of Indian artifacts. In addition, they spoke with Benjamin O'Fallon, Auguste Chouteau, John F.A. Sanford, and Kenneth McKenzie, all of whom had had experience on the big, muddy Missouri and knew the Indian people whom Maximilian and his men would encounter. The prince was fortunate in charming this sector of St. Louis citizenry, for they were not only knowledgeable about the West but could help him realize his goals. They assisted him as he decided on his itinerary, dissuading him from making a direct overland journey to the Rocky Mountains and urging him to take the Missouri River route instead. In addition, O'Fallon gave the prince a large-scale copy of the famous Clark map of the West and proudly showed the group Indian portraits painted by George Catlin the year before. After seeing these portraits, Karl Bodmer had beheld the very best artwork yet executed of American Indian people–that of Charles Bird King in Philadelphia, and now George Catlin's in St. Louis. Perhaps he resolved to do an even better job of chronicling Indian people, for we know that he thought very little of Catlin's artistic talent, while King's portraits were not painted on site, in the Indians' actual homelands.

On April 10, 1833, Maximilian, Bodmer, and Dreidoppel started up the Missouri on the steamboat *Yellow Stone,* the same boat that had taken George Catlin to Fort Union the year before. Once more on board the boat was Pierre Chouteau, one of the directors of the American Fur Company, this time accompanied by his wife and daughters. This year Chouteau made only a short overnight trip to St. Charles, Missouri, where he disembarked. Charles Bird King's

before. The prince was not impressed with the town, whose "first appearance is not prepossessing, as it has no steeples," he wrote in his *Travels*. "The mass of houses, however, unfolds as you approach; the environs are low and monotonous." Upon settling in, Maximilian immediately saw signs of injustice, noting that one of their neighbors "flogged one of his slaves in the public streets, with untiring arm. Sometimes he stopped a moment to rest, and then began anew." He noted that all blacks were "held in contempt by the Americans." He also saw evidence of the inequalities inflicted upon the Indians, the first Maximilian had seen. A delegation of Sac and Fox, led by Chief Keokuk, arrived in St. Louis to plead for the release of Black Hawk. As the Indians met with William Clark in his council chamber, Maximilian made careful notes about their appearance. In terms of their "physiogamy," he felt they were of the same "race" as the native Brazilians he had studied fifteen years earlier. On his visit to Jefferson Barracks, a military installation south of the city, he saw Black Hawk and the other leaders of his rebellion shackled with weights around their ankles and languishing in a cell. Several of these Indians died soon after Maximilian and Bodmer met them. Interestingly, no sketches were made o f these visits or these Indian people. U nlike George Catlin, whose conscience quickly made him a champion of the

212-213 *"View of the Stone Walls."* On August 6, 1833, Maximilian stayed on deck all day with Bodmer to watch the fantastic scenery slip by. Maximilian recalled that they "had not yet taken leave of the extraordinary sand-stone valley, on the contrary, we now came to a most remarkable place. The stratum of sand-stone, regularly bedded in low hills, runs along both banks of the river, which is rather narrow; like a high, smooth, white wall, pretty equally horizontal above, with low pinnacles on the top."

213 BOTTOM *"Rock Formations on the Upper Missouri."* The Yellow Stone *traveled up the Missouri to Fort Pierre, where after a few days' respite the prince's party boarded another steamboat, the* Assiniboin, *to Fort Union. The last leg of their trip, to Fort McKenzie, was accomplished on board a 60-foot keelboat named* Flora. *The* Flora *set out on July 6, 1833, with 52 passengers on board, including Fur Company official David Mitchell. Bodmer painted this picture when the boat was not far from Fort* Union; the boatmen were busy cordeling, or hauling the boat from the shoreline, because there was no breeze for the sail. The view included what Maximilian described as "the lofty fantastic chain of clay hills, of a whitish-grey colour, with some darker strata, or horizontal stripes, and regular perpendicular clefts or ravines." Intensely interested in science, the prince was never bored on this leg of the trip as he studied the distant hills and speculated on their geological history.

patron Kenneth McKenzie, who was returning to Fort Union, and Maj. John Dougherty, on his way to the Omaha agency at Bellevue, boarded at St. Charles; each was able to provide the prince with information about Indian affairs in the Upper Missouri region. The remainder of the ship's company consisted, Maximilian noted in his *Travels,* of "about 100 persons . . . most of whom were those called engagés, or voyageurs, who are the lowest class of servants of the Fur Company. Most of them are French Canadians, or descendants of the French settlers on the Mississippi and Missouri." The trip was a dangerous one, with snags floating down the river and threatening to tear the bottom out of the boat, and sandbars forcing frequent stops. At the

outset, the little steamboat was battered by severe thunderstorms, losing a smokestack and some of its deck cargo.

As peaceful weather returned, Bodmer sketched and made watercolors of landscapes along the route. Although he painted some of the same scenes and people as Catlin had, he rendered them with far more precision and draftsmanship, perhaps due to Bodmer's European training. In terms of portrait painting, Catlin actually had far more experience than Bodmer, but he never approached Bodmer's technical expertise. Perhaps Bodmer just had more natural ability than Catlin, for setting aside the differences in style and media, Bodmer's works are, scene for scene, portrait for portrait, superior to Catlin's; they were in fact more accomplished than those of any artist who had yet worked in the American West. Karl Bodmer painted in watercolors, a tricky and

unforgiving medium far different from oils. Mistakes cannot be hidden easily in watercolors, and white areas—such as clouds, buildings, the pupils of a person's eyes, and the feathers in an Indian war bonnet—have to be left unpainted, the stark paper itself representing white. Watercolors generally take a tremendous amount of foresight, planning, and skill to execute. Karl Bodmer proved himself a master in both landscape and portraiture during the journey. One can only imagine the excitement and wonder that the the prince felt as Bodmer's collection of pricelessly realistic scenes continued to grow.

On May 3, 1833, the *Yellow Stone* reached Bellevue, Maj. Dougherty's fur trade outpost near modern-day Omaha. The following day, at Cabanne's outpost, Bodmer painted two Omaha Indians, a father and son, while Maximilian took notes on the welcoming dance the Indians performed for them under a moonlit evening sky. Continuing along the Missouri, Bodmer painted portraits of Indians during various stops and at a Ponca village. On May 25, the *Yellow Stone* reached the Sioux agency, called Fort Lookout, where Bodmer painted Wahktageli, a Yankton Sioux warrior, who posed patiently for two days. Any superstition among the Indians about having their portraits painted seems to have ended by 1833, due to George Catlin's work among these same people. In fact, Wahktageli was so pleased with his portrait that he gave the prince his entire set of clothing and accoutrements, which became the genesis of Maximilian's important collection of Indian artifacts.

On May 30, the boat arrived at Fort Pierre, "to the great joy of all on board," noted the prince. The fort was a quadrangle of "108 paces on each side," with two blockhouses armed with cannon. During their stay, Bodmer was able to make several fine portraits of the Yankton Sioux and scenes of the Indian encampment of "thirteen Sioux tents" that was nestled next to the fort. The prince found the appearance of the Sioux men impressive and called their women "beautiful."

Meanwhile, the *Yellow Stone* unloaded her cargo and made preparations to return to St. Louis, taking on board the year's catch of

furs, including seven thousand buffalo hides. Native American and Euro-American hunters and trappers had brought a wide variety of animal hides into the various forts and trading posts along the river. In addition to buffalo, there was beaver, the formerly indispensable cash crop pelt, as well as otter, weasel, martin, lynx, fox, mink, muskrat, and deer. The era's switch from an emphasis on beaver to buffalo hides was part of a substantial change taking place within the fur trade. Beaver felt was no longer in great demand for fashionable top hats, as the Chinese silkworm and the lighter silk toppers made from it were becoming all the rage in Europe and the eastern United States. The market was changing, and fur traders were changing with it. Soon, the world of the so-called mountain men, which Maximilian and Bodmer saw in such intimacy on this voyage, would be gone forever, as the traders at Fort Pierre frankly told the prince.

214 LEFT *"A Stop; Evening Bivouac." Travel along the western rivers was rough in 1833, with few amenities. The prince was taken aback by the rude manners of the boatmen and probably hungered for intellectual companionship. Because of the dangers of the river, boats did not travel at night and were tied up on the shoreline. Bodmer painted this view of an evening encampment on October 30, 1833, when the party was headed downriver between Fort Union and Fort Clark. It is representative of the hundreds of campfire scenes the prince and his companions experienced during their two years in America.*

214-215 *Aquatint of "The Camp of the Gros Ventres of the Prairies on the Upper Missouri." This aquatint provides an excellent view of the keelboat* Flora *and the Atsina Indians coming out to meet her. It was one of a series of aquatints created for Prince Maximilian's book* Travels in the Interior of North America, 1832-1834. *The prints were constructed from watercolors Bodmer made from life, although, he often combined several different watercolors to make each aquatint a composite.*

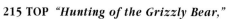

215 TOP *"Hunting of the Grizzly Bear," Lithograph After Bodmer.* While traveling the western rivers, the fur companies employed hunters to set out each morning long before sunrise and comb the countryside along the river for game to be consumed by the crew and passengers that day. When they made a kill, the hunters marked it and continued onward. When the boat rounded a bend and saw a marker, it put ashore and gathered up the meat. In this scene, grizzly bears have discovered a hunter's cache of buffalo meat meant for the boat. Men are coming toward the bears to defend what is left of it with rifles.

A small mackinaw boat can be seen in the foreground, and the Flora under sail in the background. This incident took place on July 18, 1833. The grizzly bear was killed with at least five shots from the hunters.

216 RIGHT *"Cree Woman."* Bodmer, as can be read in his diaries, realized two portraits of this Cree woman, supposed to be the wife of Deschamps, who worked as a hunter for the Fur Company. She was said to be Cree because of the tattooing on her chin.

216-217 *"Evening Bivouac on the Missouri."* This excellent view shows the mackinaw boat in which the prince's party floated down the Missouri on their way to Fort Clark in the autumn of 1833. Loaded primarily with the prince's animal and mineral specimens and Indian artifacts, the boat was probably a bit crowded. Here the men smoke t-stemmed pipes, while a large iron cook pot boils over the fire.

216 LEFT *"Piegan Blackfeet Woman."* This is an excellent portrait, despite the fact that the subject was not feeling well on the day it was painted. History is indebted to the woman's husband, who gave permission to Bodmer to paint the portrait in exchange for some paint and beads. The very typically dressed Plains woman wears a dress decorated with trade beads, cinched with a colorful sash. Although this may be her best dress and pair of moccasins rather than everyday wear, it shows the correct length for both, which worked together to cover the ankles, an area of the body that modesty forbade revealing. Women learned to do quill and bead work at an early age and competed with each other to be acknowledged as the best at their craft. Women produced decorative bead and quill-work strips and designs for the clothing of members of their extended family. By tradition, the mother or sister rather than the wife was most often the artist of a warrior's beaded and quilled shirt and leggings. All of the beaded and quilled items shown in the paintings of King, Catlin, and Bodmer were the products of the patience and artistry of many Native American women like the one depicted here.

In order to proceed further upriver, the party had to board a second steamboat, the *Assiniboin*, which departed on June 5. The boat stopped briefly at the Mandan villages and rough-hewn Fort Clark on June 18. There the travelers were treated to the rare sight of a large group of Crow Indians, who had traveled all the way from the Bighorn Mountains, in what is today Wyoming. Properly known as Absaroka in their own language, the Crow were called various other names by outsiders. They had erected seventy tepees near the fort, and this was the prince's only chance to study them. The party examined the tepees and the

"mounted warriors, with their diversely painted faces, feathers in their long hair, bow and arrows slung across their backs." Accosted by wolflike dogs in the camp, the group had to throw stones to drive the animals off, "in which some old Indian women assisted us," noted Maximilian in his *Travels*. Bodmer was able to paint portraits of several of the Crows, as well as a Blackfoot Indian, thus adding to his growing chronicle of the appearance and customs of American Indian people.

The party arrived at Fort Union on June 24, to a rousing welcome of cannon fire and musketry from the walls. Begun in 1829, Fort Union was the principal and central post of the Upper Missouri trade, supporting

Fort Cass, 200 miles up the Yellowstone, and Fort McKenzie, 650 miles farther up the Missouri. The voyage from St. Louis had taken 75 days, but the westward journey was not yet finished. Unlike George Catlin, whose westward journey ended at Fort Union, Maximilian's party was poised to continue onward. Maximilian wanted to travel into the Rocky Mountain region and perhaps farther west. Since they were at the farthest point of steamboat navigation, the next leg of their journey, to Fort McKenzie in Blackfoot country, would be on the 60-foot keelboat *Flora*. While they waited for the *Flora*'s departure, Assiniboin Indians patiently posed for Bodmer and allowed him to paint their small camp circle of tepees. He also sketched the fort itself,

situated on a flat plain, where Indians could encamp at the height of the trading season.

The *Flora* moved out into the river on July 6, this time without the chugging of a steam engine, for the Flora did not have one. Instead, the boat was propelled by its sail, or when the wind failed, it was towed by the crew, who walked on the shore or sometimes in waist-deep water, pulling the boat with a hawser tied to its bow. The crew were a rough lot, mostly French-Canadians who made their living on the river, hard-drinking and hard-cursing men with rough hands and quick tempers. Excessive heat and oppressive mosquitoes made the crew miserable as the crowded keelboat slowly made its way upstream. The prince collected animal specimens along the river

by day, but he complained in his *Travels* that the rude engagés threw them overboard at night.

The river wound through the indescribable and fantastic colors and rock formations of the Badlands. The rocks and cliffs reminded the Europeans of castles along the Rhine, while the bighorn sheep they saw were like the chamois of the Alps. The prince made comparisons between the endless silent scene before him and the Brazilian rainforest he had seen fifteen years earlier, with its thick forests and abundant wildlife. He noted in his *Travels* that in the Badlands "the silence of the bare, dead, lonely wilderness is but seldom interrupted by the howling of the wolves, the bellowing of the buffaloes, or the screaming of the

218 TOP *"Indian Woman."* *This unidentified woman was painted in the Mandan village in the spring of 1834. She wears a beautifully decorated buffalo robe for warmth. Unfortunately, the watercolor was never finished, but it nevertheless gives us a very good concept of the woman's dress and demeanor.*

218 BOTTOM *"Ninoch-Kiaiu, Piegan Blackfeet Chief."* *Ninoch-Kiaiu, "Chief of the Bears," had recently taken a new name in commemoration of his successful war raid, in which 47 Salish warriors had been killed. In mourning for his nephew, who had been killed by a member of the Blood tribe of the Blackfeet, Ninoch-Kiaiu dresses simply. He was arrogant and aggressive and as a result unpopular with those around him, both Indian and white. During Maximilian's stay at the fort, he constantly tried to get the whites to attack rival factions and tribes when they angered him.*

218-219 *"The Travellers Meeting With Minatarree Indians Near Fort Clark."* *This engraving depicts Hidatsa Indians conversing through an interpreter with Maximilian and Bodmer, the prince being the shorter man on the right of the picture, the artist being the taller man on the far right. Both carry rifles, while Bodmer also has a leather carrying case for his art supplies, to which he has attached a belt ax. While staying at Fort Clark during the winter of 1833-34, Maximilian and Bodmer were able to study the Mandan culture in depth.*

crows." Bodmer produced realistic landscapes of the region, depicting buffalo and white wolves in a far more accurate manner than Catlin had, and realistically rendering the topography, so unlike anything he had ever seen before.

The Badlands were relatively silent but full of adventure. One day as the hunters were sent out to procure meat, they came upon a huge grizzly bear, king of the American wilderness, who was eating the remains of a dead buffalo. Bodmer, who was with the group, recorded the scene just before they killed the mighty bear. The trip up the winding river from Fort Union took over a month, as they moved over and around rapids. The party narrowly escaped trouble with the Atsina (Gros Ventres) Indians, who swam out and boarded the *Flora* when it stopped briefly at their village. They

demanded gifts and nearly became violent when they were refused. "Our situation was anything but agreeable," noted the prince in his *Travels,* "for these same Indians had entirely demolished a fort, on the frontiers of Canada, two years before, killed a clerk, and eighteen other persons, besides murdering several other white people in those parts. . . . If it was their intention to treat us in a hostile manner, there was no way for us to escape." An unequal trade ensued, which kept the peace but rattled the nerves of the Europeans.

On August 9, after over a month of travel on the keelboat, the party rounded the bend near Fort McKenzie, the westernmost outpost of the Missouri fur trade. Located 650 miles upriver from Fort Union near the mouth of the Marias River, Fort McKenzie had been completed just the year before, through the permission of a treaty that Kenneth McKenzie had negotiated with the Blackfeet. Eight

hundred Blackfoot warriors greeted the *Flora* upon her arrival, in a pouring rain, firing their muskets and giving uninterrupted war cries. Several were dressed in colorful blue and red European-style uniforms, while others were in their native finery. The Blackfeet were at war with their neighbors, the Assiniboin and Cree, and sometimes the three bands of the Blackfeet, known as the Piegans, the Kahna (Bloods), and the Siksekai (Blackfeet) also fought among themselves. This made the situation a tense one at Fort McKenzie, nearly 3,000 river miles from St. Louis and far from any assistance from fur traders or any other Euro-Americans.

The fort, far smaller than Fort Union, had sides 45 to 47 paces in length, according to Maximilian. The twenty-seven Euro-American men living there were all married to Indian women. The fort contained one-story buildings with flat roofs covered in green sod, whose interior rooms were small, with dirt floors, and they had parchment in their windows rather than glass. In fact, the *Flora* had brought a shipment of glass and other improvements for the rough outpost. It was surrounded by prairie, with a chain of hills beyond.

Relations between the Indian tribes in the area were far too unsettled for the prince to continue farther toward the Rocky Mountains. In addition, the large number of Indians who had come in to barter had forced the traders to send their horses downriver, and no interpreter was then at the fort who could assist with a Rocky Mountain journey. As a result, the party stayed at Fort McKenzie during the entire month of August, allowing both Maximilian and Bodmer to study the Blackfeet in depth. The three bands all passed through the fort while Maximilian and Bodmer were in residence, trading with the Fur Company and in the process literally besieging the little fort. Maximilian noted the beauty of these people, and their extreme height, remarking upon one man who stood six feet eleven inches tall.

Bodmer carefully painted portraits of the Indians trading at the fort. The Blackfeet clapped their hands when they recognized the subject of a completed portrait. Bodmer was also able to paint Kutenai and Shoshoni people who had been captured by or intermarried with the Blackfeet, as well as landscape scenes of the distant mountains, made from the hills surrounding the fort. He also made a fine exterior study of the fort itself and of the Indian encampment outside. With great care Bodmer accurately depicted the tepees rising to various heights, depending upon family size and the status of the owners. Other artists, particularly Catlin, depicted tepees as being of uniform height and size and paid little attention to the manner in which they were constructed.

220-221 *"Fort McKenzie, August 28, 1833."*
When Cree and Assiniboin Indians attacked the Blackfoot camp outside Fort McKenzie, Fur Company officials, along with Maximilian and Bodmer, took their turns on the ramparts helping ward off the attack. The scene in this aquatint was made from the point of the view of the Indian village, when in reality Bodmer was one of the silhouetted figures on top of the wall in the background. Maximilian noted that "at break of day, we were awakened by musket-shot, and Doucette entered our room, crying, 'Levez-vous, il faut nous battre,' on which we rose in haste, dressed ourselves, and loaded our fowling-pieces with ball. When we entered the court-yard of the fort, all our people were in motion, and some were firing from the roofs. On ascending it, we saw the whole prairie covered with Indians on foot and on horseback, who were firing at the fort; and on the hills were several detached bodies. About 18 or 20 Blackfeet tents . . . had been surprised by 600 Assiniboins and Crees . . . Four women and several children lay dead near the fort, and many others were wounded. The men, about 30 in number, had partly fired their guns at the enemy, and then fled to the gates of the fort, where they were admitted. They immediately hastened to the roofs, and began a well-supported fire on the Assiniboins." The Assiniboin made it clear that their attack was on the Blackfeet and not on the white traders, but even though the Fur Company superintendent, David Mitchell, ordered his men to stop firing, some continued, and "ten or twelve of our people, among whom were Doucette and Loretto, went into the prairie, and fired in the ranks of the Blackfeet."

Not only were the paintings important as ethnological documents, but the prince's writings were equally crucial. Just as Catlin's written notes on the Mandan became priceless after the 1837 smallpox epidemic devastated the tribe, Maximilian's notes performed a similar service for the Blackfeet, who would lose an estimated fifty percent of their number in the same epidemic.

While at the fort the party witnessed a battle between Indian groups. On the morning of August 28, 1833, an Assiniboin and Cree party attacked the Blackfoot village just outside the fort. It was a short skirmish, and the more numerous Blackfeet were able to drive off the attackers, with the help of gunfire from the fort. It is possible that the prince and Bodmer helped defend the fort with rifles. Many Indians lay dead, and the Indian camp was a shambles when the

Assiniboin and Cree were finally driven off. Bodmer illustrated this battle only after his return to Europe. It is interesting that he recreated this dramatic scene from memory—and not from his subjective position in the fort, but from a hypothetical location in the midst of the fighting tribes. Historian William Goetzmann has pointed out that Bodmer's work for the prince was meant to emphasize the ethnological and rarely lapsed into a reportorial mode. He did not record the faces of the fur traders, the boatmen, or the hunters at the fort; nor did he portray many dramatic incidents of the journey in original sketches. It was only later, in the aquatint engravings he made in Europe, that the most dramatic incidents of the journey were brought to life.

The August 28 battle helped Bodmer gain more volunteers to sit for their portraits than

he could handle—after a warrior named Pioch Kiaiu, or "Distant Bear," claimed that Bodmer's portrait had kept bullets from killing him during the fighting. Subsequently, all the warriors felt that they would be invincible if they owned a portrait of themselves.

Realizing that he could go no farther west, that winter was coming on, and that they might "be attacked by the Assiniboins" at any time, which would imprison them in the fort, Maximilian decided to turn back down the Missouri River. In the courtyard of the fort the carpenter built a small "Mackinaw boat" for the prince, a flat-bottomed boat made of wooden planks. On September 14, 1833, the prince, Bodmer, Dreidoppel, an experienced engagé named Henry Morrin, and three novice French-Canadian bateaumen set out with the

221 TOP *"Pachtuwa-Chta, Arikara."*
This interesting lithograph gives us a rare glimpse
of an Arikara warrior.

221 BOTTOM *"Fort McKenzie at the Mouth
of the Marias River."* *Fort McKenzie was the
westernmost outpost of the American Fur
Company. Completed in 1832, it was 650 miles
upriver from Fort Union, and Maximilian's party
took 34 days to make the journey aboard the
Flora. Not only was the fort centered in Blackfeet
country, it was the scene of intense intertribal
rivalry at the time of the prince's visit. Due to
warfare between the Blackfeet and the
Assiniboin and Cree, the prince's ambition to
press onward to the Rocky Mountains was
never realized.*

prince's accumulated artifacts and specimens
as well as some animals, including two
caged bear cubs and a tame fox. Luckily,
they traversed the 650 miles back to Fort
Union in fifteen days, without encountering
any hostile Indians. However, their journey
was miserable in the leaky, open boat during
torrential rains, which soaked and destroyed
the prince's collection of plant specimens.
Yet they were able to observe the abundant
wildlife of the region, hear elks bugling, and
observe the fall colors.

Floating with the current, the group
stopped once more at Fort Union, where
Bodmer was able to paint several Cree men
and women. On October 11 the prince,
Bodmer, and a group of hunters from the
fort went out on a buffalo hunt, an
exhilarating event of which Bodmer was able
to make several fine watercolors. Maximilian

became separated from the rest of the group near sunset but soon caught up with Bodmer, who was calmly sketching one of the kills. The group stayed out on the prairie that night, wrapped in buffalo robes. Three days later, the first snowfall of the season fluttered down on Fort Union, and the winds of winter began to blow.

It was Maximilian's intention to spend the winter among the Mandan people, as Lewis and Clark had thirty years earlier. For a pioneering ethnologist such as himself, the Mandan were one of the most fascinating groups of Indians to study on the plains. During the mid-eighteenth century, when fur traders first began living among them, many Europeans remarked that these Indians were lightly complected and often went prematurely gray, with long white streaks mixed into their dark black hair. Legend claimed that these people were the descendants of the legendary Welsh prince Madoc, who had sailed to America in the twelfth century. Whether or not there was any truth to the belief, the prince was eager to study the Mandan people in depth.

The party made the journey downriver in a larger mackinaw boat, traveling from Fort Union to Fort Clark between October 30 and November 8, 1833. The prince could not have chosen a less sturdy and secure place than Fort Clark in which to endure the severe winter weather of the Great Plains. The fort was small and poorly constructed, and the party's quarters were even worse. James Kipp, the fur trade representative at the fort, had a two-room log cabin constructed for the Maximilian party, but its clay mortar soon cracked and failed. The bitter winters of the region could kill a man without warm clothing in a matter of minutes, and the winter of 1833-34 was even harsher than usual. As winter set in, the prince recorded temperatures of 46 degrees below zero on the Fahrenheit scale. "At night the cold was so intense," he remembered in his *Travels,* "that we could not venture to put our hands from our bodies, lest they should be frozen." The group lived in extremely cold conditions in a fort poorly stocked with food and among Euro-American people whose habits the prince considered disgusting. This was not snobbishness on his part, for he confided to his diary some of the more unsavory things that the servants within the fort and the Kipp family did that winter.

Despite the horrible conditions at Fort Clark, the prince and Bodmer were extremely

222 "Sih-Chida and Mahchsi Karehde, Mandan." *Sih-Chida was an Indian artist who was encouraged by Maximilian and Bodmer. Mahchsi-Karehde was one of the most prominent Mandan warriors.*

223 TOP "Winter Village of the Minatarees." *This aquatint shows what life was like in the Minatarees (Hidatsa) village during the winter months. On the left, two men play "Tchung Kee," while on the right, groups of men and women converse.*

223 CENTER "Ptihn-Tak-Ochata, Dance of the Mandan Women." *Bodmer's artwork captured a good deal of the ceremonial side of women's lives on the Plains. Too often, American Indian women were dismissed as mere "drudges" or "slaves" to the men. Not until more recent times has been an examination made of the place of women in Indian cultures and the importance of specific rituals and dances to women.*

productive during their five months among the Mandan. The prince detailed the Mandan customs and ceremonies, while Bodmer made beautiful portraits of them. Both men befriended many of them, particularly the principal chiefs of the tribe. One wonders how Bodmer was able to turn out such fine works of art with his hands shaking from the cold, his paints freezing in their containers, and the water itself sometimes frozen solid.

Along with his beautiful portraits and landscapes, Bodmer recorded a detailed view of the interior of a Mandan earthen lodge, which continues to be of enormous ethnographic importance. He carefully chronicled the dances and ceremonies of the Indians by making individual sketches that were later unified into panoramic scenes in the finished engravings in Europe. He also painted the symbolic cairns of human skulls and high stakes wrapped with feathers that he noted near the Mandan villages. Such shrines were places of great religious significance, and Bodmer and the prince

tried to find out as much about them as they could. Their sensitivity to detail and to the significance of individual objects and shrines shows a gift for intercultural understanding.

Bodmer's art also had an effect on the Indians' own art, which forever after was more three-dimensional than it had been previously. In general, the production of Indian art was divided along gender lines; women produced geometric patterns in porcupine quills and beadwork to decorate clothing and other items, while men represented their exploits in pictographs made in paints derived from clay, minerals, and charcoal, as well as pigments obtained through trade with Euro-Americans. These pictographs might embellish buffalo robes or the tepees of Plains warriors.

One of the Mandan people most fascinated by Bodmer's artwork was a 25-year-old man named Sih-Chida, or Yellow Feather. Sih-Chida asked the prince to draw a soldier for him, and he asked Bodmer to paint an image of a bird on his war shield.

223 BOTTOM "Mih-Tutta-Hang-Kush, Mandan Village." *This aquatint was created in Europe from an unfinished watercolor that Bodner made in the spring of 1834 at the Mandan villages. The Mandan women in the foreground are navigating the Missouri River in bullboats, excellent shallow-draft watercraft made out of buffalo hide. In the background, the summer village of the Mandans can be seen on the bluff above the river, silhouetted against the horizon.*

223

224 *"Leader of the Mandan Buffalo Bull Society."* *Both Maximilian and Bodmer were fascinated by the culture of the Mandans, just as George Catlin and Lewis and Clark had been before them. The prince noted that Mandan men had a series of six societies, which could be joined in succession as a man advanced in age. This watercolor shows one of two leaders of the Buffalo Bull Society, the last and most prestigious of the six. Leadership of this group was a high honor in the tribe, reserved for warriors who had distinguished themselves in battle. A man entering the society was usually about forty and had been a member of all the previous five societies. He had to purchase his way into the society through gift-giving. The items worn and held by this society leader possessed incredible power in the Mandan culture. The full-head buffalo mask, the*

The very fact that Sih-Chida allowed Bodmer to touch his war shield, let alone paint an image on it, shows that a bond of great trust had grown up between the two men. War shields carried great spiritual power, which could easily be lost if it was influenced by the negative power of another object or person. Sih-Chida seems to have felt that Bodmer himself represented positive spiritual energy, which might be transferred to his shield through the artwork. Sih-Chida requested that Bodmer share paints, paper, and brushes with him. With these materials Sih-Chida produced portraits of Maximilian and Bodmer, as well as a self-portrait and drawings of his friends.

Another Mandan affected by Bodmer's art was Mahtatohpa, or Four Bears, the second chief of the tribe and the principal informant of both George Catlin and the prince about the culture of the Mandan people. Mahtatohpa painted representations of his battle feats on buffalo robes, on his clothing, and on his own skin. These representations became noticeably more three-dimensional in character with the influence of Catlin in 1832 and Bodmer in 1833-34. By the time Bodmer left the Mandan, a new pictographic style had emerged. Tragically, Sih-Chida was killed in battle soon after Bodmer's sojourn with the Mandan, while Mahtatohpa died soon after the 1837 smallpox epidemic.

In late November 1833, Eager to visit the Hidatsa, Maximilian made a nine-hour hike in the bitter cold to attend a ceremony in their village, farther north along the river. Staying for several days, the prince and the artist made notes and drawings. The Hidatsa also

ceremonial lance, the wolf tails trailing out behind the moccasins, and the shield decorated with personal medicine signs all added up to a ceremonial figure of great importance and mystical power. This unfinished watercolor was later used to construct the aquatint scene of the Buffalo Bull Dance.

225 *"Buffalo Bull Dance of the Mandan Indians."* *Several figures drawn by Bodmer in the field were put together in Europe for this incredibly vivid aquatint scene, a visual summation of all the artist and the prince had learned about the culture of the Mandan. At noon on December 22, 1833, Maximilian wrote that "we heard the drums of the Indians, and a crowd of people filled the fort. At their head were fourteen men of the band of the bulls, from Ruhptare, distinguished by their*

strange costume. . . . They were closely enveloped in their robes, and had bow-lances ornamented with feathers, coloured cloth, beads, &c., and most of them had foxes' tails at their heels. Some of these men beat the drum, while they all formed a circle, and imitated the bellowing of the buffalo bulls. After they had danced awhile, some tobacco was thrown to them, and they proceeded to the village in the forest further down the river, taking off their wigs."

226 *"Hidatsa Scalp Dance."* *Maximilian and Bodmer witnessed this fascinating dance at Fort Clark on February 11, 1834. The figures are Hidatsa women, who for the dance dressed like the men, in war shirts, with painted faces and weapons. The dance was a chance for the women to celebrate the brave feats of the men in the tribe. The pole on the left holds a stuffed magpie with a scalp attached. The figures to the right are men, who are providing the music. Maximilian noted that "at two o'clock the Manitari women arrived in procession, accompanied by many children and some*

Mandans. Eighteen women, marching two and two in a close column, entered the court-yard of the fort, with short-measured, slow pace. Seven men of the band of the dogs, having their faces painted black, or black striped with red, acted as musicians, three of them having drums, and four the schischikue. . . . The women filed off in a semicircle; the musicians, taking their stand on the left wing, now commenced a heterogeneous noise, beating the drum, rattling the schischikue, and yelling with all their might. The women began to dance, waddling in short steps, like ducks. After awhile they rested,

and then recommenced, and continued dancing about twenty minutes. The director of the fort now caused tobacco, looking-glasses, and knives, from the Company's stores, to be thrown in the middle of the circle. Hereupon the women once more danced in quick time, the musicians forming themselves into a close body, and holding their instruments towards the centre. This concluded the festivity, and the whole band retired to the Mandan forest village." *These figures were drawn, as in the case of the Buffalo Bull Dance, to be included in an aquatint engraving later on.*

visited the Mandan village in the spring of 1834, which allowed Bodmer to make further sketches and some portraits of Hidatsa men, including several important chiefs.

Another story involving cross-cultural artistic influences concerns a Hidatsa named Ahschupsa Masihichsi, which translates to "Chief of the Pointed Horn." After his portrait was completed by Bodmer, Ahschupsa wanted to keep it, particularly since he was about to go out with a war party on a raid. Perhaps he feared that if harm came to his likeness, harm might come to him wherever he was. At any rate, Bodmer not only refused to give Ahschupsa the original painting, he would not make a copy either. The crafty Ahschupsa, not to be bested, retaliated by

drawing a picture of Bodmer, which he took with him on his war party. The prince noted that the likeness of Bodmer was quite good.

The ice on the river broke in April, and on the eighteenth Bodmer said farewell to his Indian friends. The prince, suffering from scurvy as a result of the poor diet he had endured at Fort Clark, had to be carried to the boat, which headed downriver for the last time. Six weeks later, the group was back in St. Louis, its skyline now augmented by the completed spire of its cathedral. The prince was dismayed to learn that many of his prized artifacts, which he had put on board the *Assiniboin*, had been lost when the steamboat burned on its return trip to St. Louis. There were still enough artifacts,

however, even after this loss, to comprise a large and respectable collection.

The prince, Bodmer, and Dreidoppel left St. Louis on June 3, returning east via New Harmony, the Ohio River, and the Ohio Canal along the Scioto River, then aboard a steamboat along the shore of Lake Erie to Buffalo, where Bodmer painted Niagara Falls. During the entire journey Maximilian continued to record the flora and fauna, as well as the geophysical characteristics of the regions they traveled through, taking specimens along the way. From Buffalo they traveled by way of the Erie Canal and the Hudson River to New York City, from which they departed for Europe on July 16, 1834, having spent just over two years in America.

227 RIGHT *"Mahchsi-Nihka, Mandan Man."* A deaf-mute, Mahchsi-Nihka was a proud warrior and a good hunter. He supplied the prince and the artist with meat during the long, cold winter at Fort Clark. He proudly posed for this watercolor in his war paint and clothing. When he was taunted by another Mandan who said that Bodmer had painted all his other subjects in their best clothes, not their battle clothes, Mahchsi-Nihka became quite agitated. Maximilian noted that "we in vain endeavoured to pacify him, by assuring him that we intended to make him known to the world in a truly warlike costume. Mr. Bodmer then thought of an expedient; he quickly and secretly made a copy of his drawing, which he brought in, tore in half, and threw into the fire, in the presence of the Indian. This had the desired effect, and he went away perfectly satisfied." In the surviving drawing, Mahchsi-Nihka holds a lethal-looking spiked war club. The small sticks in his hair commemorate the wounds or blows he received in battle.

Arriving at the French port of LeHavre on August 8, 1834, the three travelers continued on to Germany. None of them ever visited North America again.

The prince began to prepare his book, using the diaries he had kept so meticulously on his journey. But his task was difficult, for he was of the opinion that his North American trip in no way compared with the success of his Brazilian trip of 1815-17. The Bodmer illustrations were the real contribution of this trip to science, not his notes or specimens. Unable to interest a publisher in the work, the prince finally financed its publication himself. Bodmer was asked to supervise the creation of 81 aquatint engravings from his watercolors, which were included in a picture atlas. The atlas differed slightly with each version of the book, and because each aquatint was hand-colored, each of the atlas sets is unique.

In 1836, Bodmer moved to Paris, where he supervised production of the plates and mounted an exhibition of his work, the first paintings documenting American Indians and authentic western scenes that had ever been seen in Europe. Curiously, the exhibit was not well received. The preparation of the book and the prints also did not go smoothly. Bodmer, promised a share of the profits, assembled a staff of twenty artists to work on the engravings, which proceeded slowly. He also promoted sales in England and France, but he was no businessman, and he squandered the money the prince paid him while making a mess of the promotion.

As the years rolled by, not only was the book's publication delayed, but personal problems beset the artist. His father died in 1839, and his grief brought on recurrent illnesses. Bodmer's brother Rudolf was gradually consumed by mental illness, dying in 1841. At this point in his life, Bodmer—frustrated as an artist and low on funds—tried to browbeat his benefactor in terse letters when he was questioned about delays. The completed book, *Travels in the Interior of North America,* was highly priced and sold poorly. Only 1,000 copies were produced, with three successive versions, first in German (1839), next in French (1841), and finally in English (1843). Like McKenney and Hall's *Indian Tribes of*

North America and Catlin's *Letters and Notes*, the book was out of the price range of the average citizen and was purchased only by wealthy persons and institutions.

Bodmer failed in his efforts to promote the book, even when he tried to use the success of George Catlin's Indian Gallery in London and Paris to boost sales. Both Maximilian and Bodmer had nothing but contempt for Catlin's artwork, yet Bodmer was willing to try anything to turn a profit. In 1847 Bodmer turned over the engravings to the Wied estate, which published a less expensive version of the illustrations, with captions, entitled *North America in Pictures*. This book also foundered and was not a success.

After the debacle of the book's publication, Karl Bodmer had further trouble as an artist. Unable to find inspiration, he turned down offers to travel to exotic places in order to continue to paint the same bucolic scenes of his American adventure. He begged the prince for money so that he might continue his painting and receive further instruction, and Maximilian often consented to aid his friend. By early 1849 Bodmer joined two younger artists, Jean-François Millet and Charles Jacque, and took up residence in the town of Barbizon, located within the Fontainebleau forest outside Paris. He began to paint forest scenes in oils and finally received positive notices and a second prize at the 1850 Paris Salon. Now that he was moderately successful, his contacts with his old benefactor Maximilian dwindled. In 1865 they collaborated one last time on a catalogue of North American reptiles and amphibians written by the prince, which included seven engravings. The last of his adventures over, Maximilian died on February 3, 1867, at the age of 84 at his Neuwied estate.

228 LEFT *"Massika, Sauk Man."* *Bodmer's paintings of western Indians began in St. Louis. Massika was one of a group of Sac and Fox warriors who came to St. Louis in the spring of 1833 to ask for the release of the imprisoned Black Hawk. The unusual face paint worn by the warrior makes him look scarified on his cheeks, when in reality he was not. His ears are decorated with a profusion of shell beads, sometimes called wampum. Maximilian was intensely interested in these, the first Indians he had seen, and wrote copious notes about them in his journal.*

Meanwhile, Bodmer had become part of a bohemian, free-spirited community at Barbizon, where he was a familiar figure in the taverns. He lived for many years with a German woman named Anna-Maria-Magdalena Pfeiffer, with whom he had three sons out of wedlock. But this life quickly faded, and Bodmer grew more and more reclusive. His thoughts turned to the halcyon days of his North American sojourn, while his paintings depicted only European forest and animal themes. He once said to a colleague, "In Europe I have acquaintances, but over there I had friends." His days among the Indians had indeed been happy ones, and the memories of the privations he had suffered, particularly during the winter at Fort Clark, had faded into nostalgia. Perhaps Bodmer had a point, however, in saying that the Indians he encountered had been true friends. They had admired his artwork and expected little in return. They gave as well as took in their relationships, unlike Europeans, who seemed only to take, never to give. It is certain that Bodmer never encountered any human beings, with the possible exception of the prince, who were as selfless and generous as the American Indian people he met in the 1830s.

228 RIGHT *"Wakusasse, Fox Man."*
Wakusasse, who came to plead with William Clark for Black Hawk's release, wears a deer hair roach in his scalp-lock and shell beads in his ears. Maximilian noted that the Sac and Fox were "stout, well formed men, many of them above the middle size, broad shouldered, muscular and brawny. The features of the men are expressive, and strongly marked; the cheek bones prominent, the lower jaw broad and

angular; the dark brown eyes animated and fiery. . . . The Saukies and Foxes had shaved their hair off the whole head except a small tuft behind, the greater part of which was cut short, like a brush, and which terminated in a thin braid, to which was fastened the chief ornament of the head, the deer's tail, which is a tuft of hair from the tail of the Virginian stag, white, with some black hair, the white part being dyed red with vermilion."

In 1876, Karl Bodmer was awarded the Legion of Honor by the French nation. He married Anna-Maria and taught his sons to paint, although they never made reputations for themselves in the art world. He sometimes collaborated with Millet, but as the years went by, his contacts with family, friends, and fellow artists tapered off. During the 1860s, 1870s, and 1880s, he was well known as an illustrator for several French periodicals and books, mostly contributing sentimental animal scenes. He had no pupils and drifted into relative poverty as he grew older. He later moved to Paris, where

deafness, a feeble constitution, and eventual blindness overtook him and prevented him from working. He died on October 30, 1893 at age 86, frustrated at not having lived up to his artistic promise.

After the preparation of the engravings for the prince's book in 1841, 427 of Bodmer's original watercolors and sketches were stored at Neuwied castle, where they were left untouched for over a century. Shortly after World War II, a German museum official conducting research at the castle stumbled upon Bodmer's masterpieces and realized the importance of the paintings, as well as their

229 LEFT *"Massika, Sauk."* This litohgraph shows Massika, one of the first Indians that the prince had ever seen. "We did not come up to them till they were in the house," reported the prince, "and the first sight of them, which did not a little surprise me, convinced me at once of their great affinity to the Brazilians, so that I cannot hesitate to consider them as belonging to the same race."

229 RIGHT *"Wakusasse, Fox."* This is a lithograph made from the Bodmer drawing of the Fox warrior.

230 LEFT *"Noapeh, Assiniboin."* Noapeh's beautiful clothing provided an opportunity for the creation of this colorful and detailed lithograph. Bodmer's excellent ability to render the details of cultural attributes made lithographs such as this, created many months after the fact, possible.

230 RIGHT *"Psihdja-Sahpa, Yankton Sioux."* This lithograph of Psihdja-Sahpa was made in Europe from the original watercolor. Maximilian wrote of the Dakota Sioux on May 25, 1833, that, "All these Dakotas of the Missouri, as well as most of those of the Mississippi, are only hunters, and, in their excursions, always live in portable leather tents. All these Indians have great numbers of horses and dogs, the latter of which often serve them as food. The Dakotas on the Missouri were formerly dangerous enemies to the Whites, whereas now, with the exception of the Yanktonans, they bear a very good character, and constantly keep peace with the Whites."

231 *"Pehriska-Ruhpa, Hidatsa."* This lithograph presents a good example of the changes Bodmer's work underwent when converted into a different medium. Although it does not have the freshness or spontaneity of the original watercolor, it shows the figure at full length, in the midst of his dance rather than standing still. Many details of the original have been lost in the translation, but the spirit of the moment of the dance, the importance of the ceremony, and the movement of the special clothing and headdress are probably better expressed in the lithograph.

beauty. Portions of the work were exhibited in Germany and the United States in the 1950s. In 1959, the heirs of Prince Maximilian sold the entire collection to the art dealers M. Knoedler and Company of New York City, from whom they were purchased by the Northern Natural Gas Company (now InterNorth, Inc.) in 1962. InterNorth also acquired Maximilian's original travel diaries and letters, first editions of his *Travels,* and the copperplates used in the production of the atlas. Today, Bodmer's original work and the related Maximilian items are on permanent loan to the Joslyn Art Museum in Omaha, Nebraska. In addition, the Newberry Library in Chicago

has a collection of forty of the watercolors and sketches used in the production of the atlas. Nearly all of Bodmer's watercolors and sketches, covering the entire two-year trip to North America, were reproduced in a 1984 book published by the Joslyn Art Museum, *Karl Bodmer's America.*

Bodmer's watercolors are perhaps the most accurate works of art ever made of American Indians during the nineteenth century. His attention to detail in beadwork, personal symbols, clothing, accoutrements, and facial expression make these portraits precious documents of a lost world. One wonders if, in his isolation at the very end of his life, Bodmer's final thoughts were of the

Indian people he had once known on the Plains of America. Although his work was quickly forgotten after his death, an appreciation of its magnificence began with American ethnologists and scholars in the twentieth century, who realized its photographic realism and valued its attention to detail. Karl Bodmer unknowingly bequeathed a legacy to all those people, both Indian and non-Indian, interested in the cultures of these fascinating people as they existed before major Euro-American intrusions. His work in the American West was not only the highlight of his own career but the apogee of the artistic representation of the American Indian.

232 "Ho-Ta-Ma, Ponca Man." *This man was painted at Fort Pierre on May 31, 1833, and was described as living with a band of Lakotas encamped near the fort. He is dressed in a buffalo robe and has unusually unkempt hair, his locks bound with strips of leather.*

233 "Ponca Camp." *A small group of three Poncas came on board the* Yellow Stone *on May 11, 1833, and were given a ride to their encampment, which was reached on May 12. Tepees can be seen in the background of the scene, as can many members of the village on the shore. The Ponca were a small tribe related to the Omaha and lived at one time near the Pipestone Quarry in Minnesota. By the 1830s they had been displaced to an area along the Missouri River, near the boundary of Nebraska and South Dakota. They continued to live in permanent villages and farm, while they hunted buffalo seasonally.*

234 *"Psihdja-Sahpa, Yankton Sioux."*

Psihdja-Sahpa was painted at Fort Clark in January 1834. Despite the desperately cold conditions in the small room Bodmer used as a studio at Fort Clark, Psihdja-Sahpa shows his bare chest in this pose, revealing personal symbols painted there. His ears and hair are decorated with glass beads. Maximilian wrote of the Dakota Sioux on May 25, 1833, "All these Dakotas of the Missouri, as well as most of those of the Mississippi, are only hunters, and, in their excursions, always live in portable leather tents. All these Indians have great numbers of horses and dogs, the latter of which often serve them as food. The Dakotas on the Missouri were formerly dangerous enemies to the Whites, whereas now, with the exception of the Yanktonans, they bear a very good character, and constantly keep peace with the Whites."

235 *"Wahktageli, Yankton Sioux Chief."*

*Wahktageli, "The Big Soldier," was painted at the
Sioux agency on May 25, 1833. Well over six feet
tall, Wahktageli was 60 years old at the time.
A Yankton (Nakota) Sioux, his colorful garb
included headgear consisting of "long feathers
of birds of prey," wrote the prince, "which were
tokens of his warlike exploits, particularly of the
enemies he had slain. They were fastened in a
horizontal position with strips of red cloth.
In his ears he wore long strings of blue glass beads,
and, on his breast, suspended from his neck, the
great silver medal of the United States. His leather
leggins, painted with dark crosses and stripes, were
very neatly ornamented with a broad embroidered
stripe of yellow, red, and sky-blue figures,
consisting of dyed porcupine quills." Wahktageli
holds a pipe-tomahawk, a popular trade item
manufactured by the whites, in his hand. Before
the departure of the prince, Wahktageli made him
a present of his entire costume, thus starting
Maximilian's collection of Indian artifacts.*

236 *"Sioux Camp."* This scene shows the architectural solution to life on the Great Plains, the tepee. Mobile, warm, and cozy, with a good draw for smoke from the fire, a tepee was an ideal home for the Plains Indian lifestyle. Unlike tepees in the paintings of George Catlin, Bodmer's tepees all have individuality and character. Bodmer's superior draftsmanship makes his paintings nearly photographic in their fidelity to the original scene. His tepees are correctly rendered in that they all face east and are braced or "backed up" toward the West, the direction of the prevailing winds. The top of each tepee is blackened with smoke. The tepees shown are the typical, fourteen-foot-tall size, easily managed by one woman, who had to take down and erect the family tepee on her own. If a man gained more prestige and had two wives, he might dwell in a sixteen-footer. Tepees larger that sixteen feet were reserved for chiefs who conducted meetings and gatherings. They were few in number, since large tepees were bulky, difficult to transport, and heavy. Modern tepees are often larger than sixteen feet because they are covered with canvas, not buffalo hides, and therefore can be erected with greater ease. This Sioux woman uses an elkhorn scraper to take the hair off a hide and prepare it for brain-tanning. As a man walks from the back of the tepee with a rifle, two dogs look on, and a small child plays near the doorway.

237 LEFT *"Wah-Menitu, Teton Sioux."*
Wah-Menitu, "Spirit in the Water," was, according
to Maximilian, a cheerful, talkative man "who
had such a voracious appetite, that he devoured
everything which the others had left." During his
portrait session at Fort Pierre in June 1833,
Bodmer gave him vermilion paint so that he might
prepare his face. Wah-Menitu's feathers signify
coups he counted in battle. Although he wore only
one to the portrait session, he "had a right to wear
three," which Bodmer later supplied in the
drawing. Maximilian recorded information on
coups on May 30, 1833: "He who, in the sight of
the adversaries, touches a slain or a living enemy,
places a feather horizontally in his hair for this
exploit. They look upon this as a very
distinguished act, for many are often killed in the
attempt, before the object is obtained. He who kills
an enemy by a blow with his fist, sticks a feather
upright in his hair. If the enemy is killed with a
musket, a small piece of wood is put in the hair,
which is intended to represent a ramrod."
Maximilian noted that Wah-Menitu "stayed on
board [the Assiniboin] for the night; sung, talked,
laughed, and joked without ceasing; and seemed
quite to enjoy himself."

237 RIGHT *"Chan-Cha-Uia-Teuin, Teton
Sioux Woman."* Dressed in a gorgeously painted
buffalo robe later purchased by the prince, this
Lakota woman had her portrait done by Bodmer
on June 1, 1833, at Fort Pierre. The dress Chan-
Cha-Uia-Teuin wears under her robe is decorated
with blue and white glass trade beads "and
polished metal buttons, and trimmed as usual at
the bottom with fringes, round the ends of which
lead is twisted so that they tinkle at every
motion." The English translation of her name is
"Woman of the Crow Nation." Perhaps she was a
captive taken from that tribe, a common
occurrence during Plains Indian warfare.
Prisoners, especially young people, were often
adopted into the tribes of their captors,
sometimes literally taking the place in a
family group of a slain or captured child.

237

238 *"Assiniboin Medicine Sign."* *The prince and the artist saw this cairn near Fort Union in 1833, where the prince noted that "on the highest points, and at certain intervals of this mountain chain, singular stone signals, set up by the Assiniboin, of blocks of granite, or other large stones, on the top of which is placed a buffalo skull, which we were told the Indians place there to attract the herds of buffaloes, and thereby to ensure a successful hunt." The Assiniboin, once part of the Yanktonais Sioux in Minnesota, broke off into their own tribe in the 1600s, migrating to* the modern provinces of Manitoba and Saskatchewan. When they became seminomadic hunters and developed a typical Plains Indians lifestyle, they gave up making pottery and began boiling their meat in the stomach of a buffalo. The stomach was hung on a tripod. Rocks were heated in a nearby fire, then carried with forked sticks and put into the stomach with the soup or stew, raising the temperature to a boil. Many Plains tribes cooked in this fashion, but the Assiniboin received their name from the practice, for it means "Those Who Cook with Stones."

239 *"Assiniboin Burial Scaffold."* *At first glance a pastoral scene, a closer look reveals an Assiniboin burial in the foreground. Such places held immense power and were usually shunned by Indian people, who must have thought the intense interest in them displayed by Maximilian and Bodmer quite unusual. Maximilian recorded that one of the corpses "had fallen down, and been torn and devoured by wolves. . . . Mr. Bodmer made an accurate drawing of the tree, under which there was a close thicket of roses in full blossom, the fragrant flowers of which seemed destined to veil this melancholy scene of human frailty and folly."*

240 TOP *"Assiniboin Warrior."* Bodmer portrayed this young man as though he were posed out-of-doors, with tepees in the background. The man's name is lost to history, but his well-cared-for flintlock trade rifle, his elaborately decorated shirt, and his earnest expression shine through Bodmer's watercolor to make the man seem immediate and real. Unlike King and Catlin, Bodmer was able to work his way through the tribal hierarchy to paint some individuals who were neither leading warriors nor chiefs.

240 BOTTOM *"Blackfoot Girl."* This girl was another captive, a Blackfoot being raised by the Assiniboin. She was painted at Fort Union in October 1833, one of the anonymous Indian people immortalized by Bodmer.

240-241 "Assiniboin Camp." On June 30, 1833, a small group of Assiniboins set up camp outside Fort Union, and Bodmer faithfully painted the scene. The largest tepee, which dominates the center of the scene, belonged to chief and was decorated with pictographs of bears. Bodmer painted the tepees in such a way that their individual component hides can be seen. Constructed of buffalo hides sewn together with sinew, a fourteen-foot tepee usually took fourteen hides, and a sixteen-foot tepee took sixteen. Inside, a liner of nine or ten hides could be tied in place, which helped provide warmth and improve the draw of the smoke flaps at the top. The tepee cover was erected on a "lifting pole" from the back or west side, then drawn around the skeleton of lodgepole pine poles that spiraled around a tripod base. The two sides of the cover were drawn together at the front or door side on the east, then locked in place with the wooden lacing pins seen above the doorflap. Bodmer's artistry shows us the skeleton of lodgepole pines under the buffalo-hide cover, through his use of light and shadow. We also see the "ear flaps" near the open smoke vent at the top of the tepee, above the door. The ear flaps, another ingenious Indian invention, assisted the draw of the fire inside the tepee. Their position could be modified according to weather conditions by using poles that were attached to them and crossed at the back of the tepee. The uncovered skeleton of poles on the left side of the central tepee is composed of three dog travois, each made up of a pair of pine poles with a small netted platform attached. Dogs were expected to assist in moving a family's belongings from place to place by being harnessed to such a travois. Before the advent of the horse, dogs provided all the motive power for such moves.

241

242 *"Pitatapiu, Assiniboin."* This painting is important in its accurate portrayal of the bow-lance, a special ceremonial item of great power, held by Pitatapiu. Both a bow and a lance, it was carried only by the most renowned warriors of a tribe. Pitatapiu also proudly displays his war shield, "to which a small packet, well wrapped up, his medicine or amulet in horse-stealing, was fastened, and which he greatly prized." Perhaps the most personal item of equipment for a Plains warrior, a shield was decorated with symbols and colors of personal meaning to the individual. "His hair hung down like a lion's mane," wrote Maximilian of Pitatapiu, "especially over his eyes, so that they could scarcely be seen; over each of them a small white sea shell was fastened with a hair string. . . . The handle of his whip was of wood, with holes in it like a flute." Maximilian mentioned that the Assiniboins enjoyed the warm room in the fort shared by the prince and the artist, "and a number of them were always sitting with us, to smoke their pipes."

243 LEFT *"Noapeh, Assiniboin."* Most Indian portraits made by King, Catlin, and Bodmer were made with the sitter in their very best attire, and this was no exception. Noapeh's handsome war shirt, seen under his buffalo robe, is decorated with beadwork, an intricate circular quill design, paint, and human hair. His unusual headdress is composed of antelope horn shaved and smoothed until black and glossy, with a crest of clipped feathers between. Noapeh, "Troop of Soldiers," posed on June 28, 1833, at Fort Union. According to Maximilian, he was "brought in at an early hour, and stood with unwearied patience."

243 RIGHT *"Pteh-Skah, Assiniboin."* This chief, painted at Fort Union in October 1833, wears a bear claw necklace, a beautifully painted robe, and red clay in his hair. "His face was characterized by a long nose," reported the prince, "his hair smeared with clay, and his summer robe painted of variegated colours. This chief was commended as a man thoroughly to be depended upon. When the portrait was finished he received a small present." Pteh-Skah's name meant "White Buffalo Cow."

243

245 *Unidentified Man. This painting was also identified by Bodmer as a "Piegan Medicine Man," although the resemblance is again strong to the Atsina medicine man.*

244 LEFT *"Mexkemauastan, Atsina Chief."*
His rifle and bow covered in hide cases, Mexkemauastan was nevertheless a figure of some anxiety for passengers on the keelboat Flora. *A year earlier, he had threatened to shoot the superintendent at Fort McKenzie, and with his people demanding presents from the whites, he seemed a figure of potential danger. Since Mexkemauastan was a medicine man and a keeper of a holy pipe, he did not cut his hair but piled it on top of his head in this characteristic fashion. The Fur Company transported Mexkemauastan and another warrior upriver to their village on August 5 and 6, 1833.*

244 RIGHT *Unidentified Man.*
This painting was once thought to be of a Piegan Blackfoot warrior, but the decoration on the buffalo robe has led some to believe that he is an Atsina.

246 "Pioch-Kiaiu, Piegan Blackfeet."

His face smeared with blue and red paint, his prominent nose and chin featured in profile, Pioch-Kiaiu was a survivor of the Assiniboin attack on the Blackfoot camp on August 21, 1833. He claimed that this Bodmer portrait had protected him from harm, thus starting a booming business in portraits for the artist. He was described by the prince as a "good-tempered, friendly man, . . . he gave me some account of his people and some words of their language, which are very difficult to pronounce."

247 LEFT *"Tatsicki-Stomick, Piegan Blackfeet Chief."* The principal chief of the Piegan tribe of the Blackfeet, Tatsicki-Stomick, or "Middle Bull," painted his face with pigments that made it blue and red. He wore a very simple shirt with small beaded strips for his portrait.

247 RIGHT *"Natoie-Poochsen, Piegan Blackfeet."* Natoie-Poochsen was an uncle of Ninoch-Kiaiu and was also in mourning. He chopped off his hair and rubbed white clay on his hair and face. His name meant "Word of Life."

"Makuie-Poka, Piegan Blackfeet."

*Makuie-Poka, "Child of the Wolf," was the son of
Homach-Ksachkum, a Kootenai man adopted
into the tribe, and a Blackfoot mother. Makuie-
Poka is dressed in resplendent garb, brass rings
on his fingers and a profusion of glass beads and
hair pipes on his clothing and in his hair. A bear
claw necklace and feather fan complete the look
of this warrior, who has painted his face with
great subtlety.*

249 LEFT *"Piegan Blackfeet Man."* The name of this man has not come down to us, but his exploits can still be read in the fine white elkskin robe he wears. War parties, horse's hooves, bows, rifles, and bleeding adversaries tell tales of personal bravery for all to see. The man smokes a ceremonial pipe of a characteristic Blackfoot design.

249 RIGHT *"Packkaab-Sachkoma-Poh, Piegan Blackfeet."* Painted at Fort McKenzie, this man is shown wearing a blanket, with a fashionable feather fan held under his arm.

250-251 "Hotokaueh-Hoh, Piegan Blackfeet." "Head of the Buffalo Skin" holds a sacred medicine pipe in his hand, one of the tribe's holiest relics. Sacred pipes were sources of great power for the tribe and were cared for by only its most trustworthy and important members. This pipe is decorated with the feathers of many types of birds, cloth, and trade beads. While this portrait was being painted on August 12, a Blood shot an Indian man named Martin in an adjoining room inside Fort McKenzie. The Blackfoot man said that this killing was an accident. He narrowly escaped death at the hands of other Blackfeet and was driven from the fort by Ninoch-Kiaiu but was otherwise unharmed.

251 LEFT *"Mehkskehme-Sukahs, Piegan Blackfeet Chief."* One of the chiefs who greeted the Flora on its arrival at Fort McKenzie, Mehkskehme-Sukahs, or "Iron Shirt," wears a hide shirt decorated with brass trade buttons and strips of blue glass beads.

251 RIGHT *"Kiasax, Piegan Blackfeet."* Intertribal trade is not often discussed in most historical texts, which most often dwell on European trade with Indian peoples. This portrait reveals a lot about intertribal trade, since Kiasax wears a Navajo blanket from the Southwest and a Spanish silver cross from the same region. Kiasax was apparently a fascinating and unusual man. He had married a Hidatsa woman and lived with her on the Knife River. Taking a ride on the steamer Assiniboin in 1833, he traveled to Fort Union, presumably to see his relatives, but he was spooked by the intertribal tensions he perceived there and returned downriver. A friend who decided to stay was killed by a Cree warrior. Note especially the long braid of hair running down Kiasax's back.

251

252 LEFT *"Homach-Ksachkum, Kootenai/ Blackfeet."* In direct contrast to his son Makuie-Poka, Homach-Ksachkum is very plainly dressed in this portrait. He was a respected leader among the Blackfeet, despite the fact that he was born a Kootenai.

252 RIGHT *"Stomick-Sosack, Blood Blackfeet Chief."* Called "Buffalo Bull's Back Fat" by George Catlin, Stomick-Sosack was painted a year earlier by that American artist. Bodmer's painting shows the chief in a different light entirely. Maximilian translated the man's name as "Bull's Hide." Stomick-Sosack wears a Jefferson peace medal in the painting, although we are shown the reverse side with the clasped hands design and the words "Peace and Friendship." This reverse was used from 1801 until 1850. Jefferson medals were unusual, in that they were the only United States medals ever made that were not solid silver, but rather were composed of two thin sheets of silver welded together to form a front and a back with a hollow center.

253 *"Ihkas-Kinne, Siksika Blackfeet Chief."* An otter pelt tippet, an outer garment used by mountain peoples like a jacket, is worn by this Blackfoot chief. The tippet is heavily decorated with abalone shells and pewter and silver items. The prince was told that Ihkas-Kinne also owned a shirt covered with mirror fragments, which says a lot about the personal tastes and style of this particular chief. Maximilian also recorded that this brave warrior had single-handedly returned Fort McKenzie's herd of horses, which had been stolen by another band of Blackfeet.

254 TOP LEFT *"Shoshonean Woman."* The Shoshone or *"Snake"* Indians lived in the mountains of Idaho and Wyoming. This woman, who may have been a captive of the Blackfeet, eventually married an employee of the Fur Company at Fort McKenzie named Marcereau. This portrait was made on September 6, 1833, less than two weeks after the woman, whose name is lost to history, delivered a baby. Childbirth among many American Indian tribes was an event conducted in private, without the aid of friends or family or even husband. The baby was delivered by the mother from an upright, squatting position, and the woman was usually up and about that same day, expected to fulfill her usual tasks in addition to caring for the new infant. Most Plains Indian tribes practiced birth control, not to regulate population but to prevent a mother from having to look out for more than one toddler at a time. Parents tried to space their children by seven-year intervals, using abstinence as the primary form of birth control.

254 TOP RIGHT *"Piah-Sukah-Ketutt, Cree."*
*"Speaking Thunder" was a hunter for the
American Fur Company at Fort Union. He wears a
bear claw necklace and a silver medallion.
"Mr. Bodmer drew a very good portrait of this Cree
in his Indian dress," wrote the prince.*

254 BOTTOM *"Cree Woman."* *Thought to be the
wife of Deschamps, a hunter for the Fur Company,
this Cree woman had tattooing on her chin.
Incredibly heavy earrings adorn both ears, and
Bodmer thought them interesting enough to make
a detail in the upper right corner of the painting.
The portraits of these Cree people were made at
Fort Union in October 1833.*

255 *"Pachtuwa-Chta, Arikara."* *The Arikara
were feared by the whites because they had sworn
everlasting enmity toward all Euro-Americans in
the first decade of the nineteenth century. This
man was a personal friend of Mahtotohpa;
however, and visited the Mandan village in March
1834. The prince noted that Pachtuwa-Chta "was
a handsome man, but not to be depended upon,
and was said to have killed many white men."
This proud warrior wears a beautiful red buffalo
robe with painted designs, and heavily beaded
leggings and moccasins. Hidden in the crook of
his arm is a red "gunstock"-type war club. In
exchange for his portrait, Pachtuwa-Chta asked
for a picture of a bear, which Maximilian drew,
with a forest scene background supplied by
Bodmer.*

256 "Unknown Man." *This unknown man could be either Mandan or Hidatsa. He wears silver armbands and an eagle-bone whistle around his neck.*

257 "Pehriska-Ruhpa, Hidatsa." *A member of the Dog Society, Pehriska-Ruhpa posed in his ceremonial garb for Bodmer in 1834. The special headdress was designed to be seen in motion, with black magpie feathers tipped with white down, brown turkey feathers at the back, and a red plume in the center. Pehriska-Ruhpa carries a rattle made of small hooves hanging from a beaded stick. Maximilian noted on March 14, 1834, that when each of the sittings for this portrait were over, "he always took off his ponderous feather cap, and rubbed it twice on each side of his head, a charm or precaution which he never neglected." This painting is one of Bodmer's most successful portraits and a justly famous image of the American West.*

K. Bodmer

258 *"Pehriska-Ruhpa, Hidatsa."* In this pose, Pehriska-Ruhpa, whose name means "Two Ravens," wears a nicely painted buffalo robe and a bear claw necklace, and he carries a huge ceremonial pipe, profusely decorated. The beadwork on his moccasins is particularly nice and is handled by the artist in such a way that it can still be seen and appreciated over a hundred years later.

259 *"Addih-Hiddisch, Hidatsa Chief."* Addih-Hiddisch's body was not painted but was tattooed with geometric patterns on his neck, arms, and chest. He was a great warrior and the chief of the village of Awachawi. He wears a Euro-American hat, carries a trade tomahawk, and has a peace medal around his neck. A scalp-lock is attached to the tomahawk.

260 **"Awascho-Dickfas, Hidatsa."** *In this interesting portrait of the back of a Hidatsa warrior, we see the details of his beautifully painted buffalo robe, which he interpreted for Prince Maximilian. The circular pattern represented the tracks of wolf paws, the black circle in the center the wolf's den. The portrait presents a good view of the way hair was handled behind the head. Awascho-Dickfas's name means "Swallow With the White Belly".*

261 LEFT *"Birohka, Hidatsa."* *Birohka's cap, made from the hide of a rare and sacred white buffalo, and his robe, painted with the circle design of a feathered bonnet, reveal him to be a man of great standing in his tribe.*

261 RIGHT *"Ahschupsa Masihichsi, Hidatsa."* *This was the warrior who requested that he be allowed to bring his portrait with him as he went off to battle. Refused in this request by Bodmer, Ahschupsa Masihichsi countered by drawing a picture of the artist, which he retained to do with as he pleased. In the painting he carries a "gunstock"-type war club decorated with brass furniture tacks.*

262 *"Mato-Tope, Mandan Chief."* Mato-Tope was also an enthusiastic artist who learned much from both Karl Bodmer and George Catlin. Catlin, who called this second chief of the Mandans "Mah-ta-toh-pa," painted two portraits of him in 1832. This Bodmer portrait, probably painted in 1834, shows the chief once more dressed in his finest clothing, his face elaborately painted. His eagle-feather war bonnet is impressive, while he holds the special lance he used to kill the Arikara who slew his brother. The Arikara's stretched scalp adorns the haft just below the lance point. Included in Mato-Tope's war bonnet is a wooden replica of a knife, reminiscent of the knife he took from a Cheyenne warrior in hand-to-hand combat. Maximilian noted that Mato-Tope was one of their "most constant visitors," bringing along "his wife and a pretty little boy, to whom he had given the name of Mato-Berocka (the male bear). He brought his medicine drum, painted red and black, which he hung up in our room, and so afforded Mr. Bodmer an opportunity of making a drawing of it."

263 *"Mato-Tope, Mandan Chief."* This second Bodmer portrait of Mato-Tope shows the Mandan stripped and painted for battle, feathers commemorating specific deeds and wounds from battles past in his hair, body paint in place, and his favorite tomahawk at the ready. The yellow hand painted on his chest means that he had taken prisoners in battle. The horizontal lines on his arms are records of the coups he counted. The eagle feathers in his hair were symbols of coups, the split turkey feather signified an arrow wound, and the owl feathers, which are dyed yellow, indicated his membership in the Dog Society. The six painted wooden sticks with brass tacks in the ends represented bullet wounds this great warrior endured. During the winter of 1833-34, Mato-Tope and Karl Bodmer became especially close, Bodmer giving the Mandan gifts of paper, pencils and watercolors. Three years after this portrait was made, Mato-Tope became the principal chief of his people, but then the smallpox epidemic of 1837 decimated the Mandan; only 125 of 1,600 survived. Many sources say that Mato-Tope died in the epidemic, while Catlin stated that he committed suicide by starving himself to death after the tragic loss of his entire family. Mato-Tope's son and namesake succeeded to the position of principal chief. Mato-Tope the younger led his people to Fort Berthold in 1845, where a reservation for the remaining Mandan, Hidatsa, and Arikara was established, and where they continue to live today.

264 "Mandeh-Pahchu, Mandan."

Mandeh-Pahchu, the brother of Mahchsi-Karehde, is decked out in all his finery in this Bodmer portrait, his hair, ears, and neck decorated with beads, dentalium and abalone shells. He holds a flute, the central instrument in nonceremonial Indian music. Flutes were used especially by young men to compose and perform love songs for girls they wished to court. Maximilian recorded that Mandeh-Pahchu traded his flute for the prince's whistle. The Mandan was also interested in Maximilian's music box, thinking at first that a small man was inside performing the music.

264-265 *"Interior of a Mandan Earth Lodge."*
One of the most important paintings ever made, from both an ethnographic and historical perspective, Karl Bodmer's watercolor of the interior of a Mandan earth lodge gives us a unique view of their culture. Lances, paddles, and war shields are seen on the right, while woven baskets and pottery are on the left. The size of the structure can be understood by observing the horses on the left-hand side, who could be stabled inside the earth lodge. An extended family of five to sixteen or as many as thirty people lived inside such a lodge, which lasted for seven to twelve years before

a new lodge had to be built. "In the centre of the hut a circular place is dug for the fire," wrote Maximilian, "over which the kettle is suspended. This fire-place, or hearth, is often enclosed with a ledge of stones. The fuel is laid, in moderately thick pieces, on the external edge of the hearth, crossing each other in the middle, when it is kindled, and the pieces gradually pushed in as they burn away. The Indians are not fond of large fires. The inmates sit round it, on low seats, made of peeled osiers, covered with buffalo or bear skin. . . . The beds stand against the wall of the hut; they consist of a large square case, made of

parchment or skins, with a square entrance, and are large enough to hold several persons, who lie very conveniently on skins and blankets." In the fire pit area, with its smoke-hole overhead, a willow back rest can be seen between two of the seated figures, which include two men, a boy, a woman, a girl, and two dogs. This was the home of Dipauch, an older man who shared information about his culture with Prince Maximilian. Most Mandan men had one wife, but some had as many as four. This extended family, plus any grown sons, with their wives and children, might inhabit an earth lodge.

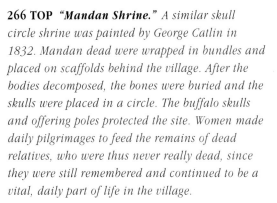

266 TOP *"Mandan Shrine."* *A similar skull circle shrine was painted by George Catlin in 1832. Mandan dead were wrapped in bundles and placed on scaffolds behind the village. After the bodies decomposed, the bones were buried and the skulls were placed in a circle. The buffalo skulls and offering poles protected the site. Women made daily pilgrimages to feed the remains of dead relatives, who were thus never really dead, since they were still remembered and continued to be a vital, daily part of life in the village.*

266 BOTTOM *"Sih-Sa, Mandan."* *Posed against a deep blue sky, Sih-Sa, or "Red Feather," was a hunter who frequently brought in game to Fort Clark. Slung behind his back is a beautiful quiver made of a mountain lion skin.*

267 *"Mandan Shrine."* *The prince was able to discover the meaning of the poles decorated with hides depicted in this Bodmer watercolor. The two poles symbolized the Lord of Life, the Great Spirit or creator; and the Old Woman Who Never Dies, who represented Mandan subsistence through corn and the buffalo. In the distance can be seen the scaffolds of the Mandan dead behind the village.*

268 "Upsichta, Mandan." *Wrapped in a warm buffalo blanket, Upsichta could be sure of his appearance with the hand mirror bound to his eagle-wing fan. A warrior whose name meant "Great Blackness," Upsichta once killed three Assiniboin enemies in one battle.*

269 "Mahchsi-Karehde, Mandan." *"Flying War Eagle" was one of the most prominent Mandan warriors, part of a small group that regulated tribal affairs. At just over six feet tall, he is every inch the Plains warrior, from the eagle feather in his hair to the wolf tails on his moccasins. A large bear claw necklace and eagle feather fan complete the ensemble. Mahchsi-Karehde was the brother of Mandeh-Pahchu.*

270-271 *"Mih-Tutta-Hang-Kusch, Mandan Village."* This excellent landscape shows not only the summer Mandan village in the distance across the frozen Missouri River, but also the stockade of Fort Clark next to it. The summer village was located on a high peninsula, with steep bluffs on three sides, which projected into the Missouri River. There were about 65 earthen lodges and several auxiliary buildings in the village. Fort Clark was the home of Maximilian and Bodmer during the winter of 1833-34. The winter village of the Mandan was located in the timbered bottomland below the bluffs, but in times of emergency the better-defended summer village could be used at any time of the year. In this scene, a party of Indian women moves firewood across the frozen ice, while men stand guard.

270 BOTTOM *"Artifacts."* This assortment of Indian artifacts includes a wooden type of war club, a horn ladle, and Mandan snowshoes.

271 TOP *"Quiver, Bows, and Arrows."* The quiver is Crow, the bow either Mandan or Hidatsa. This watercolor may have been made in Europe of some of Maximilian's collected artifacts.

271 BOTTOM *"Mandan Buffalo Robe."*
This buffalo robe copies a design by Mato-Tope.
The original robe survives today in the Linden-
Museum in Stuttgart, Germany. The vignette on
the lower left side of the robe depicts the attack on
Mato-Tope by a Cheyenne armed with a knife. In
this, his most famous battle, Mato-Tope faced the
Cheyenne chief in single combat while a battle
raged around them. They began with rifles,
charging each other on horseback. When Mato-
Tope's powder horn was shot away, the two chiefs
fired arrows at one another until their quivers
were empty. Mato-Tope's horse was killed in this
exchange, and he ran toward the Cheyenne to
fight him hand-to-hand. Mato-Tope, slashed twice
on the hand and bleeding profusely, disarmed his
adversary and killed him with his own knife. This
is the knife which was replicated in wood and
was worn in Mato-Tope's headdress and hair
arrangements. Another episode Mato-Tope related
to the prince is depicted on the robe in the upper
left-hand corner. An Assiniboin who attacked the
Mandan village fired point-blank at Mato-Tope,
but the barrel of the defective weapon exploded.
Throwing the weapon to the ground, the
Assiniboin turned to run, but Mato-Tope killed
him with the tomahawk he is holding. Each of the
pictographs could be interpreted in this way, and
each tells a story about Mato-Tope's exploits as a
warrior.

272-273 *"Mandan Dogsled."* This group of
Mandans are moving household possessions by
means of a dogsled across the frozen ice. Since the
summer village was sometimes reoccupied as early
as February or March, this view may represent part
of the seasonal move between the two villages.

Dogs were very often impressed into service.
Maximilian noted that "the inhabitants of
Ruhptare had all removed from their winter to their
summer quarters" on February 9, 1834; "they were
evidently afraid that the ice would break up early,
and the water of the Missouri rise considerably."

Although there is a great deal of pictorial and verbal information included in this book, each of the artists profiled has been examined in greater depth elsewhere, along with the historical context of Indian-white relations in which they worked. Without the pioneering work of the Smithsonian ethnologist John C. Ewers, an appreciation for the historical importance of these works of art would not be possible. For information on the relationships between American Indians and Euro-Americans, the work of Francis Paul Prucha stands out, particularly in reference to the era when Indian people were forcibly relocated. Prucha's books *The Great Father: The U.S. Government and the American Indian, American Indian Policy in the Formative Years, and Documents of U.S. Indian Policy* will all provide the interested reader with accurate and informative material on this subject. On Thomas McKenney, Herman J. Viola has written the pioneering work with *Thomas L. McKenney, Architect of America's Early Indian Policy: 1816-1830.* For Charles Bird King, Andrew F. Cosentino's *The Paintings of Charles Bird King (1785-1862)* provides the most in-depth information about the man's total body of work, including his paintings of non-Indian subjects. William Treuttner's *Natural Man Observed: A Study of Catlin's Indian Gallery* is the most comprehensive study of Catlin's paintings to date; it includes a complete catalogue of more than 400 of the artist's known works. For Karl Bodmer, the most definitive book has to be the excellent catalogue compiled by the Joslyn Art Museum, *Karl Bodmer's America*, with an introduction by William H. Goetzmann, annotated reproductions of Bodmer's complete North American work by David C. Hunt and Marsha V. Gallagher, and a biographical sketch of Bodmer by William J. Orr. The original writings of Maximilian, Catlin and McKenney are also available in modern reprints. Specific books used in the creation of this volume are listed below.

Introduction: Three Artists Meet the West

Anderson, Gary Clayton and Alan R. Woolworth (eds.) *Through Dakota Eyes: Narrative Accounts of the Minnesota Indian War of 1862* St. Paul: Minnesota Historical Society Press, 1988.

Black Hawk *An Autobiography* Donald Jackson (ed.) Urbana and Chicago: University of Illinois Press, 1955.

Debo, Angie *A History of the Indians of the United States* Norman: University of Oklahoma Press, 1970.

Ehle, John *Trail of Tears: The Rise and Fall of the Cherokee Nation* New York: Doubleday, 1988.

Filler, Louis (ed.) *The Removal of the Cherokee Nation: Manifest Destiny or National Dishonor?* [Original documents relating to the removal of the Cherokee] Malabar, Florida: Robert E. Kriegar Publishing Company, 1962; reprinted 1988.

Foreman, Grant T*he Five Civilized Tribes: Cherokee, Chickasaw, Choctaw, Creek, Seminole* Norman, Oklahoma: University of Oklahoma Press, 1989.

Goetzmann, William H. *Army Exploration in the American West, 1803-1863* New Haven: Yale University Press, 1959.

Jensen, Richard E., R, Eli Paul, and John E. Carter, *Eyewitness at Wounded Knee* Lincoln, Nebraska: University of Nebraska Press, 1991.

Linethal, Edward T. *Sacred Ground: Americans and Their Battlefields* Urbana: University of Illinois Press, 1991.

Nabokov, Peter, ed. *Native American Testimony: A Chronicle of Indian-White Relations From Prophecy To The Present, 1492-1992* New York: Viking Penguin, 1991.

Prucha, Francis Paul *The Sword of the Republic: The United States Army on the Frontier, 1783-1846* Lincoln: University of Nebraska Press, 1986.

Walter, James R. *Lakota Belief and Ritual* (ed. by DeMallie and Jahner) Lincoln: University of Nebraska Press, 1991.

Charles Bird King: Portraits for the Record

Cosentino, Andrew F. *The Paintings of Charles Bird King (1785-1862)* Washington, D.C.: National Collection of Fine Arts, Smithsonian Institution Press, 1977

Dunlop, William *History of the Rise and Progress of the Arts of Design in the United States,* 3 volumes; originally published 1834, reprint of 1965 edited by Alexander Wykoff; New York: Benjamin Bloom, 1965.

Elliot, Jonathan *Historical Sketches of the Ten Miles Square Forming the District of Columbia* Washington, D.C.: J. Elliot, Jr., 1830.

Ewers, John C. *Artists of the Old West,* Garden City, New York: Chanticleer Press, Doubleday, 1965; 1973.

Horan, James D. *The McKenney-Hall Portrait Gallery of American Indians* New York: Crown Publications, 1972

McKenney, Thomas L. *Memoirs, Official and Personal* Lincoln: University of Nebraska Press, 1973.

Prucha, Francis Paul *Sword of the Republic: The United States Army on the Frontier, 1783-1846,* Lincoln: University of Nebraska Press, 1969.

Viola, Herman J. *Thomas L. McKenney, Architect of America's Early Indian Policy: 1816-1830* Chicago: Swallow Press, 1974

Viola, Herman J. *Diplomats in Buckskins,* Washington: Smithsonian Institution Press, 1971.

George Catlin: Rescuing the Indians from Oblivion

Berkhofer, Robert F., Jr. *The White Man's Indian,* New York: Vintage Books, 1978

Catlin, George *Letters and Notes on the Manners, Customs, and Condition of the North American Indians,* two volumes, London: Published by the Author at the Egyptian Hall, Picadilly, 1841; reprinted by Dover Publications, New York, 1963.

Catlin, George *Catlin's Notes of Eight Years' Travels and Residence in Europe, With His American Indian Collection,* two volumes, London, 1848

Catlin, George *Life Amongst the Indians, A Book for Youth* New York, 1867; London: Lampson Low, Son & Co., 1861.

Catlin, George *O-Kee-Pa: A Religious Ceremony* London, 1867; reprinted by Yale University Press, New Haven, Connecticut, 1967.

Cooper, James Fenimore *The Prairie* New York: Signet Classic/New American Library reprint, 1962.

Dippie, Brian *Catlin and His Contemporaries: The Politics of Patronage* Norman Oklahoma: University of Oklahoma Press, 1990

Donaldson, Thomas "The George Catlin Indian Gallery," in the *Annual Report of the Smithsonian Institution,* 1885, Part 5, Washington, D.C., 1886

Ewers, John C. *Artists of the Old West,* Garden City, New York: Doubleday and Company, 1965

Haberly, Lloyd *Pursuit of the Horizon: A Life of George Catlin, Painter and recorder of the American Indian* New York: Macmillan Co., 1948.

Halpin, Marjorie *Catlin's Indian Gallery: The George Catlin Paintings in the United States National Museum* Washington, D.C.: Smithsonian Institution Press, 1965

Honour, Hugh *The European Vision of America,* a catalogue for an exhibit at the Cleveland Museum of Art, 1975, Number 298.

Matthiessen, Peter (ed.) *George Catlin's North American Indians* Penguin Books, 1989

McCracken, Harold *George Catlin and the Old Frontier* New York: Dial Press, 1959

Roehm, Marjorie Catlin *The Letters of George Catlin and His Family* Berkeley, California, 1966

Sellars, Charles Coleman, *Charles Willson Peale,* New York, 1969.

Troccoli, Joan Carpenter *First Artist of the West: George Catlin Paintings and Watercolors From the Collection of the Gilcrease Museum* Tulsa Oklahoma: Gilcrease Museum, 1993.

Truettner, William H. *Natural Man Observed: A Study of Catlin's Indian Gallery* Washington, D.C.: Smithsonian Institution Press, 1979

Karl Bodmer: "Over there I Had Friends"

Ewers, John C. *Artists of the Old West* Garden City, New York: Chanticleer Press, Doubleday, 1965, 1973.

Ewers, John C. "An Appreciation of Karl Bodmer's Pictures of Indians" in *Views of a Vanishing Frontier* Omaha: Joslyn Art Museum, 1984.

Goetzmann, William H. *The West of the Imagination* New York and London: W.W. Norton, 1986

Joslyn Art Museum *Karl Bodmer's America* Lincoln: University of Nebraska Press, 1984

Maximilian, Prince of Wied *Travels in the Interior of North America,* 1832-34, in *Early Western Travels, 1748-1846,* edited by Reuben Gold Thwaites, Vols. 22-24; Cleveland: Arthur H. Clark Company, 1906, reprinted 1966.

Rossi, Paul A. and David C. Hunt *The Art of the Old West: the Collection of the Gilcrease Museum* New York: Promontory Press, 1981.

Thomas, Davis and Karen Ronnefeldt, *People of the First Man: Life Among the Plains Indians in Their Final Days of Glory* New York: E.P. Dutton, 1976.

King. © P.C.

55 Chon-Mon-I-Case, lithograph after Charles Bird King. © P.C.

56 Chippeway Squaw & Child, lithograph after Charles Bird King. © P.C.

57 Tshusick, lithograph after Charles Bird King. © P.C.

58 Pow-A-Sheek, lithograph after Charles Bird King. © P.C.

59 Pow-A-Sheek, oil on panel by Charles Bird King. © Gerald Peters Gallery

60 top Peah-Mus-Ka, painting by Charles Bird King. © Eiteljorg Museum of American Indians and Western Art

60 bottom Peah-Mus-Ka, lithograph after Charles Bird King. © P.C.

61 top Push-Ma-Ta-Ha, lithograph after Charles Bird King. © P.C.

61 bottom Push-Ma-Ta-Ha, oil on canvas by Charles Bird King. © The Warner Collection of Gulf State Paper Corporation, Tuscaloosa, AL, USA

62 Keokuk, oil on canvas by Charles Bird King. © Gerald Peters Gallery

63 Ma-Has-Kah, oil on canvas by Charles Bird King. © Collection of Gilcrease Museum, Tulsa

64 Moa Na Honga, oil on canvas by Charles Bird King. © Collection of Gilcrease Museum, Tulsa

65 Petalesharro, oil on canvas by Charles Bird King. © Collection of Gilcrease Museum, Tulsa

66 Waneta, oil on canvas by Charles Bird King. © Gerald Peters Gallery

67 left Shaumonekusse (Prairie Wolf), oil on canvas by Charles Bird King. © Collection of Gilcrease Museum, Tulsa

67 right Ne Sou A Quoit, oil on canvas by Charles Bird King. © J. N. Bartfield Galleries

68 left Hayne-Hudjihini, oil on canvas by Charles Bird King. © Collection of Gilcrease Museum, Tulsa

68 right Ong Pa Ton Ga, oil on canvas by Charles Bird King. © Collection of Gilcrease Museum, Tulsa

69 Rant Che Wai Me, oil on canvas by Charles Bird King. © Collection of Gilcrease Museum, Tulsa

70 left Joseph Polis, oil on canvas by Charles Bird King. © Collection of Gilcrease Museum, Tulsa

70 top right David Vann, oil on canvas by Charles Bird King. © Collection of Gilcrease Museum, Tulsa

70 bottom right John W. Quinney, oil on canvas by Charles Bird King. © Collection of Gilcrease Museum, Tulsa

71 The Prophet, oil on canvas by Charles Bird King. © Collection of Gilcrease Museum, Tulsa

72 top Rant Che Wai Me, lithograph after Charles Bird King. © P.C.

72 bottom Young Ma-Has-Kah, lithograph after Charles Bird King. © P.C.

73 Naw-Kaw, lithograph after Charles Bird King. © P.C.

74 left Lap-Pa-Win-Soe, lithograph after Charles Bird King. © P.C.

74 right Waa-Top-E-Not, lithograph after Charles Bird King. © P.C.

75 Kee-She-Waa, lithograph after Charles Bird King. © P.C.

76 top Nah-Et-Luc-Hopie, lithograph after Charles Bird King. © P.C.

76 bottom Timpoochee Barnard, lithograph after Charles Bird King. © P.C.

77 top Tulcee-Mathla, lithograph after Charles Bird King. © P.C.

77 bottom Thayendanega, lithograph after Charles Bird King. © P.C.

78 Wakechai, lithograph after Charles Bird King. © P.C.

79 left Mo-Hon-Go, an Osage Woman, lithograph after Charles Bird King. © P.C.

79 right Tish-Co-Han, lithograph after Charles Bird King. © P.C.

80 right Ahyouwaighs, lithograph after Charles Bird King. © P.C.

80 left Red Jacket, lithograph after Charles Bird King. © P.C.

81 Ki-On-Twog-Ky or Corn Plant, lithograph after Charles Bird King. © P.C.

82 Yaholo-Micco, lithograph after Charles Bird King. © P.C.

83 top Paddy-Carr, lithograph after Charles Bird King. © P.C.

83 bottom Mistippe, lithograph after Charles Bird King. © P.C.

84 top Ledagie, lithograph after Charles Bird King. © P.C.

84 bottom Itcho-Tustinnuggee, lithograph after Charles Bird King. © P.C.

85 Se-Loc-Ta, lithograph after Charles Bird King. © P.C.

86 top Spring Frog, lithograph after Charles Bird King. © P.C.

86 bottom Tah-Chee, lithograph after Charles Bird King. © P.C.

87 top David Vann, lithograph after Charles Bird King. © P.C.

87 bottom John Ridge, lithograph after Charles Bird King. © P.C.

88 left Yaha-Hajo, lithograph after Charles Bird King. © P.C.

88 right Tuko-See-Mathla, lithograph after Charles Bird King. © P.C.

89 left Micanopy, lithograph after Charles Bird King. © P.C.

89 right Nea-Math-La, lithograph after Charles Bird King. © P.C.

90 Payta-Kootha, lithograph after Charles Bird King. © P.C.

91 top left Kish-Kal-Wa, lithograph after Charles Bird King. © P.C.

91 top right Ca-Ta-He-Cas-Sa-Black Hoof, lithograph after Charles Bird King. © P.C.

91 bottom Qua-Ta-Wa-Pea, lithograph after Charles Bird King. © P.C.

92 Okee-Makee-Quid, lithograph after Charles Bird King. © P.C.

93 top Shin-Ga-Ba-W'Ossin, lithograph after Charles Bird King. © P.C.

93 bottom J-Aw-Beance, lithograph after Charles Bird King. © P.C.

94 A Chippeway Widow, lithograph after Charles Bird King. © P.C.

95 Chippeway Squaw and Child, lithograph after Charles Bird King. © P.C.

96 top Pee-che-Kir, lithograph after Charles Bird King. © P.C.

96 bottom Wesh-Cubb, lithograph after Charles Bird King. © P.C.

97 top No-Tin, lithograph after Charles Bird King. © P.C.

97 bottom Wa-Em-Boesh-Kaa, lithograph after Charles Bird King. © P.C.

98 left Amiskquew, lithograph after Charles Bird King. © P.C.

98 right Mar-Ko-Me-Te, lithograph after Charles Bird King. © P.C.

99 top Wa-Baun-See, lithograph after Charles Bird King. © P.C.

99 bottom Me-Te-A, lithograph after Charles Bird King. © P.C.

100 Tai-O-Mah, lithograph after Charles Bird King. © P.C.

101 Wa-Pel-La, lithograph after Charles Bird King. © P.C.

102 Kee-She-Waa, lithograph after Charles Bird King. © P.C.

103 Ne-Sou-A-Quoit, lithograph after Charles Bird King. © P.C.

104 Kish-Ke-Kosh, lithograph after Charles Bird King. © P.C.

105 Ap-Pa-Noo-Se, lithograph after Charles Bird King. © P.C.

106 top A-Mis-Quam, lithograph after Charles Bird King. © P.C.

106 bottom Hoo-Wan-Ne-Ka, lithograph after Charles Bird King. © P.C.

107 top Tshi-Zun-Hau-Kau, lithograph after Charles Bird King. © P.C.

107 bottom A Winnebago, lithograph after Charles Bird King. © P.C.

108 Chone-Ca-Pe, lithograph after Charles Bird King. © P.C.

109 No-Way-Ke-Su-Ga, lithograph after Charles Bird King. © P.C.

110 Not-Chi-Mi-Ne, lithograph after Charles Bird King. © P.C.

111 Ne-O-Mon-Ne, lithograph after Charles Bird King. © P.C.

112 Moa-Na-Hon-Ga, lithograph after Charles Bird King. © P.C.

113 Ma-Has-Kah, lithograph after Charles Bird King. © P.C.

114 Shar-I-Tar-Ish, lithograph after Charles Bird King. © P.C.

115 Pes-Ke-Le-Cha-Co, lithograph after Charles Bird King. © P.C.

116 top To-Ka-Cou, lithograph after Charles Bird King. © P.C.

116 bottom Esh-Ta-Hum-Leah, lithograph after Charles Bird King. © P.C.

117 Wa-Na-Ta, lithograph after Charles Bird King. © P.C.

118 left Broadside Advertising "Catlin's Indian Gallery" Washington DC, April 1838. © Library of Congress, Washington

118 top right Male Caribou, oil on canvas by George Catlin, 1836. © National Museum of American Art, Washington DC/Art Resource, NY

118 top left Strong Wind, oil on canvas by George Catlin, 1834. © National Museum of American Art, Washington DC/Art Resource, NY

118 bottom right Mouse-Colored Feather, oil on canvas by George Catlin, 1832. © National Museum of American Art, Washington DC/Art Resource, NY

119 Portrait of George Catlin by William Fisk, 1849. © National Portrait Gallery, Smithsonian Institution/Art Resource, NY

120-121 Ojibwa Troupe in London, George Catlin, 1844. © Collection of Gilcrease Museum, Tulsa

122 Mandan Game of Tchung-Kee, 1832-33, oil on canvas by George Catlin, 1832-33. © National Museum of American Art, Washington DC/Art Resource, NY

122-123 Sioux Indian Council, oil on canvas by George Catlin. © Collection of Gilcrease Museum, Tulsa

124 Strong Wind, oil on canvas by George Catlin, 1834. © National Museum of American Art, Washington DC/Art Resource, NY

125 Strikes Two at Once, oil on canvas by George Catlin, 1832. © National Museum of American Art, Washington DC/Art Resource, NY

126 One Horn, oil on canvas by George Catlin, 1832. © National Museum of American Art, Washington, DC/Art Resource, NY

127 The Wolf, oil on canvas by George Catlin, 1832. Gift of Mrs. Joseph Harrison, Jr. © National Museum of American Art, Washington DC/Art Resource, NY

128 top Portrait of William Clark by George Catlin, 1832. © National Portrait Gallery, Smithsonian Institution/Art Resource

128 bottom Cock Turkey Repeating His Prayer, oil on canvas by George Catlin, 1831. © National Museum of American Art, Washington DC/Art Resource, NY

128-129 William Clark's Map of West, 1805-1838. © Yale Collection of Western Americana, Beinecke Rare Books & Manuscript Library

129 Wolf on the Hill, oil on canvas by George Catlin, 1832. © National Museum of American Art, Washington DC/Art Resource, NY

130 Rabbit's Skin Leggings, A Brave, oil on canvas by George Catlin, 1832. © National Museum of American Art, Washington DC/Art Resource, NY

130-131 Map of Travels of George Catlin, 1830-1837. © P.C.

131 St. Louis from the River Below, 1832-1833. © National Museum of American Art, Washington DC/Art Resource, NY

132-133 Arikara Village of Earth-Covered Lodges, oil on canvas by George Catlin, 1832. © National Museum of American Art, Washington DC/Art Resource, NY

133 Band of Sioux Moving Camp, oil on canvas by George Catlin, 1837-1839. © National Museum of American Art, Washington DC/Art Resource, NY

134 left Buffalo Hunt under the Wolf-Skin Mask, oil on canvas by George Catlin, 1832-33. © National Museum of American Art, Washington DC/Art Resource, NY

134-135 Buffalo Chase With Bows and Lances, oil on canvas by George Catlin, 1832-33. © National Museum of American Art, Washington DC/Art Resource, NY

135 Buffalo Chase, A Single Death, oil on canvas by George Catlin, 1832-33. © National Museum of American Art, Washington DC/Art Resource, NY

278

Fire, 1846-48, oil on canvas by George Catlin. © National Museum of American Art, Washington DC/Art Resource, NY

201 top Portrait of Karl Bodmer, pencil sketch by Loys Delteil, 1894. © Jocelyn Art Museum.

202-203 Banks of the Missouri, watercolor on paper by Karl Bodmer. © Jocelyn Art Museum.

203 left Paesesick-Kaskutau, Assiniboin, watercolor and pencil on paper by Karl Bodmer. © Jocelyn Art Museum.

203 right Sih-Chida, Mandan, watercolor on paper by Karl Bodmer. © Jocelyn Art Museum.

204-205 Map of the travels of Prince Maximilian and Karl Bodmer. © Alecto Historical Editions, London

205 right Portrait of Prince Maximilian of Wied, by Johann Heinrich Richter, 1828. © Courtesy of his Highness Prince Friedrich Wilhelm/Jocelyn Art Museum.

206-207 The Steamboat Yellow Stone, watercolor on paper by Karl Bodmer. © Jocelyn Art Museum.

206 Mouth of the Big Sioux River, watercolor and pencil on paper by Karl Bodmer. © Jocelyn Art Museum.

207 top View of the Missouri near Fort Leavenworth, watercolor and pencil on paper by Karl Bodmer. © Jocelyn Art Museum.

208 Study of an Elk, watercolor, ink, and pencil on paper by Karl Bodmer. © Jocelyn Art Museum.

208-209 White Castles on the Missouri, watercolor on paper by Karl Bodmer. © Jocelyn Art Museum.

209 bottom Nodaway Island, watercolor on paper by Karl Bodmer. © Jocelyn Art Museum.

210 Head of a Buffalo, watercolor and ink on paper by Karl Bodmer. © Jocelyn Art Museum.

210-211 Landscape with Herd of Buffalo on the Upper Missouri, watercolor on paper by Karl Bodmer. © Jocelyn Art Museum.

212 Unusual Elevations on the Upper Missouri, watercolor on paper by Karl Bodmer. © Jocelyn Art Museum.

212-213 View of the Stone Walls, watercolor on paper by Karl Bodmer. © Jocelyn Art Museum.

213 bottom Rock Formations on the Upper Missouri, watercolor on paper by Karl Bodmer. © Jocelyn Art Museum.

214 left A Stop; Evening Bivouac, watercolor on paper by Karl Bodmer. © Jocelyn Art Museum.

214-215 The Camp of the Gros Ventres of the Prairies on the Upper Missouri, lithograph after Charles Bird King. © Library of Congress, Washington

215 top Hunting of the Grizzly Bear, lithograph after Karl Bodmer. © Library of Congress, Washington

216 right Cree Woman, watercolor and pencil on paper by Karl Bodmer. © Jocelyn Art Museum.

216 left Piegan Blackfeet Woman, watercolor and pencil on paper by Karl Bodmer. © Jocelyn Art Museum.

216-217 Evening Bivouac on the Missouri, watercolor on paper by Karl Bodmer. © Jocelyn Art Museum.

218 top Indian Woman, watercolor and pencil on paper by Karl Bodmer. © Jocelyn Art Museum.

218 bottom Ninoch-Kiaiu, watercolor on paper by Karl Bodmer. © Jocelyn Art Museum.

218-219 The Travellers Meeting with Minataree Indians near Fort Clark, lithograph after Karl Bodmer. © Library of Congress, Washington

220-221 Fort McKenzie, August 28, 1833, lithograph after Karl Bodmer. © Library of Congress, Washington

221 top Pachtuwa-Chta, watercolor on paper by Karl Bodmer. © Jocelyn Art Museum.

221 bottom Fort Mckenzie at the Mouth of the Marias River, watercolor and pencil on paper by Karl Bodmer. © Jocelyn Art Museum.

222 Sih-Chida and Mahchsi Karehde, watercolor and pencil on paper by Karl Bodmer. © Jocelyn Art Museum.

223 top Winter Village of the Minatarees, lithograph after Karl Bodmer. © Library of Congress, Washington

223 center Ptihn-Tak-Ochata, Dance of the Mandan Women, lithograph after Karl Bodmer. © Library of Congress, Washington

223 bottom Mih-Tutta-Hang Kush, Mandan Village, lithograph after Karl Bodmer. © Library of Congress, Washington

224 Leader of the Mandan Buffalo Bull Society, watercolor and pencil on paper by Karl Bodmer. © Jocelyn Art Museum.

225 Buffalo Bull Dance of the Mandan Indians, lithograph after Karl Bodmer. © Library of Congress, Washington

226 Hidatsa Scalp Dance, watercolor and pencil on paper by Karl Bodmer. © Jocelyn Art Museum.

227 right Mahchsi-Nihka, watercolor, ink and pencil on paper by Karl Bodmer. © Jocelyn Art Museum.

228 left Massika, watercolor on paper by K. Bodmer. © Jocelyn Art Museum.

228 right Wakusasse, watercolor and pencil on paper by Karl Bodmer. © Jocelyn Art Museum.

229 left Massika, lithograph after Karl Bodmer. © Library of Congress, Washington

229 right Wakusasse, lithograph after Karl Bodmer. © Library of Congress, Washington

230 left Noapeh, watercolor and pencil on paper, by Karl Bodmer. © Jocelyn Art Museum.

230 right Psihdja-Sahpa, lithograph after Karl Bodmer. © Library of Congress, Washington

231 Pehriska-Ruhpa, lithograph after Karl Bodmer. © Library of Congress, Washington

232 Ho-Ta Ma, watercolor and pencil on paper by Karl Bodmer. © Jocelyn Art Museum.

233 Ponca Camp, watercolor on paper by Karl Bodmer. © Jocelyn Art Museum.

234 Wahktageli, watercolor and pencil on paper by Karl Bodmer. © Jocelyn Art Museum.

235 Psihdja-Sahpa, watercolor on paper by Karl Bodmer. © Jocelyn Art Museum.

236 Sioux Camp, watercolor on paper by Karl Bodmer. © Jocelyn Art Museum.

237 left Wah-Menitu, watercolor on paper by Karl Bodmer. © Jocelyn Art Museum.

237 right Chan-Cha-Uia-Teuin, watercolor and pencil on paper by Karl Bodmer. © Jocelyn Art Museum.

238 Assiniboin Medicine Sign, watercolor on paper by Karl Bodmer. © Jocelyn Art Museum.

239 Assiniboin Burial Scaffold, watercolor on paper by Karl Bodmer. © Jocelyn Art Museum.

240 top Assiniboin Warrior, watercolor and pencil on paper by Karl Bodmer. © Jocelyn Art Museum.

240 bottom Blackfeet-Assiniboin Girl, watercolor on paper by Karl Bodmer. © Jocelyn Art Museum.

240-241 Assiniboin Camp, watercolor on paper by Karl Bodmer. © Jocelyn Art Museum.

242 Pitatapiu, watercolor and pencil on paper by Karl Bodmer. © Jocelyn Art Museum.

243 left Noapeh, watercolor and pencil on paper by Karl Bodmer. © Jocelyn Art Museum.

243 right Pteh-Skah, watercolor and pencil on paper by Karl Bodmer. © Jocelyn Art Museum.

244 left Mexkemauastan, watercolor on paper by Karl Bodmer. © Jocelyn Art Museum.

244 right Unidentified Man, watercolor and pencil on paper by Karl Bodmer. © Jocelyn Art Museum.

245 Unidentified Man, watercolor on paper by Karl Bodmer. © Jocelyn Art Museum.

246 Pioch-Kiaiu, watercolor on paper by Karl Bodmer. © Jocelyn Art Museum.

247 left Tatsicki-Stomick, watercolor on paper by Karl Bodmer. © Jocelyn Art Museum.

247 right Natoie Poochsen, watercolor on paper by Karl Bodmer. © Jocelyn Art Museum.

248 Makuie-Poka, watercolor on paper by Karl Bodmer. © Jocelyn Art Museum.

249 left Piegan Blackfeet Man, watercolor and pencil on paper by Karl Bodmer. © Jocelyn Art Museum.

249 right Packkaab-Sachkoma-Poh, watercolor and pencil on paper by Karl Bodmer. © Jocelyn Art Museum.

250-251 Hotokaueh-Hoh, watercolor and pencil on paper by Karl Bodmer. © Jocelyn Art Museum.

251 left Mehkskehme -Sukahs, watercolor, ink and pencil on paper by Karl Bodmer. © Jocelyn Art Museum.

251 right Kiasax, watercolor on paper by Karl Bodmer. © Jocelyn Art Museum.

252 left Homach-Ksachkum, watercolor and pencil on paper by Karl Bodmer. © Jocelyn Art Museum.

252 right Stomick-Sosack, watercolor and pencil on paper by Karl Bodmer. © Jocelyn Art Museum.

253 Ihkas-Kinne, watercolor and pencil on paper by Karl Bodmer. © Jocelyn Art Museum.

254 top left Shoshonean Woman, watercolor on paper by Karl Bodmer. © Jocelyn Art Museum.

254 top right Piah-Sukah-Ketutt, watercolor and pencil on paper by Karl Bodmer. © Jocelyn Art Museum.

254 bottom Cree Woman, watercolor and pencil on paper by Karl Bodmer. © Jocelyn Art Museum.

255 Pachtuwa-Chta, watercolor on paper by Karl Bodmer. © Jocelyn Art Museum.

256 Unknown Man, watercolor and pencil on paper by Karl Bodmer. © Jocelyn Art Museum.

257 Pehriska-Ruhpa, watercolor and pencil on paper by Karl Bodmer. © Jocelyn Art Museum.

258 Pehriska-Ruhpa, watercolor on paper by Karl Bodmer. © Jocelyn Art Museum.

259 Addih-Hiddisch, watercolor on paper by Karl Bodmer. © Jocelyn Art Museum.

260 Awascho-Dickfas, watercolor and pencil on paper by Karl Bodmer. © Jocelyn Art Museum.

261 left Birohka, watercolor and pencil on paper by Karl Bodmer. © Jocelyn Art Museum.

261 right Ahschupsa Masihichsi, watercolor on paper by Karl Bodmer. © Jocelyn Art Museum.

262 Mato-Tope, watercolor on paper by Karl Bodmer. © Jocelyn Art Museum.

263 Mato-Tope, watercolor on paper by Karl Bodmer. © Jocelyn Art Museum.

264 Mandeh-Pahchu, watercolor and pencil on paper by Karl Bodmer. © Jocelyn Art Museum.

264-265 Interior of a Mandan Earth Lodge, watercolor and ink on paper by Karl Bodmer. © Jocelyn Art Museum.

266 top Mandan Shrine, watercolor and pencil on paper by Karl Bodmer. © Jocelyn Art Museum.

266 bottom Sih-Sa, watercolor on paper by Karl Bodmer. © Jocelyn Art Museum.

267 Mandan Shrine, watercolor on paper by Karl Bodmer. © Jocelyn Art Museum.

268 Upsichta, Mandan, watercolor on paper by Karl Bodmer. © Jocelyn Art Museum.

269 Mahchsi-Karehde, watercolor and pencil on paper by Karl Bodmer. © Jocelyn Art Museum.

270-271 Mih-Tutta-Hang-Kusch, Mandan Village, watercolor on paper by Karl Bodmer. © Jocelyn Art Museum.

270 bottom Artifacts, watercolor and pencil on paper by Karl Bodmer. © Jocelyn Art Museum.

271 top Quiver, Bows and Arrows, watercolor and pencil on paper by Karl Bodmer. © Jocelyn Art Museum.

271 bottom Mandan Buffalo Robe, watercolor on paper by Karl Bodmer. © Jocelyn Art Museum.

272-273 Mandan Dog Sled, watercolor and ink on paper by Karl Bodmer. © Jocelyn Art Museum.

280 Artifacts, lithograph after Karl Bodmer. © Library of Congress, Washington

P.C. means Private Collection